The Leadership Triad

The Leadership Triad

Knowledge, Trust, and Power

DALE E. ZAND

New York   Oxford
OXFORD UNIVERSITY PRESS
1997

Oxford University Press

Oxford New York
Athens Auckland Bangkok Bogotá Bombay
Buenos Aires Calcutta Cape Town Dar es Salaam
Delhi Florence Hong Kong Istanbul Karachi
Kuala Lumpur Madras Madrid Melbourne
Mexico City Nairobi Paris Singapore
Taipei Tokyo Toronto

and associated companies in
Berlin Ibadan

Published by Oxford University Press, Inc.
198 Madison Avenue, New York, NY 10016

Oxford is a registered trademark of Oxford University Press

Library of Congress Cataloging-in-Publication Data
Zand, Dale E.
The leadership triad: knowledge, trust, and power
Dale E. Zand.
p. cm.
Includes bibliographical references and index.
ISBN 0-19-509240-6
1. Leadership. 2. Decision-making.
3. Control (Pyschology) 4. Trust (Psychology)
I. Title. BF637.L4Z36 1996
303.3'4—dc20 96-28083

1 3 5 7 9 8 6 4 2

Printed in the United States of America
on acid-free paper

For Charlotte Zand

and Jacob, Emily, Trevor, Alisa, and Nathaniel

Preface

I wrote this book to probe below the suface of leadership, believing that the actions and the techniques of leaders can be described by concepts that explain why some leaders are more effective than others. Society marvels at the accomplishments of great leaders, but the elements that constitute effective leadership are not well understood. People marveled at magnetism and light until scientists penetrated the mysteries of electricity and identified its three basic variables, voltage, current, and resistance; so in this book I have tried to formulate and explain the three variables that generate the electricity of leadership: knowledge, trust, and power. These variables, I believe, illuminate the mystery of leadership; as people come to understand them, I hope that effective leadership will become more widely available.

Writing this book, like much of leadership, has been an adventure in learning. It is a pleasure to acknowledge the support, direct and indirect, that I received along the way. Warren Bennis took time from a busy schedule to read an early draft manuscript. I greatly appreciate his comments and guidance. Chris Argyris and Bill Starbuck helped me make a crucial decision about selecting a publisher, which affected the eventual format and content of this book. Ed Schein and Dick Beckhard expressed an early encouraging interest in this project, for which I am grateful.

The writings of Peter Drucker, Rensis Likert, Herbert Simon, James March, Douglas McGregor, Kurt Lewin, Michael Porter, and many others have influenced my thoughts.

My years as a consultant working with many leaders in different companies have shaped much of what I say in this book. They trusted me, and I hope that I have done justice to that trust. I especially wish to thank Joe Foster, chairman and CEO of Newfield Exploration Company, and Charles Ellis, chairman and CEO of Greenwich Associates, for the opportunity and the joy of working with them. There are many others whom I acknowledge and thank although I do not name them here either because the list would be too long or because I would be abrogating confidentiality, but they know who they are.

My colleagues at New York University, Stern School of Business, helped me find time for this project. John Dutton generously made available and discussed his vast store of materials and knowledge on anything I asked. David Rogers and Hrach Bedrosian thoughtfully rearranged my teaching schedule to give me time when I needed it. Steve Stumpf's energy and "can-do" attitude spurred me to finish this book.

One of the pleasures of writing this book has been working with Herb Addison, my editor at Oxford University Press, whose insight and guidance has been invaluable. My wife, Charlotte, has been most supportive and understanding. She cheered me along as I labored through successive revisions of the manuscript.

Great Neck, N.Y.   D. E. ZAND
April 1996

Contents

INTRODUCTION

The Leadership Triad

Effective leaders harness three forces—knowledge, trust, and power. Like three horses pulling a chariot, these forces, if coordinated and working together, provide a swift and exhilarating ride. But if one force is mismanaged or pulls against the others, the ride is bumpy and can end in disaster.

The first force in the triad of leadership is knowledge. Effective leaders know or can find out what should be done. In other words, they have vision, and they know how to fulfill that vision. They set clear, challenging goals, and they know what needs to be done to reach the goals. Triadic leaders are not omniscient—all-knowing or all-wise—but they know how to gain access to the knowledge of others, and they know how to work with people to convert that knowledge into action.

The second force in the triad is trust. People trust effective triadic leaders, giving them loyalty and commitment. Triadic leaders earn trust by disclosing relevant information, sharing influence, and competently using knowledge. They earn trust by fairness in their dealings with others—fulfilling the spirit of their agreements, sharing rewards and hard times and not abusing their power. Triadic leaders are not necessarily liked or loved although they may be. Some may be famous, such as Lee Iacocca of Chrysler or Jack Welch of GE, but they are not saints without human foibles and shortcomings. People, however, have confidence in how they will use knowledge and power.

The third force is power. Effective triadic leaders use their power appropriately. They know when and how to be directive or to delegate. They know how to review and evaluate constructively. They know how to be consultants, providing guidance rather than issuing commands.

This book examines how leaders gain the knowledge needed to make wise decisions. It describes how they build the trust that motivates people to act with commitment. It analyzes how leaders use power appropriately. Some leaders have mastered one or two of these forces, but effective leaders enhance and integrate all three. They know what should be done, they have the trust of their people, and they use power appropriately. Leadership, therefore, as we use the term, consists of the principles, skills, and attitudes that harness and integrate knowledge, trust, and power.

NEED FOR LEADERS

Organizations need leadership at all levels, from top to bottom. At the top, leaders make the broad, comprehensive strategic decisions that set the organization's long-term direction. They determine which markets to enter or leave—local, regional, national, and international—and who will be the targeted customers. They determine the character of the product line—the range of features, the quality level, and the degree of innovation. They set research policy, from pioneering in basic research and frontier applications to copying only tried-and-true products that have succeeded in the market place. They pursue distant opportunities by making decisions regarding investment in plant, marketing, research, and finance that expose the firm to risk. They design the firm's basic structure, oversee the hiring of key executives, and review the firm's performance. Top leaders' decisions are so highly leveraged and amplified that small improvements in the quality of those decisions have wide, long-lasting effects on employee well-being and on the firm's performance.

At the lower levels of organizations, first- and second-level supervisors manage the firm's day-to-day operations. They are, as the cliché goes, "where the rubber hits the road." They translate strategy into action. They see that work gets done, products are delivered, and customers are satisfied. Their leadership greatly affects the attitudes and the productivity of workers. They can almost make or break a company by how they lead the workforce and by how effectively their practical decisions respond to material shortages, equipment breakdowns, and customer demands. Like the sergeants and the corporals who lead platoons into battle, they must make critical adjustments to local conditions and terrain, keeping people together and productive. Their leadership literally gets the work done. They are a precious resource that wise top and middle managers cultivate and develop.

Middle-level managers develop short-range plans to execute strategy and coordinate work across units in the organization. Like the majors, captains, and lieutenants in an army, they lead projects and programs—self-contained, almost independent ventures critical to the organization's strategy. They spearhead the design of new and improved products, lead marketing, advertising, and promotion campaigns, oversee the installation, start-up, and maintenance of new equipment in plants, and interpret top management's strategy, transforming it into the practical details of work. Their leadership is the bridge that connects top leaders' ideas to lower leaders' actions. With the downsizing and "right-sizing" of organizations in the 1990s and the steady reduction in the number of middle-level corporate leaders, the leadership of those who remain has become more critical than ever, for it keeps the heads and the hands of organizations working together.

Many of the examples in this book describe the effects of triadic leadership by top management leaders. These examples have been chosen because they are usually dramatic, have far-reaching effects, and have been well documented. But the triadic leadership principles, skills, and attitudes that apply to top management are just as important and just as relevant to middle and lower-level managers. Organizations need competent leaders at all levels. Leadership is not mastered quickly or easily, so if one wishes to move up in an organization, one is wise to learn about and practice leadership skills in one's current position, whatever it may be. Readers will find that this book can be used profitably by those who are already in management, regardless of level, as well as by those who are interested in moving into management.

ALLSTATE AND TRIADIC LEADERSHIP

Business strategy decisions, because of their great scope and their lasting effects, illustrate the three forces of triadic leadership in action. Strategy starts as knowledge, or vision, in the form of selecting a direction—a broad course of action such as entering a line of business or a market. Effective leaders synthesize knowledge, trust, and power to develop and implement a strategic vision. Working with their staffs, they, astutely select a path and then sharpen concepts, learn from errors, and make adjustments, refining their strategy and its implementation as they go along. Consider the following case.[1]

Robert Wood, the chairman of Sears Roebuck, used to play cards with Carl Odell, an insurance agent, during their morning train commute from Lake Michigan's north shore suburbs to work in downtown Chicago. One day in 1930, Odell offhandedly suggested that Sears ought to start an auto insurance company to sell insurance by mail. That seemingly causal remark was transformed by Wood's leadership into the Allstate Insurance Company, one of the most profitable ventures in Sears's history and in the insurance industry. Wood and his staff of mail-order retailers studied the changing demographics and buying patterns of the U.S. market. They concluded that soon most families would own automobiles and that consumer mobility would revolutionize retailing, permitting shoppers to drive miles from small towns to convenient central locations. Properly located and designed, retail stores would have a greatly expanded market reach. Ownership of automobiles was growing so rapidly that Sears was already selling tires, auto parts, and tools by mail and in stores to the auto retail market. Wood had the foresight and the courage to pursue the idea of selling insurance, which, at the time, was completely foreign to Sears's product line and to its collective corporate knowledge. Wood asked Odell to write a note on how selling insurance by mail might work and had experts brief him on the intricacies of the insurance business. He concluded that selling insurance would draw on many of Sears's existing merchandising abilities. He estimated that selling by mail, without going through agents, would give Sears as much as a 20 percent cost advantage over its competitors.

Wood began sharing his vision about selling insurance, discussing it with Sears's senior managers and consulting Sears's directors. Some of those he spoke with questioned the timing of the move. They thought it wasn't smart to start a new business during a deep economic depression and doubted that there would be sufficient consumer demand to sustain a new insurance venture because family income was too low. Better to wait for an economic recovery, they said. Others were concerned that Sears had no experience in the insurance business, which was heavily regulated by laws that varied from one state to another. Wood persisted. By the end of 1930 he had convinced the full Sears board to approve the venture and Sears's investment bankers, Goldman Sachs, to guide its funding. In 1931, about a year after Odell's casual suggestion, Wood launched Sears's insurance business. Allstate, the name of Sears's popular auto tires, was chosen as the name of the insurance company. Although Allstate was licensed only in Illinois, it could write insurance in any state so long as sales were entirely by mail. (Later, to meet competitive and regulatory obstacles, Allstate began to obtain licenses in other states.)

At first, Allstate sold insurance only directly to consumers through the mail. It employed no agents although at the time most insurance policies in the United States were sold by independent agents who handled the policies of several companies. Allstate also placed advertising leaflets in Sears stores, encouraging shoppers to buy its insurance by mail. After the company had operated for several years as a mail-order vendor of insurance, studies convinced Wood and Allstate's leaders that Allstate could increase sales if it had its own agents who would sell only Allstate policies in Sears's stores in large cities. The American population was gravitating to cities, and insurance sales, Allstate's leaders believed, would eventually grow more rapidly in big-city stores than through mail-order catalogs and rural stores. Wood and Sears's other leaders transformed Allstate into an exclusive agency-company, selling its policies through its own agents at a time when the industry was still primarily using independent agents. Within three decades Allstate had become the second largest insurance company in the world.

Wood had acquired the knowledge to make a wise, strategic decision—to move into insurance using Sears's mail-order and merchandising capabilities. He had the trust of Sears's leaders and directors, who concurred with the decision and oversaw its implementation. He had the trust of Sears's bankers, who guided the funding. He used his power appropriately, discussing, consulting, obtaining concurrence, and consigning implementation as Allstate grew and adapted to its changing market environment. Allstate contributed hundreds of millions of dollars annually to Sears's earnings, keeping the retail business afloat through several decades of poor profitability. In 1993 Allstate was spun off from Sears by a stock distribution; by 1995 it had a market value of $14 billion, employed 52,000 people, and had estimated annual earnings of more than $1 billion after taxes. Who would have thought that Wood's leadership, harnessing knowledge, trust, and power, could have parlayed a casual, low-stakes card game into such an extraordinary pot of gold?

PREVIEW

This book is divided into three parts, one for each of the three forces—knowledge, trust, and power—and a concluding chapter on integrating the three forces.

Knowledge

The first part of the book, on knowledge, starts with a consideration of the new conditions of leadership. Chapter 1 discusses knowledge as the emerging weapon of competition. The chapter examines the eclipse of position power by the rise of knowledge distributed throughout organizations. It considers the challenge of gaining access to knowledge that is in people's heads, where leaders cannot see it, and examines the problem of leading subordinates who often know more than their leaders. It discusses the nonlinearity of knowledge work, which suggests that doubling the number of people assigned to a task does not double the knowledge and the insight that are brought to it. The chapter examines how these new conditions have shifted the essence of leadership from giving directions to harnessing knowledge, trust, and power.

Chapter 2, "Finding Knowledge," examines how a leader's attitudes and behavior can release or repress distributed knowledge. The chapter discusses the knowledge tune-up—the process leaders use to locate worthwhile knowledge and to check the rationality of assumptions. The chapter looks at the leader's skillful use of questions to illuminate knowledge and examines two dangerous diversions: the lure of false synergy and pseudoknowledge. It concludes with a discussion of the process of searching for new knowledge.

Chapter 3, "From Knowledge to Action," discusses how effective leaders convert knowledge to action. It looks at the problems attendant on action and the deceptive attractiveness of status-quo leadership. It examines subtle obstacles to action such as the complacency of success, unfamiliar opportunities, and cultural resistance. It analyzes the design of action and the ways leaders prepare people to act. It discusses how effective leaders improve the link between knowledge and action.

Leadership ultimately means learning and encouraging learning. Chapter 4, "Learning and Knowledge," talks about getting into a "learning groove." It examines how a leader's demands determine what people will learn. It discusses the conditions effective leaders provide to aid learning and examines the need for leaders to renew their own knowledge.

Chapter 5, "Knowledge Stress and Knowledge Workers," discusses a new phenomenon—the rise of knowledge, or mental, stress. It looks at a leader's need to manage knowledge stress in order to avoid undermining people's ability to learn and adapt. The chapter analyzes sources of knowledge stress, such as the complexity of situations, and the need to respond to multiple conflicting interests. It discusses the stress of working in a world of insecure, temporary relationships and the growing vulnerability of each individual's self-esteem. The chapter examines the characteristics of knowledge workers that create stress for leaders, such as an incessant desire to question, a drive for freedom and self-responsibility, an insatiable interest in personal growth, and a great concern for corporate morality.

Trust

The second part of the book examines the process of building trust. It looks at the determinants and the laws or principles of trust. How well people trust their leader determines how much access they will give the leader to their knowledge and commitment.

Chapter 6, "Trust and the Decision Process," defines trust and explains how it differs from amiability or affection. The chapter examines the key elements in a leader's development of trust: disclosing information, sharing influence, and exercising control. The chapter presents a model explaining how these elements flow together in a spiral of trust or mistrust. The chapter examines how trust affected the quality of decisions made during an executive simulation of a company facing serious problems. It discusses the superior productivity, creativity, and commitment of trusting leaders compared to those of mistrusting leaders.

Chapter 7, "Determinants of Trust," looks at the effects of two underlying factors on a leader's willingness to trust: personality and training. The chapter then discusses other behavioral factors affecting trust: competence, openness, and supportiveness.

Chapter 8, "Laws of Trust," discusses several enduring principles of trust: that mistrust drives out trust; that trust stimulates productivity; that mistrusting groups self-destruct; and that rapid growth masks mistrust. The chapter examines methods for increasing trust: using integrative rewards, fostering reciprocal increases in trust, and jointly analyzing a relationship.

Power

The third part of the book focuses on power. Chapter 9, "Legitimate and Decision Process Power," defines power and discusses legitimate power—the right people give a leader to make choices and resolve conflicts. The chapter examines decision process power—the leader's right to determine how a decision will be made—and analyzes the effective use of four fundamental decision processes: commanding, consulting, concurring, and consigning.

Chapter 10, "Agenda, Staffing, and Review Power," continues the discussion of legitimate power. It examines agenda power—the leader's right to determine the organization's goals, strategy, and structure. The chapter looks at staffing power—the power to select, develop, and motivate the people who will help leaders shape and implement the agenda. The chapter also discusses review power—the leader's right to examine and adjust individual performance and strategic direction to keep the organization on course—and the emergence of knowledge and trust as sources of power for individuals who often have little legitimate power.

Chapter 11, "The Power of Leaders As Consultants," discusses how effective leaders act as consultants and clients to obtain knowledge for decisions and to promote trust for implementing them. The chapter presents a model of the consulting relationship that consists of two levels: content and process. The chapter examines the consulting skills leaders need in each phase of a consulting relationship. It discusses the difficulties of being a consultant or client and ways leaders can master those difficulties.

The final chapter of the book, "Teamwork and Triadic Integration," discusses the integration of the triad of knowledge, trust, and power. The chapter describes two basic modes of leadership: production and knowledge. It describes the characteristics of different situations and discusses how to select a leadership mode that fits the situation. The chapter discusses how to integrate the triad by using a parallel knowledge mode to supplement the production mode. It describes a case in which a leader, using a lateral knowledge mode to integrate knowledge, trust, and power, built a team that successfully formulated and implemented a major strategic change in a large bank. The chapter discusses the important leadership norms of the knowledge mode that distinguish it from conventional task forces. It looks at how to blend the production and knowledge modes and at the operational realities of using a knowledge mode. The book concludes with a discussion of the characteristics of triadic leaders: wisdom, integrity, and courage.

I

KNOWLEDGE

I know nothing except the fact of my own ignorance.

Socrates

1

Leadership: The New Conditions

Leadership has changed from the days when the United States was primarily a manufacturing society. Leaders face an emerging information age in which knowledge disperses to the far corners of organizations. The old directive factory approach to leadership is no longer effective. In the past, when a few top managers and staff specialists held the organization's core knowledge, leadership could be simple and directive; leaders, working alone, could think through a problem, give orders, and expect compliance. Alone, or with the input of a few close advisers, leaders could make the decisions that governed the organization's production, marketing, and finances.

The conditions of leadership in the late twentieth century have changed dramatically. To be effective, leaders need to understand the subtle but wrenching shift that has occurred in the leadership landscape. This chapter explores the characteristics of the new world of leadership. It examines knowledge, the heavy weapon of competition, and the ways in which the advent of knowledge is eclipsing the position power of leaders. It discusses distributed knowledge and the forces diffusing knowledge within organizations. It looks at the emerging knowledge society and the characteristics of knowledge organizations. It describes the unusual features of working with knowledge, as opposed to tangible products, and the special challenges this poses for leaders. Finally, it reviews the three key dimensions of leadership in this new world: knowledge, trust, and power.

KNOWLEDGE: THE HEAVY WEAPON OF COMPETITION

Finding and processing distributed knowledge has become the heavy weapon of competition. Leaders cannot simply declare a goal such as "design a new product" or "increase market share" and expect compliance and achievement. Goals are, of course, essential, but leaders need to understand that their behavior affects how people gather, think about, and use knowledge to define and achieve those goals.

Knowledge is like intellectual quicksilver—fluid, elusive, and intangible. Understanding how people create and use knowledge in an organization requires a revolution in leadership thinking. Knowledge travels with the speed of thought but can be blocked by the smallest emotional barrier. It can enlighten the entire organization's operation, yet it can easily be concealed if people do not want leaders to see it. People throughout organizations continually acquire and create important, critical knowledge about customers, products, technology, costs, and competitors. But that knowledge can remain hidden and inaccessible to leaders. In the new world, leaders need to liberate knowledge and creative thinking at all levels and in all corners of their organizations. To compete, leaders need to move knowledge from where it is to where it can be used to define and achieve appropriate goals.

THE ECLIPSE OF POSITION POWER

In the past, formal power largely determined how effective and influential a leader could be. This is becoming less and less the case. Position power is in eclipse; even with formal power, leaders who cannot mobilize their organization's distributed knowledge and gain the trust of its employees watch in dismay as their business slips into catastrophic decline.

Many observers believe that General Motors, IBM, and American Express declined between 1983 and 1993 because, despite their position power, their leaders could not or would not access their organizations distributed knowledge or gain their trust. For years leaders watched as their competitors gained market share, but they used their formal power to divert knowledge and to downplay external threats. Position power, in other words, was used to displace, rather than seek, knowledge and wisdom. Leaders defined loyalty to mean conformity with their thinking. They demanded that subordinates agree with, and not question, their superiors' proposed action. Subordinates astutely complied, self-censoring adverse information, concealing critical analysis, and suppressing creative thinking.

General Motors's billion-dollar buyout of a major stockholder, the Texas entrepreneur Ross Perot, was a spectacular example of misdirected position power at work. Perot, a substantial owner of GM stock, became a gadfly who openly questioned management's policies at board meetings. GM's senior managers were appalled that Perot had the audacity to visit and speak to workers in plants to learn about the company's problems and possible improvements. Buying him out, they decided would silence him. Perot had observed that over the years, GM's leaders had used their power insensitively, eliciting defensiveness and mistrust among GM middle managers and employees; GM's leaders' bureaucratic responses to GM's inferior product quality, mediocre new car styling, high costs, and declining market share had resulted in lukewarm commitment from middle managers and workers. GM leaders had used their position power to protect their turf. They filtered poor results through rose-colored glasses, watching the organization's capabilities erode for years as performance slipped into catastrophic decline. The ultimate step in this process of systematically suppressing distributed knowledge was to buy out Perot, not because his knowledge was untrue but because it was annoying to hear.[1]

Leaders can no longer assume that they, either alone or with their staffs, have all the knowledge necessary to make a business successful. Environments and competition are changing rapidly, and many organizations have become large and unresponsive. Leaders need to rethink their image of leadership. The heroic fantasy of one person at the head of a column of followers shouting "Charge" as they mount the battlements is outdated. Instead, leaders need to learn to use the sensing, searching, and thinking ability of all the people within the organization. Alex Trotman, CEO of Ford, calls this reducing the "coefficient of bureaucratic drag." Jack Welch, CEO of GE, calls this "boundarylessness." Both recognize that to improve their organizations' adaptability in a rapidly changing environment, leaders need to release knowledge and gain trust at every level of an organization.

DISTRIBUTED KNOWLEDGE

The diffusion of knowledge, information systems, and bright people who can learn and think throughout organizations is shaking the foundation of traditional power-centered leadership.

Knowledgeable Subordinates

At all levels of organizations leaders are recruiting increasingly well-educated subordinates. It is not unusual for many subordinates to know more operating details, more analytic techniques, and more theory than their leaders. Organizations have become so large and so complex that subordinates have to summarize much of their activity for their unit leaders. Unit leaders, in turn, spend their time visualizing the future and integrating the work of subunits, negotiating for resources in a continual cycle of budget discussions, and representing their units in higher management's planning. Belatedly, they have discovered that these activities leave them knowing less about operations and problems than many of their subordinates. Astute leaders understand this status paradox, and effective leaders free up and mobilize their subordinates' distributed knowledge.

At Nissan, senior managers controlled the design of cars even though sales had been declining for ten years. Nissan's leaders decided to add a sports car to its line to compete against Honda, which dominated this market segment in Japan. In a major departure from past practice, which recognized that senior management might not have all the necessary creativity and knowledge, Nissan's leaders formed a new design team consisting entirely of men and women less than twenty-eight years old. The team was left on its own to make all decisions; some senior managers were occasionally invited to see the design in progress, but they made no design changes. The new car was successfully introduced; within three years Nissan dominated the segment, sales increased 500 percent, and Honda's sports model lost more than 80 percent of its market share. Nissan's leaders had sped ahead of Honda by mobilizing distributed knowledge.

Leaders, like those at Nissan, are learning that as organizations grow and environments change, jobs requiring knowledge, judgment, and discretion are distributed throughout the organization. In the new world, leaders are discovering that the dispersion of knowledge imposes limits on what they can accomplish with formal power. They need to supplement their formal power with knowledge and to seek out and integrate people who have that knowledge.

Growth of Knowledge Specialists

Competition is being reshaped by an explosive growth of knowledge and a quantum leap in the number of specialists. Leaders must now relate to specialists in finance, marketing, information systems, engineering, and human resources. These specialists know more about their specific fields than do the leaders. Yet leaders must be able to call on that staff knowledge and effectively absorb and integrate it into the work of their units. Leaders cannot use formal authority to command other people to reveal or use what they know. Nor can leaders assume that their formal power gives them greater insight and understanding than others. Formal power only gives them the right to disregard others at their own peril, as occurred at General Motors.

Many leaders have used formal authority to wall themselves off from staff. Instead of benefiting from collaboration, leaders and staff waste energy fighting each other; the leader tries to evade the staff or get help some other way, while the staff tries to get senior management to coerce lower managers to comply with staff recommendations. These conflicts occur because leaders and staff specialists mistrust each other and face off in power struggles. As a result, leaders are unable to effectively use the organization's distributed knowledge.

Knowledge Uncertainty

Market uncertainty and new product risk have increased substantially at all levels of the organization. Rapid technological developments and new approaches to marketing have shortened product life cycles, and design teams bring new products to market more quickly than ever before. Deciding what product line should be offered three years from now and predicting what competitors will be offering then are daunting challenges with a staggering range of possible answers.

Globalization has added another dimension to uncertainty. It has increased the number of competitors in a given market and the number of markets in which companies compete. Japanese, American, and European companies now compete in markets around the globe. Regional trade agreements increase uncertainty, removing trade barriers and opening gigantic market areas. The European Community and the North American Free Trade Agreement are driving companies toward acquisitions, minority investments, and joint alliances for manufacturing, marketing, and research within these regional markets.

Delineating these product, marketing, and competitive changes and predicting their effects is a continuing challenge for top management. It is unlikely that any one leader can adequately imagine or comprehend the scope and richness of these uncertainties which affect everyone in the organization. That knowledge, however, is distributed through the organization. Leaders desperately need relationships that will allow them to easily tap into other people's knowledge and thinking. They need access to the organization's distributed knowledge if they are to explore and understand this new world of uncertainties.

Cultural Diversity

The composition of the workforce is changing. It now includes people from many cultures. In the United States the workforce has expanded to include African Americans, Latinos, Asians, and women. In Europe the workforce includes many people from Africa, the Middle East, India, and the Caribbean. Globalization accelerates the trend toward diversity, by dispersing a company's manufacturing, marketing, and research functions to countries all around the world; globalization requires that leaders work with people from different nations with different histories and that they mobilize knowledge that is now distributed across and filtered through different cultures. Leaders, need to understand the values, beliefs, ceremonies, and symbolisms distributed across their diverse workforce and markets. Leadership based on knowledge and trust is more effective than leadership based on formal authority when companies are collaborating with and marketing to people from different cultures.

The Need for Balance

Knowledge is also distributed across time. Leaders need to balance visions of the future with the demands of current operations. The word "leader" has increasingly been used to mean a person with vision, someone who initiates changes that anticipate future threats and opportunities and who inspires others to follow. The word "manager" has come to mean a person who primarily administers day-to-day work, who stays largely within the boundaries of present rules and procedures. The distribution of knowledge and the flattening of organization structures, however, increasingly blurs this distinction. Leaders who think only about distant visions, without concern for current performance, become incomplete leaders. They succumb to the complacement belief that current performance will take care of itself. By overlooking the need to continually improve current performance, their imbalanced leadership leaves the organization vulnerable to lower-cost, more customer-sensitive, competitors.

On the other hand, managers who think only about current performance and who have no vision are also incomplete leaders. Although knowledge about future threats and opportunities is available, they lull themselves into the belief that so long as current operations are going well, the future will take care of itself. Competitors, however, march to a different drummer. They like nothing more than competing against a complacent organization that stands still. Operating managers need to think about vision, just as visionary leaders need to think about operations. Sooner or later, leaders need to redress any imbalance between vision and operations.

Steve Jobs, a visionary and the cofounder of Apple, the computer company, had limited concern for day-to-day operations. John Sculley was therefore hired from Pepsi Cola to reformulate marketing strategy and to improve current operations. After a brief period of harmony, Jobs and Sculley began to fight continually about the imbalance between vision and operations. Their conflict persisted and escalated until the board of directors forced Jobs out of the company. Sculley then moved to balance operations and marketing with long-term vision.[2]

Regardless of whether a person is called a leader or a manager, she needs to be concerned with the present, the future, and change. Which of these elements leaders choose to emphasize will depend on their level of management, the company's competitive position, and changing threats and opportunities in the company's environment. With knowledge and access to knowledge spreading through organizations, leaders can and should be concerned with all three elements; only the balance will vary.

THE KNOWLEDGE SOCIETY

Industrialized nations around the world are becoming knowledge societies, and the businesses that operate within them are becoming knowledge-processing organizations. In the United States a massive public education system employs almost 3 million educators to guide the knowledge development of some 60 million children and adults, beginning with project Head Start which reaches preschoolers; a comprehensive system of scholarships, student loans, student aid, and low-tuition public universities practically ensures the availability of a college education, and even graduate studies, to every student with sufficient ability and motivation. Adult education, once considered a pastime, has become "continuing education"—and is considered a necessity for those wishing to keep up with the explosive growth of knowledge.

Business organizations are driving the quest for knowledge, demanding well-educated, knowledgeable employees. Many firms require a college education as a minimum condition for employment; some pay the tuition of employees who continue their education, and some even grant full-time scholarships. Businesses are an important source of university research grants and unrestricted donations. Some firms are major creators and disseminators of knowledge in management and technology. Organizations such as General Electric and Motorola not only send leaders to universities; they also operate educational facilities and programs that rival those at the largest universities.

Effects of Social and Economic Transitions

Three hundred years ago America was an agricultural society. People worked in small, self-contained, family units. Life's major activity was farming—sowing and harvesting the fruits of the soil. Markets were limited by primitive transportation and communication systems, and large, complex business organizations did not exist—indeed, could not exist. The transition to an industrial, capital society began about 150 years ago, when isolated industrial organizations—factories—erupted on the social landscape to become key institutions mobilizing great masses of people. They contributed to the economic well-being of people far beyond the factory gates and had a greater influence on social patterns than did the governments of the largest cities and states.

This social and economic transition, though imperceptible to most of the people who lived through it had dramatic, far-reaching effects. Some of these were highly beneficial. The standard of living increased; the quantity, quality, and variety of available goods increased; leisure time increased. Other effects were not so desirable. Land was stripped; forests were laid waste; air was polluted; rivers were fouled. Perhaps most insidious of all, a subtle, new form of social indenture was devised—dedicated, unquestioning conformity to the leaders of the employing organization.

In the last decade of the twentieth century society crossed another threshold—into the information age, marked by the emergence of the knowledge organization. The labor of a smaller and smaller percentage of the population produces the necessities of life—food, shelter, clothing, and other common material goods. Less than 3 percent of the population works on farms, and less than 11 percent produces all of the nation's industrial output, while almost 30 percent goes to school. Organizations have largely mastered the tasks of production, marketing, and physical distribution, although they will continue to improve these activities, but the real opportunities in the future will belong less to people who work with their hands and feet—the pure production workers—and more to people who work with their heads—the managerial, knowledge, service and sophisticated production workers. As technology and marketing advance, organizations will seek out people with increasing knowledge, causing more and more employees to become hybrid knowledge-production-service workers.

The Knowledge Organization

The core competence of organizations is shifting to the processing of knowledge. Leaders, and their people, work with ideas and assumptions. They formulate concepts and judgments, design proposals and make decisions, and exchange, extrude, and shape knowledge. Their projections and conclusions determine the firm's present and future production and marketing activities. Profitable businesses are knowledge-intensive, and their level of knowledge cannot easily be duplicated by lower labor cost competitors elsewhere in the world.[3] This shift suggests a future in which leaders will be heading what can best be called knowledge organizations.

Knowledge organization's have several features in common. Knowledge becomes the leading edge of the competitive effort and the company's ability to apply knowledge to products and markets determines the expansion or contraction of the firm's production work force. The ratio of knowledge workers to production workers increases. The relationship between the two groups inverts; in the past the production workers supported a small number of knowledge workers, whereas now the output of the knowledge workers increasingly determines the fate of the production workers. Without knowledge workers, the production workers eventually will have no work. Leaders sense that they need to guide others in acquiring and using knowledge if the organization is to survive and grow.

The required change in leadership attitudes is perhaps the most important, but least appreciated aspect of the new organization. Leaders in an organization with distributed knowledge face unrelenting pressure to release and use knowledge. Competitive advantage in the information age is in constant jeopardy; knowledge is fluid, and creative thinkers leapfrog over existing knowledge. Leaders know that it is increasingly difficult, if not foolish, to base survival, and growth, primarily on ownership of scarce materials, on patents that will expire, or on transitory product superiority; they understand that product innovations and marketing decisions made three or five years ago rapidly lose their ability to sustain the firm.

Knowledge Work Is Nonlinear

The essence of knowledge work is that it is done in the head. It cannot be seen. It is not produced in discrete, tangible units, like cars or dishwashers coming off an assembly line. It is difficult to measure. Leaders with a traditional production, marketing, or accounting orientation find this notion difficult to comprehend and accept. The nonlinearity of knowledge work is extremely annoying and frustrating to power-centered leaders. It does not make sense, for example, to demand that a person produce twice as many bright ideas in two hours as he can produce in one hour; it is meaningless to demand that the quality of a decision made by a group of seven people be seven times as good as a decision made by one person.

Progress in knowledge work is also nonlinear. If people seem to be half way toward solving a problem after two days, for example, can leaders expect a complete solution in two more days? Will people need more than two days? Or will the pieces fall into place and sensible solutions emerge in the next two hours? At Apple Computer, a team of engineers had been working for months, with limited success, to design a controller that would make a floppy disk drive work with an Apple II computer. Then Steve Wozniak, a cofounder of Apple, tackled the problem. In a few weeks, staying up nights, he devised a brilliant solution that used only eight chips instead of the usual fifty or more. An admiring coworker called it "poetry in electronics."[4]

Leaders in an organization with distributed knowledge face a life in which productivity is intangible and resolution is uncertain. It is hard for leaders to know when people are working, what stimulates their work, and how they are progressing. Thinking, which is nonlinear, takes the world apart, adds ideas, and imagines new configurations. This process takes place people's heads, where it can't be seen unless the people choose to disclose it because they trust the leader.

Contribution Ambiguity

In this strange world of knowledge, leaders contribute by guiding others to find and use knowledge. To the casual observer this is an ambiguous, almost undetectable contribution. Are people producing useful knowledge about products, markets, and production because of, or in spite of, their leaders? When leaders make decisions and assert ideas, they blend their contributions with those of many other people. Often it is fanciful to single out the leader's contribution, let alone to cite it as the primary cause of success. Despite this ambiguity, however, leaders are crucial to finding and using knowledge.

THREE DIMENSIONS OF LEADERSHIP

Leadership in the new world has three dimensions: processing knowledge, building trust, and using power sensitively. Each dimension connects to and interacts with the others. When leaders have and use relevant knowledge, people trust them and grant them power because they have confidence that the leaders know what they are doing. When people trust their leaders, they disclose knowledge and accept the leaders' use of power. Leaders guide their people to superior results, using the knowledge their people contribute. Thus, knowledge, trust, and power are tightly coupled, circularly reinforcing each other (see Fig. 1-1).

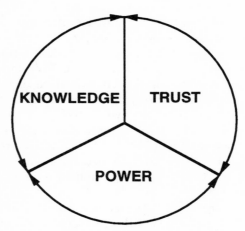

Figure 1-1 Triadic Leadership

Although leaders have the right to give orders, as in the old production organization, their effectiveness now depends on the knowledge and trust of their subordinates, coworkers, and superiors. When leaders cannot gain access to important knowledge, they make poor decisions, confusing and misleading the organization. Leaders who are mistrusted do not get the timely and well-thought-out information necessary for making good decisions or the staff commitment required for effective implementation of those decisions.

Leaders may have formal power, but without knowledge and trust they become martinets, leading people on meaningless forays. Their subordinates privately endure the hollow misuse of power, but they disconnect from the leader and from their work by lowering their commitment. They do the minimum needed to hold their jobs or leave for other jobs. Some leaders may have both formal power and knowledge, but if they are mistrusted, they too distort leadership, becoming cold, inaccessible taskmasters. Because people mistrust them, they get untimely, incomplete information and grudging, resentful implementation. They maintain control by providing tight, detailed supervision and by periodically replacing recalcitrant subordinates. They keep their units in continual states of anxiety and crisis; they mistrust their people and their people reciprocate by mistrusting them. Effective leadership in the new world depends as much on knowledge and trust as it does on formal power. A deficiency in any of these dimensions distorts leadership and reduces the leader's effectiveness.

CONCLUSION

Traditional methods of leadership were designed for supervision of factory workers. They emphasize regularity, measurement, orderly appearance, predictability, and control. When leaders attempt to enforce traditional leadership in the new knowledge organizations, they impede the flow of information, discourage creativity, inhibit adaptation, and undermine productivity. In the new world, traditional power-centered leaders often achieve the opposite of what they intended. Leaders who do not understand this new world try to remedy their declining effectiveness by using power to quash dissent and by imposing tighter controls. Caught in a vicious cycle of decreasing access to knowledge and increasing use of power, they are puzzled by the organization's unrelenting downward spiral in performance.

Leaders need to understand the new conditions of leadership. Knowledge drives competition. Knowledge is in people's heads; it is elusive, difficult to access, and nonlinear. Position power is in eclipse as leaders increasingly need to depend on others for the knowledge to make good decisions. Knowledge is diffusing across and down organizations. Organizations will continue to make products and deliver services, but the key to their survival and growth will be the ability of their leaders to find, process, and use knowledge. Leadership in knowledge organizations is the ability to harness and integrate three interdependent forces—knowledge, trust, and power. The next chapter discusses, in greater detail, the elements of finding knowledge.

2

Finding Knowledge

Organizations continuously generate new knowledge. Leaders draw on this knowledge, seeking new ideas for products, processes, and markets, sampling the best ideas, and combining them into strategies for solving problems. Leaders work on difficult problems by first finding and analyzing existing, relevant knowledge. They then turn competent thinkers loose, building relationships that smooth the flow of information. If existing knowledge does not solve a problem, then leaders must look further to locate or create new knowledge.

This chapter discusses how leaders go about finding and gaining access to useful knowledge. It looks at how the leader's attitudes and behaviors affect the release of knowledge, discusses ways to tune up the organization to find worthwhile knowledge and to clarify assumptions, and explores the leader's use of questions to illuminate knowledge. It then considers two costly diversions: the lure of synergy and of pseudoknowledge. It concludes by examining the search for new knowledge, contrasting knowledge "new only to us" with knowledge that is "new to everyone."

RELEASING KNOWLEDGE

Finding existing knowledge seems simple, but in many organizations it can be quite difficult. Existing knowledge is camouflaged and elusive. Even if leaders sense that many people know an organization's problems and have good ideas about solutions, they may find that the people resist sharing those ideas when leaders seek their knowledge.

Improvement Means Learning

For an organization to improve, its leaders must learn from the organization's errors. Poor leaders say they want to improve performance but, paradoxically, suppress the knowledge they need, becoming defensive when attempting to solve problems or improve performance. Poor leaders are inept at investigating deficiencies in a way that helps people learn and improve; they may make people fear that they will be punished if they reveal deficiencies.

Like drivers who have one foot on the gas pedal and the other on the brake, poor leaders exhort people to improve and then censure information about faulty assumptions, failing projects, and needed changes. They drive people by setting high goals but then discourage or isolate people who disclose adverse information. They punish nonconforming subordinates who offer facts, alternatives, or creative insights that diverge from those of the leader. To be politically safe, subordinates may conceal essential knowledge and resign themselves to powerlessness.

The leaders of Alldyne (name disguised*), a large producer of military air and sea equipment, decided to build commercial jet planes for the highly competitive civilian transport market. Although unfamiliar with the commercial market, they believed that the profit opportunities of this venture were worth risking hundreds of millions of dollars as long as the company maintained a "can-do" attitude. Alldyne's top leaders came from a military background and used a tight command style that said, "Don't speak unless a leader tells you to." The company's inexperience with commercial jet aircraft caused numerous design changes and delays, however, and as engineering design and model testing proceeded, middle managers could see that the cost of designing, building, and flight-testing the first two aircraft had been seriously underestimated. The final cost would be four to ten times the original estimate.

Managers began systematically suppressing information about design problems, costs, and schedule delays. They feared that their careers would be in jeopardy if they disclosed the information. They felt they had to appear to be "team players," willing to give 1,000 percent effort to overcome obstacles. By the time comprehensive information was allowed to reach top leaders and they understood its implications, a major failure was in the making. The information was no longer news; it simply confirmed what no longer could be hidden.

---

* To maintain confidentiality we shall occasionally disguise or omit a name or alter some items not material to the situation.

The company suffered a severe economic setback, its losses were so great that it was driven to the brink of bankruptcy. There were widespread layoffs, and confidence in top management was shaken. During the next two years many of the key leaders retired or resigned. Although leaders had exhorted employees to deal with obstacles, in fact they had sent a contradictory message: Overcome all obstacles to reaching goals, but don't tell us your problems. Leaders wanted improvement, but discouraged learning.

Understanding the Network

Effective leaders bind their organization into a seamless communication network. Leaders find knowledge by using existing channels, creating new channels, and updating old ones. They continually guide and monitor their network, checking who is in it, how well people are transmitting knowledge, and whose job has changed. Leaders' networks can be vast, reaching down and across the organization, connecting headquarters, divisions, departments, and sections. Each person in the network is a source, originating and transmitting knowledge. Each person senses, analyzes, creates, stores, and communicates knowledge.

Networks of people have a huge capacity to acquire, retrieve, and process knowledge. Networks operate like a complex brain, distributing knowledge throughout the organization. Just as many people use a fraction of their brain, however, so poor leaders use a fraction of their organization's knowledge and processing capacity. Effective leaders understand how to use networks to find knowledge. They understand that to prevent malfunctions that can block the transmission of information, they need to be teacher-learners.

Leaders As Teacher-Learners

Effective leaders open the flow of information by acting as teachers, planting ideas and nurturing them. Effective leaders learn by finding knowledge, and their learning becomes the foundation for successful change and improvement. Leaders help people find knowledge that identifies and properly defines the organization's problems, opportunities, and threats. As one executive put it, "It isn't the problems I know that trouble me as much as the opportunities and problems that people conceal. We can work on the ones that I know, but there is little I can do about the ones that I don't know." Competent leaders avoid two types of behavior that can undermine their effectiveness as teacher-learners: ignoring knowledge and punishing new knowledge.

Ignoring Knowledge

Poor leaders suppress, divert, or ignore existing knowledge and cause poor current performance. By withholding or ignoring existing knowledge, they perpetuate day-to-day errors and miss opportunities for improvements. Subordinates see this, for example, when a department leader does not communicate information about customer complaints to other departments, believing that it's not the other department's business or that it's not relevant. Overly competitive leaders would rather see the organization suffer than help an adversary department. When poor leaders withhold or ignore meaningful information for any reason, they decrease the organization's base of knowledge about its performance and then are surprised by the organization's uncoordinated responses.

Leaders of Bradco Electric (name disguised), a company that produced small home appliances, were struggling with a sustained decline in sales. The company's usually strong-minded and independent managers had become distant and isolated under the increased stress. Historically, company practice had been for customer relations to send a standard, courteous, public-relations letter to consumers who complained about poor product quality. Complaint letters were kept on file for 6 months, but statistics were not compiled and information about specific complaints never left the department. Managers felt that nothing would have been done with the information, so there was no reason to compile or communicate it. At the same time, orders for replacement parts from appliance repair shops were kept in the sales department. Sales managers viewed the sale of replacement parts as a high-margin, profitable business and felt it best to keep this information within the sales department. Workers in the factory who suggested changes to improve quality or to make manufacturing easier were reprimanded and told that their job was production, not product design.

Sales declined as the company's product quality began to lag behind that of competitors. To spur sales, management lowered prices and offered higher margins on its products. Despite the higher margins, distributors and retailers resisted promoting the company's increasingly inferior products. Sales continued to decline. The company struggled to survive as a marginal producer. Finally, a competitor purchased the firm for a fraction of its original value.

Leaders of each of the company's divisions had withheld or ignored critical information. Theoretically the leaders were in a network, but by not transmitting crucial knowledge they had undermined the organization's ability to respond to its customers. They had blocked the organization's ability to adapt but blamed its decline on competitors and vindictive distributors. They had ignored their customers and could not understand why customers were ignoring them. The result was a disaster for the company.

Punishing New Knowledge

Poor leaders, by isolating people with new views and punishing those who present adverse analysis, cause poor future performance. Like the proverbial ostrich with its head in the ground, they believe that if they don't talk about potential problems, they do not exist. These leaders fear that talking about difficulties will divert effort and demotivate people, so they discourage and remove subordinates who do.

Leaders of American Express, a major charge-card company, decided in the late 1980s to issue a new card, called "Optima," promoting a high line of credit for upscale customers.[1] This venture was a departure for AmEx, whose core business had been the issuance of charge cards to businesses and other upscale customers who used the cards to charge travel and entertainment expenses, rather than as a source of revolving credit. Customers paid a high annual fee for the traditional American Express card and were required to pay all balances within thirty days after their statement billing date; the charge card offered no credit.

Some managers questioned the Optima card venture for several reasons. Would it tarnish the upscale image of the traditional green, gold, and platinum AmEx cards? Would the company have to improve its ability to detect and screen out high-risk customers who would default on payments? Was the company underestimating the ratio of defaults to total charges by using the average experience of banks that had been in the credit card business for years? Would the company have to invest in a substantial collections operation to deal with defaulting card holders? Managers raising these issues wanted a more detailed analysis of the probability and the costs of higher default rates and a clearer picture of the people, funds, and facilities needed to upgrade screening and collections. Company leaders ignored or ostracized those who raised these concerns. Risk-averse naysayers, as they were perceived, lacking, the courage to pursue an opportunity, were moved out of positions of influence. Senior leaders did not conceal their displeasure with those who did not enthusiastically endorse the venture.

After the new card was issued, management's goal was to acquire new card users who would buy on credit. Optima would have to muscle aside such gorillas as Visa, Mastercard, the huge banks in the credit card business, Sears, and AT&T's Universal card. Screening criteria for new card members were gradually relaxed in an effort to gain market share. As customer defaults soon mounted to tens of millions of dollars, managers concealed and censored information about the defaults and collection problems. After incurring losses of hundreds of millions of dollars, top management finally had to suspend the card, reduce its business, and reorganize its systems. Senior leaders were replaced. The company's decision to ignore and punish those who had raised critical questions and sought new knowledge had not averted the problems. Instead, when the problems occurred, they were concealed, and leaders were woefully unprepared to deal with them.

One business executive who had been a damage control officer in the U.S. Navy, commenting confidentially on the Optima debacle, said that he is appalled by business leaders who punish inquiry and derogate adverse knowledge. He explains that "it's as if these leaders believe that if we do not talk about fire extinguishers, water hoses, or new damage control procedures, then there will never be a fire. This is an incredibly primitive superstition. In the Navy, we found just the opposite was true. The more we simulated emergencies and thought about new ways to deal with them, the more we decreased the likelihood of fire and the better prepared we were to deal with it if it occurred." He goes on to ask, "Would you want to fly in a plane whose pilot could not think about or practice what to do if an engine failed because his company's leaders punished such adverse thinking?"

Dependence and Learning

Leaders' attitudes toward dependence on others greatly affect the release and use of knowledge. Leaders cannot shed their dependence; they can only learn to use it constructively. In today's complex, fast-changing organizations, leaders must depend on others for knowledge, learning, and action. The leaders' attitudes toward that dependence determine whether they are confident or arrogant leaders.

Confident Leadership

Like the lion that sniffs the wind and cocks its ears to sense what is happening, confident leaders are acutely tuned to their surroundings. They can sense when they are encouraging others to disclose, analyze, and communicate knowledge. Confident leaders are comfortable with their dependence on others for knowledge. They do not deny or disguise that dependence; they use it to stimulate progress and teamwork. They learn with their employees.

Coworkers find it exciting and enjoyable to share knowledge with confident leaders, certain that they will get a fair hearing and that everyone will be better off for having explored different perspectives, and options. Confident leaders do not agree with everything they hear, but they know how to disagree without demeaning or undermining their subordinates. Subordinates observe and value this attitude and gradually learn to treat each other with similar confidence.

Arrogant Leadership

Arrogant leaders resent or deny their dependence on others. They condescend to receive knowledge by intimidating others. They resist learning, dismissing the views of others as clearly inferior to their own. People find it discouraging and joyless to share knowledge with such leaders. Coworkers and subordinates supply only the information specifically requested. People are fearful of presenting new views, so they withhold their knowledge of problems and their creative insights. The arrogant leader complains that people are withholding information and does not understand why. As one subordinate put it, "When you get hit with a baseball bat, you learn to duck." Having been subjected to intimidation, many subordinates often displace their frustration by berating and intimidating others. They soon find themselves practicing arrogant leadership, resenting their dependence, rather than confidently using it to find knowledge and to learn with their colleagues.

THE KNOWLEDGE TUNE-UP

Like getting a car engine to run efficiently, competent leaders tune-up their organization's search for knowledge by asking basic, hard-nosed questions that are not easy to answer and often cannot be answered completely. But leaders continue to ask them to improve their organization's search for distributed knowledge.

The questions flow in a logical circle, each leading to the next, ultimately returning to the beginning: What knowledge is worthwhile? What are the key assumptions? Who has, or should have, this knowledge? Who should receive it? What are leaders expected to do with it? What changes would improve the collection and dissemination of existing knowledge?

What Knowledge Is Worthwhile?

Leaders in the new age of information and instantaneous global communication are increasingly assaulted with masses of useless data. At the same time, they are poorly informed about relevant issues. Leaders start each day facing a mass of reports, briefings, inquires, meetings, memos, news items, express mail, e-mail, and voice mail. Effective leaders cut through the communication deluge and focus on worthwhile knowledge.

Having worthwhile knowledge reduces a leader's uncertainty about the correctness of important decisions. Knowledge that does not reduce uncertainty is redundant or irrelevant. Poor leaders insist that worthwhile knowledge consist entirely of facts, so they compulsively gather facts with little regard for relevance or priority. They intimidate subordinates, quizzing them on irrelevant minutiae while major problems go unexamined.

Effective leaders know that worthwhile knowledge takes different forms, all of which help to reduce uncertainty. Worthwhile knowledge can be information about past events or a concept that helps leaders interpret events. It can be a model that concisely represents reality or an analysis of the pros and cons of a proposal. It can be questions that illuminate thinking or a theory about causes and outcomes.

Leaders of Unimed (name disguised), a hospital buying group, were negotiating with a medical products manufacturer about price, volume, and exclusivity terms for the purchase of a large volume of single-use, disposable medical supplies such as irrigation syringes, suction catheters, and respirator tubing. Unimed represented several hundred large hospitals in a voluntary association, much like a buyers cooperative. Depending on the terms negotiated with the manufacturer, the member hospitals would buy all, some, or none of their supplies through Unimed. Historically, most hospitals had individually negotiated price-volume agreements with the manufacturer or with medical supply distributors.

Unimed's leaders asked what knowledge would best prepare them for the negotiation and reduce their uncertainty. They concluded that since the hospitals were their clients, they would need information about past hospital purchases and prices. Without this information, Unimed's leaders might agree to prices higher than those the hospitals had negotiated on their own. The leaders convinced member hospitals to provide information about their volume of purchases and net prices paid for each product for the past several years.

Unimed's leaders thus entered the negotiation with invaluable price data and a detailed model of the manufacturer's price-volume schedule. Armed with this knowledge, they negotiated an agreement for prices that were as good as, or better than, those previously obtained by the largest single hospital. To obtain the lower prices, Unimed agreed to a "committed volume"; it would deliver a specified minimum percent of the volume purchased by all of its member hospitals during the contract period. Unimed's leaders were pleased with the agreement because they could offer member hospitals top-quality products at prices better than those that most hospitals could obtain alone, provided that member hospitals bought most of their volume through the buying group.

The negotiated agreement greatly increased the value of hospital membership in Unimed and strengthened the member hospitals' commitment to buy through the group. The leaders of the manufacturing company were also pleased because the agreement enabled them greatly to reduce their sales efforts with the hundreds of hospitals in the Unimed group. The manufacturer passed some of these savings to Unimed in the form of lower prices. All parties—the manufacturer, Unimed, and the hospitals—were satisfied and diligently implemented the agreement. By identifying and gathering worthwhile knowledge, Unimed's leaders had reduced their uncertainty and made better decisions for themselves, their member hospitals, and ultimately for their supplier.

What Are the Key Assumptions?

In most complex situations, there are things that leaders cannot know. It may seem paradoxical, but worthwhile knowledge identifies the important unknowables. Leaders understand that they need to make assumptions about important unknowables. *The danger is not that leaders make assumptions but that they do not know what assumptions they are making.* Effective leaders and their people identify what is unknowable in order to discover their key implicit assumptions.

Making Rational Assumptions

Wise leaders ask their people to identify and describe as best they can what they do not know. In doing so, they are looking for implicit assumptions in knowledge. After identifying these important unknowns, wise leaders search for a rational basis for whatever assumptions are made about the unknowns. Effective leaders know that reasonable assumptions are based on more than a coin flip, a look in a crystal ball, or a reading of tea leaves.

Leaders of Cotran (name disguised), a pipeline company that supplied natural gas from the south central United States to the Northeast, planned to expand into the north central states, where one competitor had a dominant share of the market. Cotran's managers believed they could gain a share of the market by supplying gas to a segment of customers at a lower price and more reliably than the established competitor. The managers and their staffs spent several months analyzing the gas supply, transportation, marketing, and the financial aspects of the proposal.

Near the point of decision, the company's president asked what important things were still unknown about this project. A series of items was identified, and one item triggered extensive discussion: How would the competitor react? It had been assumed that the competitor's costs would, on average, be similar to those of Cotran. It had also been assumed that the competitor would therefore be reluctant to retaliate by starting a price war, since this could pressure the competitor to lower prices to its other customers as well.

Stimulated by the president's questions, the managers and their staffs searched for a basis for their assumptions. They discovered, hidden in the footnotes of public documents disclosing the competitor's past mergers and acquisitions, that the competitor had substantial, long-term gas supply contracts at prices far below those negotiated by Cotran. The crucial assumption that the competitor would not, or could not, retaliate because of high costs was clearly not valid and Cotran clearly needed to consider revising its plans. Eventually, Cotran entered the market on a much smaller scale than originally planned, focusing on small customers to avoid a direct confrontation with the large, established competitor. Cotran was able to establish and maintain a niche in the new market. The president's questions about managers' assumptions had averted what could have become a costly, escalating price war that would have destroyed the expansion project.

Monitoring Assumptions

Assumptions are like a moving tennis ball. Tennis players must keep their eyes on the ball if they are to position themselves correctly to take advantage of competitors' moves. Business, leaders must continuously monitor the assumptions underlying their important decisions. They must track competitors' actions, the business environment, and company performance to ensure that those assumptions are still appropriate. When analysis shows that assumptions are no longer valid, effective leaders need to develop alternative plans to fit the new assumptions. The monitoring of assumptions is an extremely valuable form of knowledge. It alerts leaders to critical changes in their environment and to new opportunities.

The leaders of Compaq, a manufacturer of personal computers, could not know what new products IBM, the company's major competitor, would introduce, so they had to base their product strategy on a key assumption—that IBM, because of its reputation and its market dominance, would set the product standards that customers would use as a benchmark for evaluating competitors' products. On the basis of this key assumption, Compaq's leaders formulated a follower, high-quality, product strategy—Compaq would wait for IBM's new product introductions; shortly thereafter, Compaq would introduce its own new products with higher quality and more features than IBM's.

For several years, Compaq's leaders acted on their assumption that IBM was the product leader. During this period PC technology and performance improved dramatically, costs dropped, many firms marketed IBM compatibles, and consumers became sophisticated buyers of PCs. At the same time, IBM's conservative product innovation and deteriorating financial performance eroded its product leadership position. After reassessing the situation, Compaq's leaders concluded that their original assumption about IBM's leadership was no longer valid. IBM was becoming simply another competitor in the pack, and its leadership could be challenged. Acting on this new assumption, Compaq's leaders moved to a product leadership strategy, introducing new products with increased performance and better quality ahead of IBM. Compaq took the innovation lead, and its sales grew rapidly.

A few years later, as IBM-compatibles continued to improve in quality and low-priced PCs jumped in market share, Compaq's leaders had to reassess another assumption—that consumers would support a two-tiered PC market, one with high prices and the other with low prices. Compaq's leaders concluded that they again would have to change a key assumption, consumers would no longer support a two-tier market now that technology had made low-priced PCs reliable. Compaq's leaders changed their product strategy from selling computers with high prices and top quality to selling computers with average prices and slightly better-than-average quality. Compaq lowered its manufacturing costs, enlarged its distribution system, and dropped its prices. It took the market share lead in what had become by 1994 a multibillion-dollar market.[2] By continually monitoring their assumptions, Compaq's leaders had generated worthwhile knowledge that led to superior, strategic decisions.

QUESTIONS ILLUMINATE KNOWLEDGE

Questions can spark new ways of looking at the company's operations and the assumptions underlying leaders' decisions. By asking the right questions, effective leaders can focus attention on hitherto unquestioned aspects of organizational performance.

GE's corporate leaders strongly supported sales growth and decentralization during the 1950s and 1960s. Division leaders enthusiastically proposed opportunities for investment, and headquarters supplied the capital. GE pursued an ever-widening array of products, markets, and businesses, from home appliances such as toasters, irons, washers, and refrigerators to mainframe computers, nuclear power plants, and jet engines. Although company revenues grew, profits remained relatively flat. Division leaders explained that profits were not growing because they were in an investment phase. In the near term, they said, more funds would be plowed into the business than would be earned, but after five to seven years their divisions would gain market share and profits would grow. In hindsight, these years were a period of profitless growth with flat earnings that were projected to rise rapidly in the future like a hockey stick. GE's leaders had become deeply committed to financing division growth and were reluctant to question division strategies and decisions so the company, although profitable, was a below-average performer.

Ultimately, corporate leaders began to ask a perturbing but critical question: What businesses should GE not be in? This disturbing question radically shifted the corporation's culture from freewheeling, decentralized growth to deliberate, carefully analyzed retrenchment. Division leaders resented the corporate leaders' skeptical, probing questions about growth, profitability, and return on investment. The question "What businesses should GE not be in" sparked other questions: Should the same investment and performance criteria be used for all businesses? Should there be different investment hurdle rates for different businesses? How should GE assess the attractiveness of an industry? What is the best way to get out of a business?

During the next two decades GE's leaders struggled with answers to these questions. They sold, contracted, or dissolved almost one hundred product lines and businesses. Revenue growth continued, and corporate profitability and return on investment improved significantly. By asking searching questions, GE's corporate leaders had helped create the knowledge to improve performance.

Focusing the Search

Competent leaders focus their search by pinpointing the kind of knowledge they need. They ask two focusing questions: What conditions is this decision sensitive to, and how much of a change in these conditions would warrant changing the decision?

Leaders of Polychem (name disguised), a large chemical company, were negotiating a new contract with a major customer that purchased 20 percent of their plant output. For the past ten years the industry had been operating at capacity, and manufacturers had obtained favorable prices.

Recently, however, several competitors had completed new plants that substantially increased industry capacity. At the same time, total demand had not grown as rapidly as had been forecast.

Polychem's leaders asked: What conditions should their price, volume, and quality decisions be sensitive to? They concluded that it was essential to operate their plant above its break-even point. Loss of this major customer could drive capacity utilization to the break-even point or below. The advent of excess industry capacity had made underutilization a real threat, especially since the competitors, with their new, unused capacity, would probably cut prices and pursue customers aggressively. In the past, Polychem's leaders had been concerned about how big a price increase they could negotiate. Now, however, they concluded that they should focus on the threat of falling prices and on ways to keep their plant operating above its break-even point in an industry with excess capacity.

Polychem's leaders concentrated on developing creative options that would retain their large customer under the new conditions. Gradually they shifted the focus of the negotiations from a fixed-price contract to index-based pricing using a weighted index of market prices they had devised and a price adjustment mechanism. After some haggling over details, the customer accepted the contract. Polychem and the customer agreed to a base price that would be adjusted at the end of each quarter if the price index fell outside a specified range above or below the base price. With this arrangement, prices would lag slightly behind any long-term trend whether up or down. Polychem had decided that it was better to accept some risk of declining prices rather than to lose the customer and operate below its break-even point. The customer did not feel locked into a fixed high price if prices dropped and was willing to accept some risk of higher prices if the index rose. Polychem also sweetened the deal by reducing the minimum volume the customer would have to take before incurring penalties for "underlifting." By focusing their search on the sensitive elements of their important decisions, Polychem's leaders retained an important customer and the customer retained a reliable supplier.

Questions Unlock New Possibilities

A good question starts a branching process that opens up new thoughts and possibilities. Good questions lead to other questions that open up new perspectives. Asking a good question, paradoxically, depends on having enough knowledge to know what is a good question. To ask good questions about business strategy, marketing, finance, chemistry, or medicine, for example, one needs some knowledge of the subject. Effective leaders keep asking sharp questions that unlock new possibilities by continuing to learn about the knowledge that has been developed in the different areas of their business.

Competent leaders know and use an extensive body of knowledge about business strategy to frame questions. A partial tree of questions (see Fig. 2-1) illustrates the branching process that flows from the growing knowledge of strategy. We encourage readers who may not be familiar with the literature of business strategy to explore it.[3]

Business strategy can be divided into four areas: assessing the business environment, analyzing the business situation, examining alternative strategies, and implementing the chosen strategy. Effective leaders continually update their knowledge of these areas so that they can ask relevant questions. Assessing the business environment, for

Figure 2-1 A Partial Tree of Strategy Questions

example, branches into a wide set of questions: What is the industry structure? What is the target market? Who are the competitors? What are the relevant trends? What are the threats and opportunities? Each of these questions branches again into other sets of questions, as portrayed in Figure 2-1.

The benefits of having leaders in companies like General Motors, IBM, and American Express ask these questions are enormous. These questions are difficult to answer, but competent leaders ask them because if they do not pursue the branches emanating from them, they give away their business to competitors who do ask the questions.

Triggering the Growth of Knowledge

Worthwhile knowledge sets off penetrating questions encouraging curious minds to explore new concepts. Competent leaders understand that new insights follow a jagged path, that knowledge explodes in unexpected places. Chance events, such as Robert Wood's exposure to the idea of selling auto insurance by mail, and even failures can spark imaginative people to release a treasure of worthwhile knowledge. A series of such events led to the discovery of penicillin.

Laboratory workers trying to cultivate a pure strain of bacteria complained to their colleagues that an impurity was continually killing their sample. They kept searching for a more sterile medium, one without the impurity, so that their bacteria would grow. Alexander Fleming's inquiring mind, however, viewed their failure from a remarkably different perspective. Instead of trying to eliminate the impurity, he reasoned that if he could isolate and identify it, he would have found a natural substance that might also destroy bacteria in humans. In the end, Fleming was able to isolate and identify the mold antibiotic that became known as penicillin. Fleming's wild idea that a natural substance, such as a mold, could kill bacteria spawned a worldwide search for other natural bacteria-killing substances in plants, trees, and animals, a search that goes on to this day; Fleming was awarded the Nobel Prize for his discovery. Fortunately, Fleming worked in an organization whose leaders understood that information even about a failure could trigger explosive insights in inquiring minds.

Unknowables and Learning

Like a diver perched at the tip of a high diving board, leaders have to leap into the unknown or else turn around and abandon their project. Leaders understand that some knowledge is so costly that they have to treat it as an unknown. Leaders would like to know, for example, whether a new product will succeed or fail before they introduce it. They can do marketing research and investment analysis, but, like all forecasts, these are imperfect. When the cost to know, in terms of time, money, and people, exceeds the value of the additional information, then leaders must make their decisions on the basis of the knowledge they have, even though there is a risk of failure. If they do fail, effective leaders learn from their failure and try again.

When the leaders of Apple designed their first portable computer, determining what characteristics of weight, bulk, and battery operating cycle consumers would accept was costly and difficult. As a result, Apple's first portables were a disaster. Weighing a "truss-busting 16 pounds," the portables were too heavy and ran on batteries for too short a time. [4] Customers avoided them like a proverbial rotten apple, and Apple's leaders had to write off a large inventory of unsold portables. Several years later, however, Apple's leaders redesigned their portables and introduced a line of "notebook" computers weighing less than seven pounds that set a new standard for portables and captured substantial market share. Apple's leaders had used their best information when designing their first portables, and they had failed. They learned from that failure, increased their knowledge, and introduced winning products.

DIVERSIONS

The Lure of Synergy

Synergy, like a pot of gold at the end of the rainbow, dazzles leaders by suggesting that two organizations will create additional value by dovetailing their activities, reducing costs and creating additional income. In theory each organization has something the other needs; together they should be more productive and more profitable than they are separately. In the real world, some combinations generate an opportunity for synergy, but many do not. Poor leaders, in pursuit of growth, succumb to fanciful exaggeration, tossing aside rationality, as if by wishing for synergy they will make it come true. They believe, naively, that they can increase income by spreading their organization without limit across an ever-widening set of products and businesses. Competent leaders, however, understand and respect knowledge of their organization's core competence and the limits of what their people can do. Synergy has become a mystical incantation, casting a spell over poor leaders who dismiss information about the limits of their organization's capabilities. They demand that people achieve synergy despite the realities of poor fit, strained resources, high costs, and limited benefits, insisting that commitment overcome all obstacles.

Leaders of Bowman (name disguised), a large, diversified financial services company, were dazzled by the possibilities for synergy created by their takeover of a small Swiss bank that catered to an elite, super-wealthy clientele. After acquiring the Swiss bank, Bowman's leaders were euphoric over the opportunity to sell their investment products to their new, wealthy clients.

Synergy fever, however, pushed aside serious examination of the acquisition and overshadowed some important limitations. Bowman's failed to appreciate that superwealthy clients, uninterested in the details of financial transactions, trusted their private bankers to make the best decisions for their portfolio. These private bankers steadfastly resisted Bowman's hard-sell efforts to convince them to put clients into investments that might benefit Bowman more than their clients. Fearing that they would lose their clients' trust, the bankers refused to buy high-risk products inconsistent with their clients' conservative risk profiles. Bowman's leaders, demanding greater commitment and loyalty, held meetings and sent memos pressuring the bankers to place Bowman products in client portfolios. Eventually, most of the key private bankers left, taking their loyal clients with them. Bowman reaped little benefit from the acquisition. Bowman's leaders had been lured by their own vague, puffed-up claims of synergy. Accepting and repeating embellished assertions, they did not ask the searching, practical questions that would have revealed the poor fit between the acquisition and Bowman's product and service strategy.

Pseudoknowledge

Competent leaders know that they need to protect time to think—to clarify issues, visualize future trends, and adapt creatively. The great danger is that they may get bogged down in pseudoknowledge, a miasma of readily available, easy-to-process, but irrelevant data. Leaders are flooded with masses of redundant data and spend their time preparing and discussing reams of reports about irrelevant or trivial issues. Pseudoknowledge does not clarify issues or help leaders make decisions. It insidiously absorbs the leader's most valuable resource— the ability to think.

Poor leaders are forever in search of more data to maintain their confidence. Subordinates, sensing this need, feed it by regularly sending doses of redundant data. When faced with new information, poor leaders rarely change their decisions. They rely on pseudoknowledge as a way of life, denying and evading disconfirming information because they cannot accept the fundamental changes that follow from it.

Leaders, in many organizations spend much of their time filling out reports that supply other leaders with redundant data. Executives and professionals in one research laboratory estimated that they spent up to 80 percent of their time preparing and polishing reports telling leaders what they already knew. Over a period of ten years, to stem the laboratory's declining productivity in patents and significant breakthroughs, leaders had added layers of managers, reports, and reviews. Executives and professionals were being smothered by a reporting system that left them little time or energy for asking relevant questions or thinking about new opportunities. Eventually, new leaders reorganized the laboratory into a flatter structure and cut the report system to the bare essentials. Over the next five years, freed from the lure of pseudoknowledge, new leaders brought the laboratory to its highest level of productivity ever.

Meaningless Organization of Data

Weary travelers in the former Soviet Union used to tell a story about a farmer in a small village who asked the ticket seller at the local railroad station, "When is the next train to Leningrad?" The ticket seller replied, "We haven't received a train schedule for three years, comrade, but I will be happy to give you a copy of an impressive report on rail shipments of grain, dairy, and cattle last year." Like the traveler, leaders are continually frustrated by reports, churned out to impress people, that are irrelevant to what the leaders need to know. Computers generate masses of data, but people determine how the data are analyzed and reported. Many reports are not used until leaders redesign them so that they are relevant to the leader's decisions.

The headquarters finance department of a large oil exploration company routinely sent each division a thick monthly report on all material purchases. The report was a standard general inventory report detailing the beginning inventory of hundreds of items, the monthly purchases, the amounts used, and the ending inventory, but division leaders rarely used it. They were interested in drilling, operating, and trouble costs for each specific well in their division's territory. The reports were not organized to provide this information, so division leaders devised their own special report system for estimating and controlling drilling costs in different geological formations. Using this system, division leaders were able to control costs and compare the relative efficiency of the various contract drillers they employed. Division leaders had to define their interests and direct their staffs to organize reports so that they were meaningful to the leaders as they made their decisions for their divisions.

SEARCHING FOR NEW KNOWLEDGE

New Knowledge Shifts Competitive Power

Leaders seek new knowledge that challenges conventional thinking, alters the status quo, and changes the distribution of competitive power. By investing in creating and using new knowledge, leaders precipitate drastic shifts in where and how organizations compete. Consider the following examples, one historic and the other recent.

The monarchs of Spain supported Columbus's voyage, which tested the concept of a round earth when most people believed that the earth was flat. The commercial goal was to find a new trading route to the Orient, one that would eliminate the long, perilous overland journey to Asia. Although Columbus did not find a new route to the Orient, the new knowledge gained from his voyage drastically changed international competition. His voyages spurred acceptance of the round-earth concept, precipitating an upheaval in political and economic relations among European nations. National leaders began investing in strategies of exploration and colonization in the western hemisphere. Spain, Portugal, Great Britain, and France sent expeditions to find and colonize new lands. New knowledge had shifted international competition to naval efficiency and power, triggering an era of exploration that changed the wealth of nations and moved the leaders of Spain to the front of the race.

Leaders of MCI, the telecommunications company, provide a recent example of the use of new knowledge to shift competitive power. MCI's leaders bypassed the communications giant AT&T and entered long-distance telephone service by using new microwave transmission and satellite technology that transmitted voices and data over long distances without requiring miles of copper cable. First, MCI targeted high-volume customers, such as government agencies and large companies, providing point-to-point service between customers' offices in major cities. Then MCI's leaders expanded by marketing their services to medium-sized and small businesses. Finally, MCI's leaders offered long distance service to residential customers, using microwave technology, after winning the right to connect to local telephone networks. Since AT&T had a monopoly granted by government legislation, MCI's leaders had to spend millions of dollars in legal costs to obtain regulatory and court permission to use the new technology. MCI's leaders were able to use new technical knowledge in ever-widening markets as AT&T's monopoly position was gradually dismantled by the courts and by legislation. Over a period of twenty-five years, MCI's revenues grew from less than $100 million to more than $10 billion, and AT&T's market share declined 25 percent. MCI's leaders had persisted with new knowledge, eventually shifting the distribution of competitive power, and revolutionizing the telecommunications industry.

"Knowledge New Only to Us"

Knowledge is the springboard to progress and competition. Existing knowledge makes firms productive and competitive today, but new knowledge determines how productive and competitive they will be tomorrow. To compete in tomorrow's markets, leaders seek two types of new knowledge: knowledge new to them but known to others, and knowledge new to them and also unknown to others. Leaders need different approaches to these two types of new knowledge. Effective leaders use a strategy of acquisition when knowledge is new to them but known to others. They search for existing knowledge by discussing their needs with their staff, observing what other firms are doing, hiring specialists or consultants, and searching the literature. Leaders often negotiate licenses or form joint ventures to get knowledge that already exists.

Leaders of Garret (name disguised), a company producing custom-built trucks, decided to enter the market for railroad passenger cars. Anticipating a need to replace aging rail cars and a growing global demand for passenger rail service, they set as their goal an increase in revenues and better use of their manufacturing resources. They did not have the engineering skills to design and test light-weight, high-speed rail cars, however. Garret's leaders initiated a global search for the knowledge they needed. Ultimately, they negotiated licenses to use the rail car designs of a European and an American company. After acquiring the new design knowledge through these licensing agreements, Garret's leader won several large rail car contracts, enabling the company to expand its manufacturing capability into a new field.

"Knowledge New to Everyone"

When knowledge is completely unknown—that is, new to a business's leaders as well as to everyone else—leaders must invest in a creation strategy. They need speculative thinking, imaginative leaps, and original insights to invent new knowledge. Creating new knowledge is an investment in people who make no contribution to current output. Creative people are not productive today, and often years pass and millions of dollars of additional investment are needed before the results of their creativity are converted into productive output. Effective leaders understand and accept that creating new knowledge is a risky investment. When creating a new drug or exploring for oil, for example, there is more than a 50 percent probability of failure. Leaders cannot know if any single investment in creating new knowledge will be successful, but effective leaders know that without such investments their company surely will not be successful tomorrow.

Routine Work Obstructs New Knowledge

Effective leaders carefully manage the relationship between creative people and production people. Creativity has an irregular rhythm and an unpredictable pace that conflicts with the steady routine of production. Routine is the enemy of new knowledge. People do not create new knowledge while working within the structured and tight time schedules that run factories.

Creating new knowledge is an excursion into the unknown. It requires freedom of thought and a willingness to question conventional wisdom, an ability to connect unrelated ideas, and the energy and motivation to concentrate on a problem for long periods, often to the exclusion of everything else. Creating new knowledge is different from acquiring new knowledge, and often the two tasks must be performed by different people. Acquiring new knowledge from others relies on negotiation skills, which are quite different from creative skills. Negotiation depends on sensitivity to others and on awareness of differences in power. Creativity depends on almost the opposite—an ability to concentrate on a problem without sensitivity to others and an indifference to power that might inhibit the pursuit of unconventional ideas. Leaders need to support studies of how their organizations stimulate, create, and absorb new knowledge and how they themselves create and absorb new knowledge. We further discuss the leader's contribution to creating new knowledge in chapter 4, "Learning and Knowledge."

Motivation and New Knowledge

Poor leaders want the benefits of new knowledge but not its dislocations. On the surface, acquiring new knowledge is deceptively straightforward—simply search for it, and obtain it from the people who have it. But acquiring new knowledge arouses mixed feelings. Poor leaders want to avoid appearing weak or dependent when they look for knowledge. At the same time, leaders who have new knowledge are often reluctant to share it, not wishing to see their power diminished or fearing they will not get credit for their contribution. As a result, leaders in the same company often conceal new knowledge from each other as diligently as they do from competing companies.

Resistance to New Knowledge

Effective leaders understand that acquiring new knowledge arouses conflicting forces of resistance and attraction. Resistance takes several forms. People may say that since the acquired knowledge is not theirs and they did not invent it, it is suspect. If they did not think of it, it cannot be relevant, or it won't work in their particular situation. Some people need to maintain an image of superiority, elevating their prestige by lowering their opinion of the person or organization that is the source of the new knowledge. Disdain prevents them from seeing the merits of someone else's new knowledge. If they admit that the new knowledge has merit, then they have to revise their self-images and raise their opinion of the source. Commenting on the resistance of General Motors's leaders to new knowledge, one executive said that the automobile industry was arrogant but that General Motors had made a science out of arrogance.

Poor leaders resist acquiring new knowledge, fearing that higher management will see them as inadequate and will replace them. Poor leaders put their self-interest above the interest of the organization, resisting new knowledge if they believe it will reduce their power. For example, poor leaders often resist upgrading information systems that would decrease their department's clerical work, reduce their staffs and diminish their power, even though the upgrade would make the organization more efficient and productive.

Attractions to New Knowledge

Effective leaders soften and redirect resistance by tapping the forces that attract people to new knowledge. Concern about falling behind competitors is probably the greatest force motivating leaders to obtain new knowledge. If the organization lags too far behind its competitors, it may not survive. Effective leaders dramatize this competitive lag, giving their employees personal experience with the superiority of competitors' products and services. They make the competitive gap come alive. Shortly after Lee Iacocca became CEO of Chrysler, for example, he hired Hans Matthias, a former Ford executive, to improve the quality of Chrysler's products, which many considered the worst in the industry. "[Matthias] would go to the plants every morning and pull five units off the line at random. Then he'd bring in a new Toyota and ask the guys to look at the difference. Pretty soon he had the foreman saying: 'Hey, our cars are really bad.'"[5] By demonstrating the competitive lag, rather than making speeches, Chrysler's leaders jarred the complacency of production people and increased their receptivity to new knowledge for improving quality.

The credibility or reputation of the source of the new knowledge is another important source of attraction. Effective leaders introduce new knowledge by pointing to the capable, forward-looking reputation of the source. They know that people with doubts resolve them in favor of new knowledge when they believe it comes from a highly credible source. For example, Jack Welch, CEO of General Electric, and General Electric's managers have achieved high credibility for their management skills. Motorola has achieved high credibility in the area of training and development skills. Leaders of other companies frequently visit, consult, and refer to GE and Motorola when introducing new knowledge about management and the development of managers.

People are attracted to new knowledge when they can use it to demonstrate their competence, increase their adaptability, and achieve a greater sense of competence. Having demonstrated the benefits of new knowledge, they are given greater responsibility, earn promotions, and increase their power and influence. Effective leaders use these attractions to offset resistance, offering more responsibility, jobs of greater scope, and higher compensation to motivate people to find and use new knowledge.

SUMMARY

Knowledge continually diffuses through organizations, where it often rests unused or is deliberately concealed until it is lost. Effective leaders understand that seeking improvement means learning. They help people find knowledge by continually reducing barriers to communication in organizational networks and by supporting teaching and learning based on relationships of constructive interdependence. Effective leaders find worthwhile knowledge by asking relevant, incisive questions in ways that encourage people to search and learn and systematically probe unexamined assumptions. They focus the search for knowledge by pinpointing the central problems facing the organization. They use questions to open new possibilities, and they continue their own learning so that they can frame better questions. Effective leaders puncture vague claims of synergy and avoid the lures of pseudoknowledge. They insist that reports organize knowledge so that it is relevant to the decisions that have to be made. They also use new knowledge to shift the level of competition, acquiring knowledge that is known to others and investing in creating knowledge that is unknown. They know that routine work obstructs creative thinking, so they don't load people with routine and then berate them for being uncreative. Finally, effective leaders know how to build the attractions and offset the resistance, to new knowledge.

Finding knowledge is an essential leadership skill. Converting knowledge into performance is an equally critical skill that we discuss in the next chapter.

3

From Knowledge to Action

Action transforms knowledge into products and markets. Without action, knowledge lies dormant, dispersed through the organization, waiting for leaders to channel it into goods and services. Effective leaders act by using knowledge to define goals and to mobilize people. They convert knowledge into business strategies, investment plans, and coordinated performance to make new, better, and less costly products and to provide employment to millions of people. Leaders' actions earn a return for risking capital and build a surplus that funds growth and cushions adversity. Before effective leaders can act, however, they must face, and overcome, many obstacles.

This chapter begins with a discussion of those obstacles—the conflicts that can obstruct action by pulling leaders in different directions. We then explore the risky attraction of status-quo leadership—sticking with what is done now and increasing the firm's vulnerability to competition. We look at hidden obstacles to action: success that breeds complacency, unfamiliarity that blocks action, a resistant organization culture, and negative attitudes toward technology. We examine how leaders design effective action by asking probing questions about how well decisions will fit customer needs, company goals, productivity, vision, and social obligation. We look at how leaders prepare people for action, and conclude with a discussion of linking knowledge to action.

ACTION DILEMMAS

When leaders want to act, they face three potentially immobilizing dilemmas. First there is options conflict. Leaders need to resolve conflicts, among organization factions over preferred solutions. For each problem, some people will favor radical change, some will favor small, incremental steps, and some, usually the largest group, will support the status quo. A fourth group may be noncommittal, preferring to sit on the fence waiting to see which way the leader leans and then tagging along.

There may also be conflicting views of the competition. Leaders need to appraise competitors' threats and estimate what actions competitors will take. Some subordinates and staff will see competitors as invincible warriors that the company dare not challenge or provoke; some will see them as dull-witted dinosaurs, ponderous, slow-moving, and easily outmaneuvered; a third faction will see competitors as wily foxes, clever and evasive but not infallible.

The third dilemma is vision conflict. Leaders need to formulate and continually revise their vision of the organization's goals and strategy in a changing environment. Some advisers will have dazzling visions of glorious opportunities with markets ripe for picking; others, firmly rooted in the present, will see no opportunities beyond what the firm is doing today; a third group may see a dire future with cutthroat competition and markets collapsing in a deluge of excess supply as demand dries up. Still others will vacillate, unable to imagine a link between today's reality and tomorrow's vision.

Effective leaders manage these action dilemmas: conflicts about options, differing estimates of competitors' strengths, and conflicting visions of the future. Leaders must harness the energy in these conflicts into a sensible, coherent course of action.

STATUS-QUO LEADERSHIP

Many leaders manage the dilemmas of action by maintaining the status quo. When conditions are stable for long periods, status-quo leaders can float on a wave of moderate prosperity. Their inaction, however, increases the risk that the firm's reputation will erode, causing customers to move to innovative competitors. Status-quo leaders postpone acting on knowledge until forced to; ultimately, when conditions turn against them, few of them have the acute sense of timing and the adaptability to make the radical changes needed to cope with the new circumstances. Such adaptability is usually contrary to their nature as status-quo leaders.

The Danger of Underestimating Competition

Status-quo leaders are inclined to underestimate competition. Competitors, a critical force beyond the leader's control, have their own visions, goals, and strategies. Status-quo leaders assume that competitors will allow them the luxury of postponing action on existing knowledge. Competitors, however, are not obligated to let status-quo leaders act at their convenience; indeed, they have just the opposite obligation.

In the 1970s the leaders of Ford were asked to approve a project to develop a minivan. Much had been learned about the characteristics that consumers wanted in a minivan since Volkswagen's introduction of a low-cost, lightweight, minimally equipped microbus that was popular with young families and college students during the 1960s. Ford auto designers knew from extensive marketing research that people did not like the high-step entry into minivans, nor did they want to straddle the drive-shaft hump running along the middle of the floor from the front-mounted engine to the rear-wheel drive.

Consumers with families, the target market for minivans, were especially concerned about the safety of the old VW microbus, which had mounted its engine in the rear to solve the drive-shaft problem. With the engine mounted in the rear or between the front seats as in commercial vans, the driver and the front passengers had no protection in the event of a head-on collision. These passengers would absorb the full impact of the crash, with potentially fatal results. All of this critical information was available to Ford designers, who had concluded that using a front-wheel drive, instead of a rear-wheel drive, would solve most of the problems.

Ford's leaders, and Henry Ford II in particular, however, rejected the project. They fired Harold Sperlich, a talented designer, who had zealously championed the minivan project and apparently had offended senior management (Sperlich was later hired by Chrysler). Ford's leaders had made a clear decision to continue the status quo. They would not convert existing knowledge into a product.

A year later, Lee Iacocca, President of Ford North American Operations and a major contender for the position of CEO, was also fired by Henry Ford II. Before leaving, however, he obtained permission to take a copy of the minivan marketing research, knowledge that Ford executives considered of little value. Iacocca became CEO of Chrysler, where he heroically cobbled together a package of creditor refinancings, labor givebacks, dealer supports, and government loan guarantees that rejuvenated the near-bankrupt company. In the midst of this financial and managerial bedlam, Iacocca reached down into the Chrysler organization for Sperlich. Together with Chrysler's design staff, they mounted the minivan project. The leaders of Chrysler, a faltering competitor of Ford with a small share of the market, had decided to act on existing knowledge, rather than stay with the status quo. Chrysler invested in minivan research and introduced the first successful front-wheel-drive minivan in 1983. Chrysler's minivans quickly displaced station wagons as the leading product in the market. Ford and GM, playing catch-up, belatedly introduced truck-like, rear-drive minivans that retained the handling characteristics and the unattractive features of commercial vans. GM did not introduce a front-drive minivan until 1989, and it was a fiasco, selling fewer than 82,000 units in 1993, after five years on the market. Ford's first minivan, a rear-drive vehicle introduced in 1985, reached peak sales of 188,000 units in 1988, and it did not introduce a front-drive minivan until 1992, almost ten years after Chrysler's first minivans appeared.

Ten years after introducing its first minivan, Chrysler still had about 50 percent of the minivan market. By 1994 minivans accounted for a quarter of all Chrysler vehicle sales and an estimated two thirds of its record profits of several billion dollars. The total U.S. market for minivans quadrupled from about 250,000 units in 1984 to more than 1 million by 1993. That year, Chrysler sold almost 570,000 vans. By the end of 1993, Chrysler had sold a total of 3.7 million minivans in the ten years since their introduction. In the same period, because their leaders had continually misjudged the market and offered minivans with inferior features, Ford and GM had each sold only 1.4 million units.[1] Iacocca's leadership had harnessed the action dilemmas of options conflict, estimates of competition, and vision conflicts. He had effectively acted on knowledge, achieving spectacular success in the minivan market and leaving Ford and GM leaders in the dust because of their status quo leadership.

Preparing Action Options

When effective leaders follow the status quo, they astutely invest in action options to supersede the status quo so they are ready when they have to react. Status quo leaders need to be prepared with action options and to know how to implement those options quickly when competitive conditions change. As one executive put it, "It wasn't raining when Noah built the ark." Effective leaders are often wary of status-quo leadership, however, preferring to avoid the severe handicap of trying to catch up after a late start.

HIDDEN OBSTACLES

Several factors can obstruct the leader's ability to act. Often hidden and elusive, these potential obstacles are complacency born of success, lack of familiarity with some aspects of the business, corporate culture, and fear of technology. Effective leaders analyze and integrate these factors into their action plans.

Success Breeds Complacency

A successful current strategy can be a major obstacle to action. Many leaders succumb to the narcotic effects of success. They assume that success anoints them with invincibility, permitting them to behave as if they and their organization are invulnerable to competitors. They become complacent leaders of the status quo, not realizing how restricted their vision is. On one hand, leaders of a successful firm with a large market share may resist introducing new products, fearing that they will displace sales of existing products. On the other hand, intoxicated with success, they may labor under the illusion that they will continue to dominate the market without being challenged by competitors.

The leaders of IBM dominated the market for large computers for decades and resisted introducing mini- and microcomputers that could do much of the work done by large central processing units. IBM relied on its reputation, its large installed base of equipment, and customer reluctance to switch to new suppliers. IBM's leaders were geared to making and selling a small number of large, high-margin, high-priced computers directly to business and to government buyers. They abhorred the prospect of selling hundreds of thousands of small, low-margin, low-priced computers through non-IBM dealers to small businesses and consumers. Their past success impeded their ability to act on existing knowledge. IBM continued to dominate the shrinking mainframe market but missed the explosive growth in mini- and microcomputers. As customers shifted to competitors' products, IBM's leaders paid dearly. The company took multibillion dollar writeoffs, and the price of its stock plunged by almost 67 percent. IBM's glorious half-century history of avoiding layoffs was shattered as the company let go tens of thousands of employees around the world. Success had blunted IBM's leaders' ability and willingness to act on existing knowledge.

A failing or mediocre strategy drives leaders to act on knowledge. The leaders of General Motors, for example, knew how to lower costs and improve quality for years, but they made little use of their knowledge. Only after suffering a prolonged loss of market share and huge losses did GM reluctantly concede that its status-quo, high-cost, low-quality strategy might not be working. Prior success had diminished GM's ability to adapt; its continuing reliance on what had become a failing strategy aroused the board of directors to replace the chairman. GM's leaders then finally began to act on their available knowledge, stemming GM's losses and painfully inching toward improved profitability, but with a much smaller market share.

Effective leaders enjoy and celebrate success, but they realize that success is fragile. They know that success requires continuous attention and adaptation if it is to be sustained. Despite success, effective leaders constantly coax, cajole, and challenge their people to reach for new knowledge, higher goals, and new levels of performance.

Lack of Familiarity Blocks Action

When the majority of headquarters leaders come from one division of a company, they often do not understand or see value in proposals originating in other divisions. The leaders of one multibillion-dollar conglomerate came from divisions that made and sold mechanical equipment for the construction, automotive, and agricultural markets. They were unfamiliar with the conglomerate's other divisions in the oil, gas, and financial services businesses, which had very different products, markets, strategies, and cultures. Headquarters leaders had difficulty understanding and assessing plans and proposals from the unfamiliar divisions. They also felt a strong allegiance to their former divisions and championed their interests, rather than the corporation's overall interests. As a result, headquarters systematically limited the resources available to the unfamiliar divisions, allocating the funds to the familiar but poorer-performing divisions. The financial services division did not get the support or investment it needed so it was sold at a loss of millions of dollars. The oil and gas divisions were eventually sold for billions of dollars to pay off the huge debts accumulated by the poorly performing equipment divisions. Leaders had diverted cash flow and liquidated the assets of unfamiliar divisions to support familiar but poor-performing businesses. They had been unwilling and unable to take the actions necessary to sustain unfamiliar but higher-performing businesses.

Effective leaders compensate for lack of familiarity by maintaining open access to people in all divisions. They rotate leaders into learning assignments in unfamiliar divisions and encourage the dissemination of best practices across divisions.

Corporate Culture Sets the Tone

Effective leaders assess how well their intended actions fit the organization's culture—the values and beliefs that people have about what is proper. If necessary, they take steps to change the culture to facilitate strategic actions.

The culture of Citibank, a major, money-center bank, historically emphasized the value of commercial clients and corporate banking. By the late 1970s, however, competition in commercial banking was intensifying. Corporations had become financially sophisticated and had begun to use foreign banks and nonbank sources to meet their financial needs. A crisis was also looming concerning Citibank's potentially troubled loans to less developed countries. Consumer banking, which presented a growing opportunity, was nonetheless disparaged.

To overcome the entrenched cultural resistance to the retail business, the bank's leaders organized consumer banking as a separate unit and hired a cadre of managers and marketers from consumer goods companies. Although these people had no background in banking, they came from cultures that highly valued understanding individual consumers and marketing to them. Marketing specialists became key members of management and all levels of management attended seminars in marketing financial services. Over a period of several years the leaders gradually changed the culture of the bank to one that could value and serve the individual consumer, as well as the corporate and institutional client. The change in culture enabled the bank to capture a major share of the retail business, and the retail business eventually earned profits that exceeded those of the commercial business, sustaining the bank through a period when it wrote off billions of dollars for losses in nonperforming foreign and commercial real estate loans.

Effective leaders understand that people can listen to knowledge, but they will not act on it if it violates their culture. Culture moderates the ability to act, so leaders systematically circulate among their people, learning their values and beliefs and shaping the organization's culture to facilitate strategic action.

Fear of Technology Can Block Innovation

A leader's ability to act on knowledge depends on people's attitudes toward technology. People have different views of how technology should contribute to work and life. They want to know if technology will free them to enjoy the good life or if it will doom them to a life of drudgery and insecure employment. Union members have different attitudes toward technology and work than do leaders, professional specialists, and nonunion members. These differences affect the leader's ability to use existing technical knowledge.

Leaders of a major newspaper knew about "cold type" technology for years, but the printers' union would not allow them to use it. With "cold type" technology, printers could use computers to compose articles and full pages of a newspaper, much like the word processing and desktop publishing that are routinely done on personal computers. Cold type was much faster, cleaner, and more flexible than the existing "hot type" linotype process. It was also much less costly and required less skilled labor.

Although the newspaper's advertising volume and circulation had been growing, rising costs had eaten away its profitability. For years there were grievances, strikes, and physical violence. Finally, after acrimonious negotiation and threats to close the newspaper, management was able to convert its technical knowledge into action. In return for the right to freely use the new technology, the company agreed to lifetime job security for the printers. Attrition would occur only through retirement and voluntary separation. The company leaders got the full benefits of cold type only after they had found a way to deal with the printers' fears of being displaced by the new technology.

Introducing new technology is a major competitive weapon, so effective leaders win the commitment of their workforce to the planned introduction of technology. Leaders are able to communicate the dire competitive consequences and the threat to employment if workers block the use of new technology while competitors can freely introduce it. This communication takes place over a long period in a cooperative relationship. Together, leaders and workers plan a phased introduction, with retraining and minimal displacement of the work-force. On the other hand, if the firm's labor relations history has been antagonistic, then effective leaders must confront the harsh knowl-edge that the firm and its ability to provide employment will be doomed if workers succeed in blocking the use of new technology while other companies use it.

DESIGNING ACTIONS

Moving from knowledge to action is a conversion process, similar to converting latent electrical energy into productive work by means of an electric motor. Leaders would prefer rational, well-thought-out conversion decisions, but when little is known or controllable, effec-tive leaders use questions to feel their way. They probe ambiguity, continually asking questions and clarifying assumptions. We thus come back to one of the leader's key skills, one that we introduced in Chapter 2—asking questions to illuminate knowledge and action.

Framing Questions

Effective leaders systematically analyze conversion decisions by asking penetrating questions. They continually probe concepts and examine key assumptions at critical points in a plan of action. The following questions, and their derivative questions, are examples of the probes effective leaders use when moving from knowledge to action.

• *What customer's needs and wants does this action attempt to satisfy?* Who is "the customer"? What are his relevant needs and wants? How may customers and competitors change before the firm acts?

Lee Iacocca's leadership of Chrysler's sweep of the minivan mar-ket stemmed from uncannily accurate answers to similar questions about customers. Chrysler targeted a life-stage group—the young family—at a time when this view of customers was in its infancy in the auto industry. The prevailing psychodemographic concept of sta-tion wagon customers was "conservative, middle-aged, and middle income." Chrysler's leaders identified the needs of the target cus-tomers (young families) for space, safety, and convenience for chil-dren and adults. Chrysler then produced a minivan that designers derisively called a box on wheels but that, better than any other vehi-cle, met the customer's primary need—utility. By recognizing that utility should take precedence over style in a consumer vehicle, Iacocca and Chrysler's other leaders departed radically from the indus-try's common wisdom: "Style sells cars, not utility." Iacocca also cor-rectly anticipated the slow reaction of Ford and the diminished adaptability of General Motors. Chrysler's competitors were still trying to get to the starting gate when Chrysler was already halfway down the track. Chrysler's leaders had asked and answered the questions about customers superbly.[2]

• *How will this action contribute to the organization's goals?* Can leaders define the organization's goals clearly? Can leaders ensure that they and workers know and agree with the goals? Can leaders accurately predict the outcomes of the proposed actions? Can leaders foresee how each outcome will contribute to each goal?

Poor leaders formulate broad, vague goals that, under a flimsy rationale of synergy, permit a string of imprudent, uncoordinated actions. Leaders of American Express, basically a charge card and travel services company, for example, proposed a goal of becoming a "financial" supermarket." Over a period of several years they acquired an insurance company, an investment banking company, a retail brokerage company, and an overseas international bank. They had great difficulty understanding and integrating these businesses and eventually, because of the corporation's poor, uncoordinated performance, downsized, sold, or spun off each of the acquisitions.

The connection between AmEx leader's ambiguous goals and their actions was tenuous and unclear. The phrase "financial supermarket" was catchy but vague. The idea of one-stop shopping, as in a food supermarket, was never realized because AmEx was unable to integrate its services sufficiently to convince customers to use more than one or two of the available services. There were also serious, unresolved internal obstacles. Many of the acquired businesses catered primarily to commercial customers and large institutions, not to individual consumers. Leaders of these businesses had little interest in individual consumers or in each other's target customers. There was also concern that sharing customers across businesses would confuse and complicate the primary selling relationships.

AmEx leader's goals had been so broad that they amounted to a hunting license to acquire anything remotely related to financial services. In practice, the leaders were pursuing unbridled growth. They had answered poorly the questions about predicting outcomes and how these outcomes contributed to the company's goals. Ultimately, the leadership was replaced, and the new CEO, Harvey Golub, readdressed the question of goals. He set the clear, limited goal of strengthening the company's core business, travel-related services (charge cards, travelers' checks, travel arrangements), rebuilding the American Express brand, and reducing, divesting, or spinning off all unrelated, poor-performing businesses. With that goal he began the slow process of returning the company to profitability.[3]

• *What is the productivity and cost efficiency of the proposed action?* What is the long-term forecast for costs and financial results? What will be the relevant developments in technology, competitor behavior, and legal regulation? What is the economic outlook and how will it affect results? Answering these questions requires that leaders make a giant leap of faith. Effective leaders usually have the same data about future trends as their competitors, but effective leaders seem to have two remarkable characteristics: the wisdom to interpret information correctly and the courage to march boldly into the future.

We return again to Iacocca and the Chrysler minivan. When Iacocca became CEO of Chrysler in 1978, the company was in desperate financial condition, within a hair's breadth of bankruptcy. Chrysler, however, had the minivan's critical component: the front-wheel-drive engine and transmission that it was using in Dodge and Plymouth subcompacts. Chrysler's designers, working with Sperlich, the former Ford executive who had been fired for pushing the minivan concept, combined Sperlich's and Iacocca's concepts with Chrysler's knowledge of front-wheel drives.

Developing the minivan and modernizing Chrysler's plant in Ontario to build minivans cost $700 million, a staggering commitment for Iacocca to make when the company was about to collapse under the weight of creditor defaults. Iacocca had approached Volkswagen to help finance the minivan's development and jointly produce the vehicle, but he was turned down, so he scavenged the funds by postponing the development of other vehicles. Iacocca's answer to the productivity questions was a resounding yes—the minivan project would be a worthwhile investment, in his vision of future developments. But the saga does not end here.

By the end of the minivan's first year, 1984, sales had grown to 190,000 units. This was far beyond Chrysler's most optimistic predictions, pushing the Ontario plant to operate at close to full capacity. Chrysler executives vividly recall the heated controversy that followed. It was a classic example of the option conflicts and the vision differences in the action dilemmas discussed at the beginning of this chapter. The question facing Chrysler's leaders was: Should Chrysler invest hundreds of millions of dollars to expand production of minivans, its new, untried product? It would cost up to a half billion dollars to equip another plant to make an additional 250,000 minivans. Would this be a productive investment, a wise use of Chrysler's limited funds? Most Chrysler executives, including Sperlich, opposed the investment. They felt it was too risky, given Chrysler's shaky financial condition. If the minivan was a flash in the pan and sales plateaued, as many executives feared, then Chrysler would be left with a huge inventory of unsold minivans and a useless plant at a time when Chrysler could not absorb a severe financial loss. Iacocca persisted and prevailed. His projections and estimates were prescient. Thanks to Iacocca's answers to the productivity questions in 1984, Chrysler was still out front ten years later riding its minivan caravan while competitors were jockeying for a distant second place.[4]

• *How does the proposed action fit into the organization's plans?* What are the organization's plans? Can leaders clearly describe the firm's business, what they want it to be, and its competitors? How well will the expected outcomes fit the organization's plans? Leaders know that today's actions usually conform well with near-term plans in familiar situations, but when leaders depart from familiar businesses and conditions, they enter uncharted waters. Poor leaders start with a plan but get distracted and lose sight of their core business.

Leaders of Sears Roebuck, the large national retail firm, acquired a stock brokerage firm, Dean Witter Reynolds, and a real estate brokerage company, Coldwell Banker, in 1981. Sear's leaders' vision was that the acquired firms would round out their financial services strategy. Sears would increase Dean Witter's sales of securities and Coldwell's sales of real estate by giving them access to customer traffic in its vast retail store system, as had been done years ago with Allstate. Skeptical Wall Street wags dubbed the plan "socks and stocks."

When the projected growth in securities and real estate sales to customers in retail stores was not realized, the store's financial centers were cut back. Sear's leaders, however, were so focused on the new ventures and on finding synergies with the acquired financial service businesses that they paid insufficient attention to the firm's core retail business—no one was minding the store. The retail business floundered, losing market share and position to nimble, aggressive competitors such as Wal-Mart, Kmart, Toys "R" Us, and Home Depot. Sear's market share dropped 25 percent, slipping from first to third position in the retail industry. Sear's leaders eventually spun off the Dean Witter financial services group and sold the Coldwell real estate business. They essentially returned the company to retailing, where it had been years earlier, but in a much weaker condition. To get costs under control and improve earnings, Sears eliminated 48,000 jobs to reduce costs by $2.5 billion within two years.

Sears's leaders' plans had not sufficiently considered how the Dean Witter and Coldwell acquisitions would divert energy from the retailing business and change the fundamental character of Sears. For years, Allstate insurance and the acquisitions contributed earnings that masked the retail operation's declining profits. As a result, Sears leaders could postpone confronting the poor performing retail business, which at one time had contributed 50 percent of Sears profits.[5] Ultimately, Sear's leaders had to come back to the basic planning questions: What is this firm's business? What should it be?

• *What are the human and social effects of the proposed actions?* Can leaders define and measure the human and social cost of the action? Do they wish to consider the human and social consequences of their decisions?

Leaders of a chemical company decided to invest in plants to manufacture plastic pipe. After years of complaints and legal proceedings, it was found that workers exposed to the chemical fumes and plastic dust in the company's factories had a higher than normal incidence of several malignancies. The company's leaders had not measured levels and effects of exposure, had not provided respiratory equipment to workers, and had not installed adequate ventilation systems until regulatory agencies imposed fines and threatened to close the plants for long-standing violations of health and safely regulations.

Effective leaders consider the human and social costs of their actions. They find ways to measure and mitigate those costs. They do not delay corrective action until forced to act by litigation or by government intervention.

In summary, when designing actions, effective leaders ask: What customer needs will this action satisfy? How will it contribute to company goals? How will it affect productivity? How well does it fit into overall plans? What are its human and social costs?

PREPARING FOR ACTION

Action that fits the situation and wins commitment requires preparation. Effective leaders continually invest in developing themselves and their people, preparing for action through rotational assignments, simulations, and opportunities to relearn the customer's view.

Rotation

Like living in a foreign country to learn its language and culture, rotation across assignments and divisions is one of the most effective leadership development methods. It works well because adults learn primarily from their personal experience of hands-on doing and observing rather than from passively listening to lectures. Rotation prepares leaders and their staffs for action in several ways. It exposes them to different approaches to converting knowledge to action, giving them a repertoire of leadership knowledge and skills. It allows them to experience firsthand how actions in one department affect other departments and to build relationships with people in different departments who become part of their network for solving problems in the future.

In a food processing company, for example, leaders regularly rotate through manufacturing, marketing, and research. Rotation has enabled leaders to create and market new food products and upgrade slow-moving products much faster than their competitors. In an electronics company, product design managers and manufacturing managers rotate across their departments, greatly improving product quality and lowering manufacturing costs. In a consumer goods company, marketing research managers and sales managers routinely rotate into each other's area. Rotation has increased the relevance of information from marketing research and has improved the ability of sales to use research information productively. Rotation prepares people for action by reducing the barriers and boundary conflicts between departments that can obstruct leaders' efforts to convert knowledge to action.

Simulations

People usually see actions from the point of view of their department or specialty. Many actions, however, such as pricing, product design, and capital investments, cut across departments and specialties. In complex, interdependent organizations, leaders need to understand how their actions affect other departments. Top leaders constantly struggle against suboptimization—the tendency for leaders to do what is best for their department without regard for possible adverse effects on the performance of others.

Companies cannot rotate every leader into other departments to increase their appreciation of departmental interdependence, so other leadership development methods are necessary. Simulations are one such method. In a simulation, leaders take roles in different departments in a speeded-up replication of decisions that ordinarily would take months or years. Simulations help leaders quickly see and appreciate how an apparently simple action in one department can precipitate a complex string of problems and adjustments for other departments.

A major automobile company, for example, puts engineering, manufacturing, and marketing leaders into a five-day simulation that reproduces the interdepartmental repercussions of apparently minor design changes. Leaders experience how minor proposals such as decreasing car weight by fifty pounds, increasing engine power 5 percent, or adding two inches to rear passenger leg room sends shock waves of unforeseen problems ricocheting through the organization. Decreasing a car's weight, for example, requires changes in braking, steering, and suspension systems that alter the car's handling and feel. Increasing an engine's power affects these systems and also requires changes in engine mounts and chassis strength, which increases costs. Adding two inches can change the wheel base, the entire body frame, glass areas, and upholstery. In the simulation, leaders experience in quick time the problems of performing their own assignments, trying to coordinate with other departments to adjust for supposedly small design changes while struggling to meet deadlines for producing and marketing a new model. Participants come away from the simulation with a much greater appreciation of how design changes affect different departments and a clearer picture of how people can help or hinder each other. Leaders and their staffs are better prepared to take actions that improve quality and reduce completion time when working on model changes and new car projects.

Relearning the Customer's View

Effective leaders make sure they know how customers view and use a product before converting knowledge to action. Poor leaders say that they know their customers, but this is often self-serving rhetoric. For years in one automobile company, for example, few, if any, leaders ever purchased or serviced their automobiles in the outlets their customers used. As one executive said, "One of the perquisites of being in this business is that you avoid those hassles and inconveniences." His remark revealed, more than he realized, his condescending view of customers and lack of interest in knowing what it meant to be a consumer of his company's products. Despite the talk about getting close to the customer, leaders still need to relearn what it means to be a consumer.

A motorcycle company, for example, requires its leaders to be "mystery shoppers," continually learning and reviewing what it means to be a customer. Senior executives periodically shop their products and competing products at different outlets. They then meet to analyze what they learned from their different experiences, continually updating their views of customers and distribution channels. In a laundry products company, few, if any, leaders have ever done their own laundry. They have no experience using their products as consumers use them. The company requires leaders, at all levels up to the president, periodically to relearn how consumers use laundry products. At least once a year, each leader dons casual clothes and, with a marketing researcher, spends a day visiting and doing laundry with sample consumers in the consumer's home.

These relearning experiences shatter many myths about how convenient it is to use a product or how well it works. Products, markets, and competition change, offering consumers new options. Effective leaders continually relearn personally what it means to be a customer. They diligently seek realistic, up-to-date, personal knowledge about being a customer to prepare themselves and their staffs for taking action.

LINKING KNOWLEDGE TO ACTION

When leaders act on knowledge, they run into delays and errors during implementation and deal with inadequate resources and unforseen bottlenecks. To head off and solve these problems, leaders link knowledge and action by soliciting the early involvement of people, managing boundary conflicts, using radial organization, and encouraging problem-centeredness.

Encouraging Early Staff Involvement

Leaders want knowledge to flow smoothly into action, but linear thinking and a desire to suppress differences can get in the way. When leaders want to introduce a new product or change a manufacturing method, they design a plan and then selectively involve people at different stages. Decisions about whom to involve, and when, are critical. Leaders know that the later they involve a person, the less useful is her input. Prior decisions freeze more and more of the project, reducing flexibility and decreasing the choices available for people later in the chain.

Effective leaders know that in a speeded-up, competitive environment they need to involve people with different perspectives in the early stages of a design, marketing, or manufacturing project. Cross-functional teams greatly shorten the time from concept to introduction of a new product. Automobile companies used to take three to five years to design and introduce a new product. Now, with cross-functional teams, some do it in less than two years. Computer companies used to introduce higher-performing models in five years, then in three years, now many companies can field new models in less than a year.

Effective leaders form design, manufacturing, or marketing teams comprising people with different perspectives from the start. Poor leaders, however, form new-product teams that include only people concerned with engineering design. They then sequentially hand the project to manufacturing, marketing, and accounting. Typically, in this sequential process, manufacturing finds that it can't make the product unless critical parts are redesigned, marketing can't sell it because it omits important features that competitors already have, and accounting says it costs too much to be sold at the low price marketing has set. So the project recycles over and over again, kicked back and forth across the specialties, as each introduces new problems in each cycle. The process results in debilitating delays, incurs enormous costs, and undermines morale. Effective leaders know that to compete in a rapidly changing environment, teams need to include all relevant points of view from the outset if they are not to be blindsided by major oversights. Leaders need people who think early, continually, and together about manufacturing and costs, financing and pricing, distribution and promotion, consumer use and product repair, and product disposal and environmental impact.

Managing Boundary Conflicts

When leaders act, they increase stress in the organization. Leaders want tasks performed and work coordinated. They want deadlines met and costs controlled. Converting knowledge to action increases stress at departmental boundaries and precipitates conflict. Effective leaders facilitate action by managing these boundary conflicts.

Leaders know that there is a subtle but crucial mental boundary separating operating people from knowledge people. The people who "do" are in one group, and the people who "know" are in another group. "Staff" people are separate from, and loosely coupled to, "line" people. Functional experts, project managers, and brand managers are ambiguously connected to operating managers. Tension occurs at these boundaries when leaders initiate action. Line and staff, project managers and brand managers continually battle over who has final authority to decide and act. Effective leaders, however, do not let territorial disputes determine actions. They focus on the critical issues: What are the right questions? What are the best answers for the organization? Poor leaders, however, get trapped in boundary conflicts.

The Coordinator

Some organizations appoint a coordinator, liaison agent, or integrator to manage boundary conflicts. The person in this position needs to understand how to link knowledge to action or else she may become an additional obstacle. Incompetent coordinators are ignored or, at best, humored. Their poor leadership, however, complicates and ultimately can stop the conversation of knowledge to action.

A large research and development company, for example, appointed a "coordinator" with formal authority over a research group and a product development group. Each group attempted to form a coalition with the coordinator against the other group. To maintain harmony, the coordinator gave each group the impression that he was on its side. His behavior confirmed the idea that there were "sides". Each group increased its intransigence, believing that it was simply a matter of getting the coordinator to "straighten out" the other group.

To extricate himself, the coordinator practically eliminated all meetings between the groups, ordering all communication to go directly to him. He would decide how to resolve all differences. Both groups became frustrated and angry. They communicated only the information he requested. Frequently, this information was not adequate or relevant for the action decisions that had to be made. Coordination deteriorated with the decline in interdepartmental communication. New products were delayed, and several companies that had contracted for research withheld payments, complaining that results did not meet the terms of their contracts. Instead of linking knowledge to action, the coordinator had escalated conflicts and then became an additional obstacle. Effective leaders are wary of appointing coordinators, but when they do, they monitor them carefully. Leaders know that instead of facilitating the linking of knowledge to action, unskilled coordinators escalate boundary conflicts, forcing decisions to be made with inadequate information and lowering performance.

Using Radial Organization

A radial organization is a temporary, ad-hoc group of people brought together by and radiating from a person with an urgent problem. The problem requires knowledge, skills, and coordination across different departments and several levels of an organization. A radial organization gives leaders and their people direct, rapid access to the knowledge they need enabling them to respond quickly to problems that are ordinarily lost in the organizational maze. When a product or marketing plan does not work as planned, the problem is usually referred up the chain of command. The formal organization, however, is often a maze of dead-end delays and walls of self-justification. Instead of helping, it obstructs the leader's access to knowledge.

At one machinery manufacturer, when production had difficulty assembling parts that according to engineering design should have fit together, the problem was passed up the authority ladder in manufacturing. Leaders scrupulously observed the chain of command, solving the problem was secondary. Issues moved up the manufacturing chain of command, across to engineering, then down in engineering. Simple difficulties escalated into complicated political battles, and solutions languished while lower-level leaders defended their behavior to superiors. Manufacturing and engineering became intransigent enemies, each overreacting to legitimate inquiries as if they were being accused of gross incompetence.

It was difficult to convert knowledge to action. Manufacturing costs were high because of spoilage, scrap, excess work in process, and low-quality output. Manufacturing and engineering resigned themselves to these conditions, saying it was all in a day's work. Leaders continually skirmished about production problems and ponderously ground out solutions. They wasted energy running in and out of dead ends in the organizational maze they had created. Financially, the company struggled along as a marginal performer. Its leaders would have been much more productive if they had allowed production foremen to call a meeting of people from engineering, quality control, purchasing, and accounting to deal with problems as they arose.

Effective leaders understand and use radial organizations to offset the debilitating effects of the hierarchical maze. In a radial organization, when a leader has a problem whose solution depends on knowledge held by other people, the leader can consult and meet the others directly, regardless of where they are in the organization. Leaders are not forced to pass issues up and down the chain of command when they can solve problems simply and quickly by direct consultation. The machinery manufacturer's production foremen needed a radial organization to deal with their problems. They did not need more hierarchy, a new organization structure, a coordinator, or stricter adherence to the chain of command. Radial organizations help leaders convert distributed knowledge into action by circumventing bureaucratic drag; they let leaders focus on the problem rather than on a structure.

Encouraging Problem-Centeredness

Effective leaders use radial organizations because they are problem-centered rather than territory- or structure-centered. They reward problem solving and results, rather than preservation of territory and obedience to structure. This is not to say that structure is unimportant, but when structure impedes problem solving, then leaders should give precedence to the problem.

Effective leaders focus on solving problems expeditiously. In a fast-changing environment leaders need rapid access to knowledge so that they can take timely action. Effective leaders move across functional boundaries and levels of authority to bring the best thinking to bear on a problem without undermining the structure or getting trapped in territorial battles. When effective leaders sense that their knowledge of what is happening in design, manufacturing, or marketing is deficient, they dip down into the organization and move across departmental boundaries. They initiate joint action and solve problems by working directly with their people. They use radial organization to focus on a problem-centered approach for linking knowledge to action.

SUMMARY

Effective leaders manage the dilemmas of action by harnessing option conflicts, different estimates of competition, and vision conflicts. They understand the comfort of status-quo leadership, but, unlike poor leaders, they foresee and avoid the destructive results of resting on the status quo. They lead their organizations through the traps of complacency, lack of familiarity, resistant corporate culture, and fear of technology, which impede action.

Effective leaders design actions by posing critical questions: How well do actions meet customer needs? Fit company goals? Improve productivity? Fit overall plans? Meet social obligations? Effective leaders are relentless in finding superior answers to these questions. Poor leaders neglect these questions or develop superficial answers. Effective leaders prepare themselves and their people for action through rotation, simulations, and relearning the customer view. Effective leaders link knowledge to action by seeking the early involvement of people with a wide range of relevant knowledge, managing boundary conflicts and paying close attention to the competence of coordinators, and using radial organization to solve problems that would otherwise disappear in the organizational maze. Finally, they focus on problem-centeredness and demonstrate this in their own behavior.

Organizations and boards of directors are less and less willing to pay the costly price of poor leadership. They demand that leaders learn to adapt and use knowledge, which is the topic we discuss in Chapter 4.

4

Learning and Knowledge

The new competitive battlefield is knowledge, and the leader's weapons are concepts and insights. To succeed, leaders need to be life-long learners who skillfully and continually encourage their people to learn. Competitor's attacks start with ideas, so effective leaders know that to forge ahead they must constantly stimulate the learning and knowledge that will lead to tomorrow's superior products and services. Effective leaders nurture and manage intellectual capital because in the end that is what determines the quality of the organization's physical and financial capital. Without creative insights and knowledge skills, as GM and IBM discovered during the 1980s, even the best equipment, supported by large pools of capital, will be defenseless against wise, nimble competitors.

Learning and knowledge are critical assets that concern effective leaders, and they are even starting to affect accounting practices. A proxy for the value of learning and knowledge occasionally appears on a balance sheet under the euphemism "goodwill," an ambiguous, catch-all account for the premium a buyer pays for the "going-business" value of a company in excess of its book value. Accounting is beginning to sense that ignoring an organization's learning and knowledge omits a serious asset—its intellectual capital. Accounting societies have convened task forces to study the problem: "The components of cost in a product today are largely R&D, intellectual assets, and services. The old accounting system which tells us cost of material and labor, isn't applicable."[1] Some day, accountants may agree on how to value intellectual capital, but, in the meantime leaders need to manage learning and use intellectual capital now.

This chapter looks at the leader's new role—helping people to learn by getting the organization into a learning groove. It then discusses the leader's critical function of framing the demand for knowledge, because the leader's demands largely determine what people will learn. Next, it examines the need for the leader to provide the special conditions that support learning—supporting creative deviance, mastering existing knowledge, protecting unstructured time, and encouraging new perspectives. Finally, it looks at the need for leaders to learn and renew their own knowledge if they are to avoid the knowledge obsolescence that undermines their organization.

THE LEARNING GROOVE

Effective leaders exercise people's intellectual muscles, continually stretching them to reach for new opportunities that require new knowledge. Leaders know that each increment of learning increases the organization's flexibility. Effective leaders guide the organization into a "learning groove," making adaptability second nature.

Banc One, a superregional bank, began in the late nineteenth century as City National Bank, an unpretentious local bank in Columbus, Ohio.[2] Around 1960 new leaders propelled the bank into a groove of spectacular learning and growth. The new leaders set out to make Banc One an adaptive, nimble Tiffany of retail banking. They hired the best people, delegated, innovated, and remade the bank into a learning organization. The first task was to learn about the bank's customers. John G. McCoy, the bank's president and later its CEO, created a new advertising department, directing its newly hired leader, John Fisher, who was not a banker, to find out what customers wanted. Fisher helped the bank's leaders translate customer knowledge into superior service and create a new image that grew deposits from $140 million to more than $400 million in less than a decade.

The next task was to learn about technology and internal operations. The bank's leaders set aside 3 percent of annual earnings to study the use of technology to improve customer service and bank efficiency. They introduced one of the earliest versions of the automated teller machine (ATM) in 1969, and by 1972 the bank was the first in the United States to have ATMs in every branch. Continuing to push learning, the bank's leaders were the first outside California to introduce credit cards, doing so in 1966. They used their knowledge to sell data processing services to other banks. By 1989 they were a major data service center, processing 3.2 million of their own cards and another 3.5 million for third parties.

Using what they had learned about technology and service, Banc One's leaders were ready to stretch again. In 1976 they took a path-breaking step that put them in the middle of the financial services revolution. The bank became the processor for Merrill Lynch's new Cash Management Account (CMA); customers could access their brokerage account funds directly by using a debit card or checks provided by Banc One. This pioneering alliance hastened a revolution in products and delivery that changed the boundaries of the U.S. financial services industry. The bank's leaders continued to push the learning frontier. They established an innovation group outside the bank's mainstream operations to work on new ideas such as toll-free twenty-four-hour telephone service, improved checking and deposit service at the bank's many affiliates, and home banking through personal computers and telephone.

The leaders transformed Banc One from a modest, single-state bank into a superregional bank. Their learning and adaptability were so effective that they successfully integrated more than forty acquisitions between 1969 and 1989. Regardless of its financial attractiveness, an acquisition was made only if Banc One felt that the new affiliate had high-quality, adaptive leaders. Banc One considered leader learning so vital that some acquisitions were made when the financials were not highly attractive but the leaders were. The leaders of each acquisition, with rare exception, were kept in place to manage and operate their units. Each acquisition was assigned a "mentor" bank of similar size and market; leaders of the mentor bank and its departments transferred their learning and knowledge by visiting the acquired bank several days a month, and leaders of the acquired bank in turn visited the mentor bank and other banks in the Banc One system. Banc One also installed its comprehensive information and performance measurement systems in each new affiliate so that the affiliate's leaders could compare their bank's performance to that of other banks in the system and learn from the high performers. Banc One's leaders were exceptionally successful in helping new affiliates learn and adapt; on average, they increased acquisitions' return on assets a remarkable 66 percent.

Starting with assets of less than $2.8 billion in 1979, Banc One's leaders successfully grew the bank to more than $26.5 billion by 1989. They increased net income at more than 18 percent compounded annually during those ten years. By 1989 the bank had 17,000 employees, fifty-six affiliate banks, and close to 600 offices. Banc One had the highest return on average assets of the country's fifty largest banks in 1988, making it by that measure an outstandingly profitable performer. The leaders had also endowed Banc One with a deep pool of leadership talent distributed throughout the entire bank. Banc One's leaders had moved the bank into a learning groove, making it one of the most productive and profitable banks in the country.

DEMAND GUIDES LEARNING

Effective leaders ask for knowledge that stimulates and guides learning; poor leaders ask for reports on stale facts and little more. Asking for knowledge is an essential part of the leader's new role, because the knowledge that leaders demand determines what people learn and discover. People may occasionally stumble on new knowledge by accident, but most learning is driven by what leaders request.

There are two theories about how new knowledge is discovered—serendipity and demand. The theory of serendipity says that new knowledge comes from intelligent insight into chance events; for example, Charles Goodyear discovered vulcanization after accidentally dropping rubber into a fire, and Alexander Fleming discovered penicillin after hearing his fellow researchers complain about an impurity that was destroying their bacterial samples. Demand theory, in contrast, says that new knowledge comes from a systematic search and analysis done in response to a specific demand for knowledge; for example, people learned how to design orbiting spacecraft, moonlanders, and supersonic aircraft because that's what their leaders demanded.

Serendipity was an attractive explanation when science was less advanced, education was limited, and there were few large organizations to support major research projects. Until the early 1900s, people usually worked in small companies or alone. They had little education, few resources, and limited capital. Knowledge was quite primitive, and much of it resulted from trial-and-error efforts that had little theoretical foundation, so when a person learned something new it seemed accidental. There will continue to be occasions when an individual working alone suddenly sees knowledge that has eluded others. In a complex knowledge society, however, demand theory more accurately describes reality. This means that the leader's demand for knowledge becomes the principle determinant of what people learn and discover.

Leaders face a difficult question: What new knowledge do they want? There is much they do not know. Given limited resources, what do they want to know? People find mainly the knowledge leaders demand, and little more, so the leader's decision regarding what knowledge to search for is critical. How leaders define a problem or an issue becomes the frame that determines what knowledge people will find. Effective leaders select and frame problems appropriately.

The leaders of AT&T, for example, demanded a system that would obviate a projected insatiable need for human operators as telephone traffic grew. AT&T foresaw the explosive growth of the information industry and the globalization of business. The leaders' demands resulted in a system of direct, touch-tone dialing, area codes, country codes, and switching centers that permitted callers to reach parties around the world without the need for a human intermediary. Without the knowledge that led to these developments, phone companies would have had to interview a million or more people a year to hire enough operators for the projected growth in traffic. Even with more favorable assumptions, the interviewing, record keeping, and management of so many people would have been overwhelming. By properly framing their demand, AT&T leaders guided the learning that obtained the knowledge for a quantum jump in system capacity and efficiency. People found knowledge that eliminated the insatiable need for human operators because that's what AT&T's leaders asked for.

Poor leaders select and frame problems poorly. They demand tangential knowledge, knowledge that has lost its purpose. The leaders of Polaroid, for example, demanded a system for self-developing motion-picture film just as electronic camcorders were entering the market. Eventually Polaroid developed such a system, but it was obsolete before it left the laboratory. Leaders had misdirected learning. The company lost millions of dollars in this ill-fated venture, and its leaders, including the company's founder, were replaced. Polaroid's leaders had pursued a hobby, self-developing film, without regard for the desires of its customers and the actions of their competitors.

Effective leaders realize that they are responsible for what their organization learns. What leaders demand, and how they frame those demands, determines what people learn. Treating that responsibility casually can cost the organization its future.

CONDITIONS FOR LEARNING

When leaders pursue learning and search for knowledge, they lose the stability, order, and predictability they rely on in their daily work. Instead, they enter the amorphous, unpredictable world of insight and discovery. Learning—that is, creating, absorbing, and mastering new knowledge and skills—is a delicate, highly variable process that requires special conditions. To encourage learning and adaptivity, effective leaders initiate and support the following special conditions: creative deviance, mastery of existing knowledge, unstructured time, and new perspectives.

Creative Deviance

To create new knowledge, such as new products or ways of improving current performance, means to depart—often radically—from conventional knowledge. People have to sift through many half-formed concepts and irrelevant ideas before they find an occasional nugget of worthwhile knowledge. Ventures in imaginative thought depart from what is known and accepted, they must, if they are to be useful additions to what is known.

Effective leaders understand that the creative process differs from its output, the creative product. The process flourishes in a climate that encourages deviant ideas. They also understand that many ideas will be generated but few will pass the test of rigorous critical analysis. Effective leaders are not perturbed by false starts. They are prepared for vigorous argument today in favor of concepts that may be discarded as worthless tomorrow. They do not expect the orderliness and predictability of routine operations.

3M and Creative Deviance

The inventors of the "Post-it," the notepaper that sticks to a page and peels off without tearing the page or the note, had the benefit of leaders who encouraged creative deviance. The Minnesota Mining and Manufacturing Corporation (3M), with sales of $14 billion in 1993, has introduced more than 60,000 new products and markets as many as 100 new products a year. The company's output spans a wide range of products, including pressure-sensitive tapes, adhesives, abrasives, electrical products, photographic supplies, building materials, medical and dental products, and office supplies.[3] The leaders at 3M support creative deviance throughout the company. Leaders encourage and sustain a powerful culture for creative thinking. At the center are product champions, or advocates for new ideas, some of whom are legendary heroes in 3M's history. They carry an imaginary banner—"ardore est quotidiam" (to be a zealot is normal). These champions are fanatically dedicated to ideas that most people would think are deviant and even crazy. The leaders of 3M understand that champions are monomaniacs in love with a concept, tenaciously persisting with understated grace, keeping a spark of interest alive for years, despite organizational indifference and resistance. They know what it means to be a champion, because practically every leader has been a champion. By now, it is second nature for leaders to accept, respect, and nurture creative deviance. Everyone one meets at 3M is a potential product champion. In this culture, not to challenge and stretch knowledge seems abnormal.

The company has a creative-deviance policy that allows scientists to use 15 percent of their time, almost one day a week, to pursue interesting personal projects outside their regular assignments. Leaders periodically review scientists' notebooks. Some leaders may be skeptical, but no one stops these projects or for that matter closely tracks adherence to the 15 percent rule. The leaders have built this unstructured time into their culture and feel that close monitoring will defeat its purpose of stimulating creative deviance.

Leaders expect 3M's fifty divisions to generate 30 percent of sales from products that did not exist five years ago. This leadership policy stimulates a hectic, almost inexhaustible demand for creative deviance in all divisions. Product champions roam freely through this huge, internal market. First, they present their idea to their bosses. If a boss does not support the ideas, then the champion can personally market it to other divisions in his or her group. If none are interested, the champion can market the idea to the other divisions. If none accept it, then the champion can market to the New Business Ventures Division, which is home to the most far-out ideas.

What if nobody buys, including the New Ventures Division? In 3M culture it is almost a commandment that leaders shall not kill creative deviance. They may delay, divert, or decrease support for an idea, but they do not kill it outright. Leaders know that ideas wax and wane as they proceed through laboratory concept, product development, manufacturing, and marketing. When support for an idea ebbs, leaders believe that's when they discover who is really interested; that's when zealots carry the flag and mount the barricades. Neither leaders nor champions are dissuaded by reduced support or failure; they forge ahead, patiently developing and further refining their ideas.

The company's leaders have the marathon runner's long-term pacing and perspective. They do not exhaust themselves with quick dashes for success or withdraw from the race at the first obstacle. They expect that ideas may take ten to twenty years to go from concept to market success. Leaders expect deviants to fail, just as the leaders themselves did when they were champions. Deviants who stumble are not exiled; they continue to learn and persist with their idea. Leaders have patience, confident that one day 3M people will adequately understand the pieces of the puzzle—customer needs, product concept, design, manufacturing, and marketing—and will know how to assemble them into a successful product.

Leaders at 3M do not discard an idea when it seems to have a small potential market. Eliminating the small-market hurdle has made the company extraordinarily receptive to creative deviance. Leaders have found that they often cannot foresee the long-term potential of a market. They have learned that growth often depends on customers finding new uses for a product or asking about a need that can be met by a 3M innovation. Masking tape, for example, was invented at 3M in the 1930s when company salesmen who sold abrasives to the auto industry reported that auto manufacturers were having difficulty preventing paint from running on two-tone cars. A young technician, Richard Drew, a legend in the company, came up with the idea for masking tape. Initial demand for the tape was modest, but since that time the demand for masking tape has grown beyond the wildest predictions.

Leaders at 3M believe that anyone, not just scientists or product developers, can be a creative deviant. When Scotch Tape—clear tape with adhesive—was introduced, it was used to seal industrial packages. Sales were satisfactory but not extraordinary. Then a sales manager, John Borden, another legendary figure at 3M, devised a dispenser with a built-in cutting blade, and sales took off. The lesson: Anyone, anywhere, can be a creative deviant. Volunteerism is also essential to creative deviance, in the view of 3M's leaders. After an idea is accepted, leaders form a new venture team, composed only of volunteers. Leaders do not want halfhearted, reluctant rowers pulling on the oars when ideas hit rough seas.

Over a period of ten years the leadership culture supporting deviance worked its magic in the creation of the ubiquitous Post-it notes. It started when a 3M chemist, Spencer Silver, created a new adhesive polymer while fooling around with different mixtures containing a new monomer developed by Archer Daniels Midland. The new material was tacky but not "aggressively" adhesive. It was more cohesive than adhesive, so it stuck to itself better than to other substances. The historic goal at 3M was to create stronger, more durable adhesives; scientists routinely discarded weaker adhesives as useless. Silver, however, was entranced by his new, tacky adhesive, although it had no discernible application. He nursed it along for almost five years, visiting other divisions to describe the properties of his strange mixture. He had a solution in search of a problem.

Arthur Fry is one of many deviants who contributed to this new 3M legend. It all began quite innocently. Fry was constantly losing the strips of paper he inserted in his church hymnal to locate songs during choir practice. He made the unlikely creative leap of putting Silver's mild adhesive on the page locator strips. That was the take-off application. After several years of additional conceptualization, laboratory work, and product development, Fry and his team designed machines that could place the mild, tacky adhesive on flat sheets of paper. Designing the production equipment was a major exercise in creative deviance at 3M, where engineers were world-class experts in designing machines to affix strong, not weak, adhesives to rolls of material, rather than to flat sheets of paper.

Creative deviance was evident too in the marketing that saved the Post-it from an early burial. The note pads were test-marketed in four cities. The results were bad, and the product was on the verge of being dropped. Two 3M executives, Geoffrey Nicholson, division technical director, and Joseph Ramey, vice president of division marketing, who had been patrons of the project, could not believe the test results; they had seen people in 3M's offices get hooked on the little Post-it notes. Before the product was lost in a deluge of negative marketing reports, they decided to do their own test-marketing. They visited and spoke to end users in Richmond, Virginia, one of the test markets. They introduced themselves in offices and banks, handed out the little pads to secretaries, middle managers, and vice presidents, and watched the people try them. They saw the same immediate addiction they had seen at 3M as people began sticking them everywhere. Nicholson and Ramey had confirmed what they suspected all along: Talking about the pads and putting them on store shelves would not sell them. You had to give away samples so that people could use them.

The next step, known at 3M as the Boise Blitz, was a massive giveaway of samples in Boise, Idaho, to test the "sampling" theory.

The reorder rate was 90 percent, more than double the rate of any prior highly successful office product. Since then, Post-it sales have grown to an estimated $300 million a year, and another legend has entered 3M's culture. Leaders and product champions consistently encouraged creative deviance and learned how to use a quirky, tacky adhesive to paste hundreds of millions of dollars on 3M's annual earnings.

Mastery of Existing Knowledge

Competent leaders do not waste resources reinventing the wheel. Creating new knowledge builds on what is known, so effective leaders encourage their people to master existing knowledge.

Robert Oppenheimer, the atomic physicist who led the Manhattan Project, which harnessed the explosive power of atomic energy, often said that adding to knowledge in physics was not as difficult as most people thought. He said that first one must learn the language of the subject—the mathematics, the concepts, and the experiments, all of which were available knowledge. This might take time and dedication, but after it had been done, the process of adding to knowledge in physics, he said, was about the same as it was in any other field.

Although Oppenheimer, with characteristic modesty, understated his talents, his point still stands. Mastering existing knowledge is the foundation for advancing knowledge. Competent leaders encourage their people to know the content and the boundaries of existing knowledge—its theory, methods, technology, and findings—so that they can use it to reach beyond current limits.

There is a romantic belief that ignorant people, unencumbered by knowledge, make breakthroughs, stumbling through failed methods because they do not know any better. Occasionally, such people do indeed make breakthroughs. Breakthroughs are made more often, however, by persistent people who master existing knowledge and use what they know.

The computer disk drives that are now taken for granted as a commonplace product might not exist if it weren't for the knowledge mastered by a persistent renegade group of researchers at IBM and their leaders. At the time this project began, disk drives were little more than a concept and some primitive, inefficient models in a laboratory. Magnetic tape drives were a proven commercial product, much faster, more reliable, and with much greater storage capacity than any feasible disk drive.

Evaluators recommended discontinuing the disk drive project because they did not believe that the disk drive could be developed into a commercially viable product or that electromechanical read-write arms could be controlled with sufficient precision and speed to read and write data reliably. They believed that synchronizing the read-write arm with data on a spinning disk posed insurmountable problems and that a disk of reasonable size could not store enough data to be useful. Senior managers concluded that the effort was futile, so they withdrew funding for the disk drive project.

The researchers, however, had mastered so much knowledge about disk drives that they were able to convince their local leaders to sequester funds and permit them to bootleg their research without senior management's knowledge. A few years later, the disk drive was introduced and became a highly successful product for IBM and for the industry. A senior executive, commenting on this episode several years later, said, "I hate to think of where we would be today if our controls were as good as we like to think they are."

Unstructured Time

Because insight, new ideas, and consensus building follow an irregular, disjointed path, effective leaders give their people unstructured time to pursue creative activity, freeing them from routine, repetitive activities that dull the senses.

This is not to say that a regular work schedule is not necessary. Quite the contrary. People who discover new knowledge follow a regular work schedule regardless of whether they feel creative. They work excessively long hours, however, when facing an intractable problem or teeming with ideas on the brink of a breakthrough. They cannot turn work off arbitrarily. Creative thoughts come in machine-gun bursts, at night, on weekends, regardless of whether people are in the office or at home. They pay a high price in terms of restless nights, family stress, anxiety, and high blood pressure and need time to recuperate and rearrange their thoughts after intense episodes that frequently turn out to be false starts.

Unstructured time is time in which structure—that is, goals, concepts, and methods—emerges as people explore and work. It is not time without work. Effective leaders guard unstructured time; it is their investment in learning and the creation of new knowledge. They do not neglect near-term, measurable output, but they do balance routine, programmed activities with unstructured time for themselves and their people. They periodically attend mind-stretching programs outside their organizations at which they discuss such things as Who are we? What is our business? What are our strengths and weaknesses? Where are we going? Who are our customers? How can we improve what we do? What would make working here more enjoyable? Effective leaders often put people in new, challenging situations. They rearrange tasks and tune individual schedules to fit a person's learning and creative rhythm. Poor leaders demand structure for all activities, and they get it so long as people repeat what they already know. But effective leaders push into the unknown, using unstructured time to learn and grow. They know that what people learn in unstructured time today creates the structure for tomorrow's work.

New Perspectives

Effective leaders understand that when people view a situation from new perspectives, they learn and discover new knowledge. People from marketing, engineering, manufacturing, and finance, for example, see product design problems differently and create different solutions. Effective leaders expose people to different perspectives, encouraging them to generate and build on new insights.

Leaders introduced a new perspective when they asked, "How would I see this product if I had to repair or service it?" They learned that consumers wanted reliable, easy-to-repair products. Manufacturers began to build better quality products, and consumers voted in the marketplace, buying products that needed fewer repairs. For many years, however, the leaders of General Motors thumbed their noses at this perspective. Their policy was to find and correct defects after consumers brought the cars back to dealers and complained about breakdowns. GM leaders felt that it was more important to introduce new models on time. The complacency of this "king of the hill" perspective was finally challenged when Japanese manufacturers such as Toyota and Honda introduced high-quality cars that rarely needed repairs. Consumers flocked to purchase them, and GM, which at one time dominated the market, watched its market share drop from 55 percent to 35 percent. GM took multibillion-dollar write-offs, closed underutilized plants, and laid off hundreds of thousands of workers as it lost market share to its rivals. GM's leaders eventually heard the message, but whether they can master the customer's perspective and catch up to their competitors is still an open question.[4]

In a mass-consumption society with a growing population, competent leaders are beginning to introduce yet another perspective: "How would I see this product if I had to dispose of it?" Waste disposal has become a national problem, and manufacturers will increasingly be responsible for disposal of their products. In Germany, for example, the government and auto manufacturers have been collaborating since 1991 to phase in the reprocessing of junked vehicles. Consumers will return their discarded cars to the company that produced them. Volkswagen operates a plant that disassembles, shreds, and pulverizes a VW in two man-hours.[5] German auto company leaders, adapting to this new perspective, have started to design new cars with more recyclable parts and less nonusable waste. The lesson of this new perspective has spread, and British, French, and other European auto makers are beginning to design cars for better recycling, even before their governments force them to.

Tactics for New Perspectives

Effective leaders use various methods to encourage people to take unusual points of view. Leaders often ask people to imagine military, political, or biological analogies for business problems. The leaders of a small company competing against large rivals, for example, asked, "What would you see if you were a small military force? How would you deal with the situation?" The new perspective brought a flood of responses: attack their flank, use guerrilla tactics, avoid a head-on attack that could wipe you out, withdraw and build resources until you can mount a credible attack, attack at night, probe for weak spots, use propaganda to demoralize their supporters, build support with the population in your local area, and look for a breakthrough weapon. The leaders translated these responses into a strategy of opening stores in small areas not served by large competitors, much like the original strategy of Wal-Mart.

Leaders may ask people to view a problem from the perspective of an insect, a tree, a flower, or some other element of nature. Natural organisms have characteristics and behavior that provide new insights into problems. Leaders of one food-processing company with branded products that competed against many other brands asked, "What would you see if you were a bird or flower in a meadow? How would you differentiate yourself?" The ideas from this new perspective led to colorful, distinctive packaging and a new line of exotic, foreign-recipe frozen foods.

Leaders may ask people to imagine that they are the real object. A team working on a new surgical dressing, for example, was asked "if you were an open wound, what would you see? How would you feel? What would you want?" People said that as a wound they would want protection from trauma and bacteria, access to a healing atmosphere, and a soothing, easy-to-remove shield. This new perspective led to development of an aerated, nonstick dressing. Effective leaders systematically shift perspective because they see again and again that people find creative solutions to problems when they alter their points of view.[6] Poor leaders freeze in one perspective. They look at a situation in one way, get blocked, and cannot find their way out.

Heterogeneous Groups

People with different concepts of a problem spark new insights. Competent leaders form groups with heterogeneous members to encourage the exchange of ideas. They know that people who think differently provoke others to learn. Productive scientists, for example, regularly sample new perspectives by discussing their problems with experts in fields other than their own.

Leaders know that groups of people with diverse backgrounds can be troublesome when they lapse into jargon or focus on defending trivia. Heterogeneous groups are rewarding, however, because they can turn conventional knowledge upside down so that people see what was previously hidden. Intellectually high-powered groups, brain trusts, think tanks, or policy councils, as they are variously called, are rich mines of learning and new knowledge.

KNOWLEDGE RENEWAL

Effective leaders need to renew their knowledge continually to avoid undermining key decisions and misleading their organization. Poor leaders lag in knowledge and greatly damage their organization. Leaders ultimately have the formal power to make decisions, but their understanding of knowledge and its implications affects the quality of their decisions. Poor leaders who do not continually renew their knowledge become personally obsolete and undermine their organization's competitive position They drift into knowledge obsolescence, not realizing how their power multiplies the destructive effects of their lagging knowledge.

The financial vice president of an electronics company had not kept up with new developments in financial theory and practice. He had hired several bright business school graduates with experience using mathematical models and computers for financial analysis. The vice president could not understand the knowledge these people attempted to use for the company's benefit. He resisted their changes in reporting and financial analysis, which would have substantially improved the firm's cash management and inventory polices as well as the quality of the firm's capital investment decisions. These methods were commonplace in competing organizations.

There was disappointment and high turnover among the new hires. The vice president's decision to ignore their sophisticated financial analysis led to excessive inventories and inappropriate pricing. He dismissed the analysts' risk analysis of several proposed marketing and manufacturing investments because he had difficulty understanding their logic and models. These investments later undermined the firm's profitability. In financial distress, the company was purchased by a larger organization. Leaders of the new parent company gradually assumed control of the finance area and began to see the serious problems caused by the financial vice president's knowledge obsolescence. He was eventually replaced and the department was reorganized. In this case a poor leader with substantial formal power had not renewed his knowledge. His firm was producing state-of-the-art electronics, but his financial knowledge obsolescence had kept the firm in the dark.

Renewal, Not Expertise

Leaders usually lag behind their people as specialized knowledge advances. If they do not, then they are probably settling for mediocre subordinates or in some way inhibiting their growth. Effective leaders, however, continue their learning, keeping the knowledge gap between themselves and their people within workable bounds. They do not expect to be experts, but they continually acquire new knowledge and problem-solving skills in order to understand the advice they receive and to project its implications. They acquire knowledge to visualize risks and take timely steps to diminish them. Poor leaders in contrast lag in knowledge. They use their power to circumvent their need to learn and to avoid people whose knowledge they do not understand.

Knowledge Arrogance

Few things are as offensive as the complacent expert who "knows it all." Leaders face a new phenomenon—the arrogance of knowledge. Many specialists claim great certainty for their models and mathematical abstractions, but leaders must be rooted in the subtle complexity of the real world. Poor leaders misunderstand models, expecting one-to-one correspondence between the real world and the model. Specialists often contribute to this misunderstanding; many are more concerned with impressing each other with their mathematical sophistication and elegant theories than with communicating with leaders.

Effective leaders renew their knowledge to keep abreast of how theory points to practical action. They may be impatient with arrogant specialists and their theories, but they have learned to listen to them in order to ferret out answers and guides to action. Effective leaders understand that the conceptual gap between them and knowledge specialists strains their relationship. They often see knowledge workers as naïve and conceited, whereas specialists often see leaders as unsophisticated and self-protective. Each can obstruct and frustrate the other, and their relationship, although intended to infuse knowledge, can degenerate into unproductive skirmishes. Effective leaders prevent destructive escalation of this conflict by continually renewing their knowledge. They are not intimidated by the surface arrogance of knowledge workers. Competent leaders support the search for knowledge that may not have immediate application, knowing that it helps ensure that the firm will be prepared when its products are out of date and competition intensifies. They know that they have a right and an obligation to ask for explanations of assumptions and theories. They ask for pilot tests and demonstrations to help them judge when to use knowledge that they may not fully understand.

Leaders of a major bank formed an internal management science (MS) group to study the bank's management of its asset portfolio. At first, the MS group had difficulty communicating with the bank's leaders. Over a period of years, however, the bank's leaders guided the MS group into demonstrating the benefits of using its models to manage the bank's portfolio. The bank's leaders gradually implemented the MS recommendations, significantly improving the bank's performance. Although not management scientists, the bank's leaders continually upgraded their knowledge through seminars and visits to other organizations. They came to understand, in general terms, how MS models were designed and tested, acquiring enough insight and confidence to support the MS group for years and continually proposing additional situations for its study. The leaders of the bank had productively managed a sophisticated MS group, learning how to apply MS knowledge to propel the bank to becoming one of the top ten performers in the industry.

Effective leaders expect to use their formal power even though their specialized knowledge may be limited. They explore their knowledge limitations and learn enough to understand what they need to know. Poor leaders, failing to renew their knowledge, succumb to knowledge arrogance and incur high costs. In recent years, a number of major organizations, such as Procter and Gamble and Hallmark, and localities such as Orange County, California, have lost millions of dollars through poor investments in financial derivatives. Some of them are suing their investment bankers, claiming that they were insufficiently informed of the risks. Here is a classic illustration of leaders whose lagging knowledge, real or feigned, exposed their organization to serious risks and who then blamed someone else for the costs of their knowledge obsolescence.

SUMMARY

The core of the leader's new role is to foster learning in an organization with distributed knowledge. Leaders help people learn by continually putting them in situations that stretch their knowledge and thinking. Their demands—that is, how well leaders select and frame problems and opportunities—largely determine what people will learn. Effective leaders can frame problems appropriately, as in AT&T's approach to solving its burgeoning need for operators, or poorly, as in Polaroid's futile foray into instant motion pictures.

The leader's function is shifting from getting things done by hierarchical direction to growing intellectual capital by insightful, supportive guidance. Leaders need to provide the conditions that foster learning if they are to build an adaptive organization. The first condition, creative deviance, requires that leaders have a tolerance for curiosity and differences. It also requires patience with zealots and a willingness to persist when success is not immediate. The second condition, mastery of existing knowledge, helps leaders avoid useless rediscovery and lets people know where the boundaries of knowledge are and where to push the envelope. The third condition is unstructured time, which frees people from repetitive routine and lets them learn and think creatively. The final condition, new perspectives, uses creative thinking techniques and heterogeneous groups to jog people out of fixed, single-minded views. New perspectives help people learn about consumer needs and product design and about how to make better competitive use of knowledge. Effective leaders also renew their knowledge, ensuring that they do not lag too far behind their people and obstruct progress or expose their organization to unnecessary risk. Leaders know that they need to learn if they are to keep up with the learning and growth of their people.

In the next chapter we look at an important change in the context of leadership. A new kind of stress is emerging that inhibits the learning and knowledge needed to compete; it is called knowledge stress. What are the sources of knowledge stress? How has the growing reliance on knowledge changed the character of the workforce and its attitudes toward leaders?

5

Knowledge Stress and Knowledge Workers

Leaders involved in a competitive race for knowledge need to be aware of two fundamental factors that affect leadership in the late twentieth century. First, there is the incessant, almost frantic drive to acquire and use knowledge before one's competitors. This drive for speed produces a new kind of stress—knowledge stress. Leaders need to know the sources of knowledge stress so that they can manage its debilitating effects on learning and adaptation. The second critical factor is the character and attitudes of the workforce. Today's workforce consists of increasingly sophisticated thinkers and users of knowledge who have distinctive views and attitudes about the role of the leader, their work, and themselves. In this chapter, we first talk about the stresses of knowledge work: complexity, ambiguity, multiple influences, temporary relationships, and vulnerable self-esteem. We then explore the special characteristics and attitudes of knowledge workers: a desire for freedom to question, independence and self-responsibility, a quest for personal growth, and a concern for corporate morality.

THE SPREAD OF KNOWLEDGE STRESS

Knowledge stress is not exclusively a white-collar problem. It has spread to blue-collar work that is continually upgraded by organizations to include a heavier knowledge component. Leaders increase knowledge stress when they enrich production jobs or rotate production workers across jobs. They increase it when they organize people into interdependent work teams or install computer networks in the workplace, when they build advanced technology factories that flexibly produce a wide line of products, and when they empower workers, giving them discretion and responsibility, and then demand that workers participate in quality management. Leaders increase knowledge stress when they reengineer work or push for continuous improvement in every step of production.

The boundary between knowledge work and production work is eroding. Technicians (so-called gray collars) constitute the fastest-growing class of workers in the information age. They have substantial education and credentials, and leaders expect them to exercise knowledge and judgment. Most technicians have specialized training, many have four years of college, and an increasing number in health services, biotechnology, and electronics have advanced degrees. U. S. workers with broad job titles such as engineering technician, computer programmer, clinical laboratory technician, science technician, and paralegal already number 20 million. By 2005 it is estimated that they will represent one fifth of total employment.[1]

Effective leaders understand that as they increase the learning and knowledge components of work they subject people to multiple, severe sources of stress. Each source alone is troubling; cumulatively they can be overwhelming. Knowledge stress decreases people's ability to focus and diminishes their performance. It can cause or aggravate a constellation of health problems. Competent leaders understand that the context of work has changed and that they need to alleviate and manage the following sources of stress: situational complexity, ambiguity, multiple sources of influence, temporary relationships, and vulnerable self-esteem.

Situational Complexity

Leaders and their staffs face turbulent, complex global situations each day. Forces around the globe interact, affecting product, market, and investment decisions. China may be opening or closing its markets; Japan may be softening or hardening its stand on trade; inflation may rise or fall; the Federal Reserve may tighten or loosen interest rates. This environmental complexity is compounded by the complexity of the options available to meet it. Leaders can select goals from among a wide array of possible markets, products, manufacturing methods, and financial arrangements. Often, as they pursue multiple goals, they belatedly discover that some goals are contradictory, such as getting a product to market early and producing it efficiently. Leaders may have to change their priorities in response to customer demands or competitors' actions. Leaders need continually to create and evaluate alternative products, prices, and markets. Rarely can they devise an option without facing some undesirable side effects. Some options may increase debt and raise the firm's break-even point; some may require closing plants and laying off people; some may change the distribution system and arouse the resistance of dealers. Whatever leaders decide, the results will be affected by competitors pursuing their own goals and interests. Complexity escalates as people work on several projects simultaneously. While they work, projects change and new crises erupt continually. Effective leaders understand that people pay a heavy mental and emotional price as they try to juggle and adapt to this complexity.

Ambiguity

Ambiguity is another component of knowledge stress. Often people cannot see how things fit together. One executive in a mid-sized electronics company described the ambiguity of identifying a stable product-market niche in his industry this way: "It's like searching for a black cat in a dark room when you're not sure that the cat is still in the room." In the new global competition, people face heightened ambiguity, and many leaders feel that they are chasing the black cat that may not be there. Leaders cannot definitely say that their actions are the sole cause, or the principal cause, of the results they measure. Some outcomes result from what they have done, but others may have occurred despite what they have done. Conjectures about cause and effect are riddled with ambiguities, amplifying leaders' stress when they have to make decisions in the future.

When Citibank's profits improved in 1993 after several years of huge losses, some people said that it was due to a change in leadership. Others said that leadership had eviscerated the bank by draconian layoffs and cuts in expenses. Some said that the low interest rates paid on deposits were the key because they gave the bank a low-cost source of funds. Others said that interest rates were not critical because loan volume was down. Others said that the key was the bank's ability to generate earnings by charging consumers high interest rates on credit-card debt. Still others said that it was the banking regulators' forbearance while the bank scrambled to obtain capital to improve its unacceptably low reserve position. Some said it was all of these factors plus others that they couldn't identify. Ambiguity like this forces leaders to make decisions as best they can with incomplete information and fuzzy concepts. Effective leaders understand that ambiguity is a major part of knowledge stress. They do not add to that stress by demanding that their staffs find certainty in simple cause-and-effect relationships that are unrealistic and may not even exist.

Multiple Influences

Many people with different interests see their leaders and their organization as targets to be influenced. Leaders need to collect and understand the views of these different interests. The quality of decisions often depends on that knowledge. In addition to listening to their formal superior's, for example, leaders need to listen to high-level managers in other parts of the firm. They need to listen to functional specialists in marketing, production, and human resources; to customers, suppliers, and union officials; to regulatory agencies, legal advisers, and environmentalists. All these parties have, or claim to have, a right to influence decisions. The struggle to address and to balance these conflicting interests and claims is a major source of stress.

Temporary Relationships

People live on a merry-go-round of temporary relationships. Leaders expect people with knowledge to move to where they are needed, for as long as they are needed. Leaders and their people are expected quickly to form, and then to dissolve, task forces or project groups. Theoretically, they should be able to work effectively, instantaneously, in cross-functional design teams or production teams that disappear after a product is marketed. Everyone is supposed to know how to work in a disposable group, building and ending relationships with the ease of going through a revolving door. Downsizing should not trouble people; they are supposed to be cool and unaffected as they watch their careers disappear. People shield themselves from this miasma of emotional turmoil by not getting close to others. Inwardly, however, they pay a heavy price. They live with the anxiety of impermanance and imminent disposability. Effective leaders help people cope with these feelings by giving them an anchorage, a shelter from the storm of temporary relationships.

Vulnerable Self-Esteem

In knowledge-driven competition, people rise and fall with their ideas. Knowledge and insights have become people's primary contributions. Even the best people, however, occasionally propose poor ideas. Effective leaders have learned to separate their evaluation of an idea from their evaluation of the person who proposed it. Leaders know that when they reject an idea, the person who proposed it often feels that his or her self-esteem has been attacked. They carefully control people who persistently undermine the ideas of others and play a game of "one-upmanship." Poor leaders, however, turn underminers loose to taunt and intimidate people.

In sum, effective leaders understand that knowledge stress disrupts performance. They know that it is painful to their people and costly to their organization. They pay attention to the sources of knowledge stress and manage them so that people can continue to work effectively.

UNDERSTANDING KNOWLEDGE WORKERS

It is hard to lead if you do not understand whom you are leading. Effective leaders understand the concerns and attitudes of people who work with knowledge. The diffusion of knowledge across the organization and down to the factory floor is changing the attitudes and culture of the workforce. People who work with knowledge often seem obstreperous because they value freedom to question, independence and self-responsibility, personal growth, and corporate morality. Effective leaders understand and productively channel these attitudes; poor leaders misunderstand and attempt to suppress them.

Freedom to Question

People who work with knowledge want the freedom to ask questions. They prefer to use the discovery method: If you don't know, find out yourself by using your own reasoning ability. They like to develop their own theories and to invent their way out of a problem. They question the status quo and challenge authorities. They can be very confronting, pointing out discrepancies between what people say and what they do. They strongly believe that learning depends on being free to ask questions. They feel that it is reasonable to ask leaders to explain the rationale for their decisions.

Poor leaders feel that people with these attitudes are dangerous. They believe that people who ask questions or seek information, "that shouldn't concern them" can disrupt the organization. They suppress questioners and try to keep them under tight control. Effective leaders, in contrast understand these attitudes and rise to the questions. They use the challenges as springboards to involve the questioners in continually improving performance.

Self-Responsibility

People who work with knowledge expect to take responsibility for themselves. They see themselves as independent professionals trained in a strong code of internal standards and therefore as not needing close supervision. Their knowledge, they believe, gives them the right to participate in decisions. It also gives them a heightened sense of obligation, and duty, because they understand how easily things can go wrong. They often prefer to work in teams that are self-managing. Many began taking self-responsibility at an early age, and they expect to be treated as responsible people after joining an organization.

Poor leaders put such people in a double-bind. On one hand they demand that people take greater responsibility. On the other hand, they trample on the need for self-responsibility by treating people as if they were irresponsible and unreliable. Effective leaders respect the need for independence and self-responsibility. They challenge people by clearly defining goals and then saying, in so many words, "You are on your own; do what is necessary to make the project succeed."

Personal Growth

Some cynical leaders think that people should grow on their own time. People who work with knowledge, however, have tasted the excitement of learning, and they want opportunities for personal growth at work. They look for challenges that keep them alert. They want to stretch and learn. They have a continual need for education that feeds their hunger for new knowledge and skills. Effective leaders arrange for such people to attend at least one course or development program each year to expand their intellectual horizons and give them tasks that keep them intellectually sharp and that use their full capabilities. People who work with knowledge may complain about overwork, but deep down they relish the intellectual challenge. Poor leaders on the other hand, assign repetitive, unchallenging tasks to these people. They offer little support for external education and severely demotivate them.

Corporate Morality

People who work with knowledge are accustomed to handling concepts. They can see the big picture as well as its parts. They see organizations as part of a larger social fabric, and they are concerned about socially responsible leadership. They are wary of mischievous leaders who hide in a corporate cocoon of narrowly defined self-interest. They are appalled by leaders who conceal the dumping of toxic waste, knowingly pollute waterways, or exploit public lands; they are repelled by leaders who deny accountability for hazardous products or violate employee civil rights; they are angered by leaders who use financial manipulations and then walk away from catastrophic leveraged buyouts after sacrificing the livelihoods and savings of thousands of people.

   People who have a significant component of knowledge in their work are especially attentive to the morality of leadership. They are embarrassed when leaders engage in deceptive practices or promote social inequities. Knowledge workers bring their theories of political economy and social justice to work. They know that corporate and government leaders are fallible and need guidance in controlling destructive practices and correcting injustices. They expect leaders to operate the organization legally and morally. Poor leaders say it's no one's business how they run their companies. They look aside when there is unethical behavior and shift blame when it is uncovered. Effective leaders accept responsibility and root out illegal and unethical behavior.

SUMMARY

Knowledge stress has become an important obstacle to performance. Creating and acquiring knowledge—that is, learning—increases knowledge stress and can decrease performance. Effective leaders understand and manage the sources of knowledge stress: complexity, ambiguity, multiple influences, temporary relationships, and vulnerable self-esteem.

Organizations are populated with a new type of worker—people accustomed to thinking, learning, using knowledge, and solving problems. Effective leaders understand that people who work with knowledge have special characteristics and attitudes. The knowledge workforce thrives on freedom to question, personal growth, self-responsibility, and corporate morality. They are demotivated by autocratic, controlling, socially indifferent leaders who misunderstand these characteristics.

The leader's role is a challenge because of the need to master the three elements of leadership—knowledge, trust, and power—and their interplay. All three components, of course, are present in each situation, but for analysis and discussion we have separated them. In Part I we have explored the knowledge component. Underlying our discussion there has been an implicit assumption that people trust their leaders and each other. Trust allows leaders to tap into the organization's distributed pools of knowledge and creates the commitment that leaders need for effective implementation. In Part II we focus on trust. What is it? How do leaders build it? What are its determinants?

II

TRUST

The only way to make a man trustworthy is to trust him,
and the surest way to make him untrustworthy is to distrust him
and show your distrust.

Henry L. Stimson

6

Trust and the Decision Process

Trust enriches relationships, fostering cooperation, creativity, and commitment. Mistrust weakens relationships, bringing to them suspicion and deception. Part of the leader's task has been, and continues to be, working with people to find and solve problems, but whether leaders gain access to the knowledge and creative thinking they need to solve problems depends on how much people trust them. Trust and trustworthiness modulate the leader's access to knowledge and cooperation.

Leaders distill their attitudes and impressions into one powerful belief: how much they can trust other people. Others, in turn, make their own estimates of how trustworthy the leader is. The quality and the implementation of decisions ultimately depends on how much leaders and those they work with trust each other. When they trust one another, decision quality and implementation improve. When they mistrust, decision quality and implementation suffer.

Leaders sense that they trust some people more than others, but they underestimate the corrosive effects of their mistrust. Leaders rarely discuss their mistrust with the other person; instead, they act on it. Avoiding an examination of mistrust does not diminish its effects; rather, it disguises them, making them difficult to trace and less subject to control. Leaders need to understand the meaning and the effects of trust if they are to improve how they make decisions and the quality of those decisions.

Poor leaders acknowledge that people are a valuable resource but still see their primary resources as funds, plant, equipment, products, and inventory. Each person in an organization, however, is a treasure of information, knowledge, and curiosity. Each has imagination and creativity. Each is a source of commitment, loyalty, and affection. Each has the ability to analyze, learn, and master new knowledge. Each can acquire new skills and teach them to others. Human brainpower and adaptability are awesome resources but they are hidden under layers of mistrust and defensiveness. Only by gaining trust can leaders open a path to the knowledge and abilities within each person. The increases in productivity, creativity, adaptability, and commitment that result can be astonishing.

In this chapter we discuss the meaning of trust, giving the term a precise definition to avoid the common misunderstandings of casual usage. We explore how trust relates to vulnerability and control and how it differs from friendship or affection. We examine how leaders express their trust through three elements: information, influence, and control. We present a spiral model of the trust process, showing how these elements influence the rise and fall of trust. We then describe a study, based on the spiral model, in which business executives, some with high and some with low trust, worked on a common business problem. The study demonstrates that high-trust leaders collaborate with their employees to make creative business decisions and increase commitment to their organization, whereas in identical situations, leaders who mistrust make inferior, self-protective decisions that decrease employee commitment to the organization. The chapter concludes with the surprising finding that the several hundred executives who took part in this study had little insight into how trust, or lack of it, had affected their behavior and decisions.

MEANING OF TRUST

Poor leaders disregard the effects of trust because they misunderstand what trust means. When questioned, they usually say that trust means friendliness. They say it is a feeling of affection, an expression of good will. In jest, some say, "It's a warm, cuddly feeling." Trust, however, should not be confused with affection. The terms are quite different, and a leader's failure to appreciate the difference causes much difficulty.

You may have affection for but not trust in another person. A parent, for example, may love his ten-year-old child but not trust the child to drive the family automobile. On the other hand, you may trust your life to another person even though you have no affection for her. A passenger in a commercial plane, for example, may trust the pilot but have no affection for her. In short, trust and liking are not the same. They do not necessarily occur together.

Competent leaders vary their trust according to the task, the situation, and the trustworthiness of the other person. Affection may or may not increase with trust. This is not to say that consideration and sensitivity to the other person's needs are unimportant. It is only to say that trust differs from affection and amiability.

TRUST DEFINED

Trust is quite complex, so we give a comprehensive definition before looking at its components. *Trust consists of a willingness to increase your vulnerability to another person whose behavior you cannot control, in a situation in which your potential benefit is much less than your potential loss if the other person abuses your vulnerability.*

By vulnerability we mean the possibility of being harmed. Harm can take many forms—embarrassment, inability to do what you had planned, higher costs, prolonged delays that waste your time, and in extreme cases, loss of life. The element of control is also critical. You increase trust—your exposure to possible harm—to the degree that you cannot (or do not) control the other person's behavior. Clearly, the more you control the other's behavior, the less you can be harmed. It is meaningless to say that you trust someone whose behavior you control completely. For the remainder of this discussion we shall therefore assume that you have, or decide to exercise, little control over the other person's behavior.

The next component in our definition of trust consists of benefits and losses. You increase your vulnerability to another person because you expect some benefit: completion of a job, attainment of a valued goal, or some reward. Your level of trust is indicated by the relationship between the value of the benefit compared to your potential loss. Your trust is high when the potential benefit is small compared to the potential loss.

The last part of the definition is the probability that the other party will abuse your vulnerability. When you trust, you depend on the other party's "good" behavior. Why do you trust others when the potential benefit is small compared to the possible loss? You trust because you believe that there is little probability that the other will, deliberately or accidentally, abuse your vulnerability. For example, you trust pilots because you believe that they will not deliberately hijack or crash the plane. You trust them because you believe that they are physically fit, well disciplined, and sufficiently trained to cope with possible emergencies.

Our definition of trust, then, has these components: *high vulnerability, low control, modest benefit, high possible loss, and belief that the other person will not abuse your vulnerability.*

ELEMENTS OF TRUST

People express trust, or mistrust, through three elements of behavior: *information, influence,* and *control.* Leaders communicate trust by how they disclose information, share influence, and exercise control.

Information

The flow of accurate, timely information is critical to a productive relationship. Leaders show trust by disclosing information. They increase their vulnerability to another person when they reveal information about their goals, alternatives, and intentions and when they disclose problems or discuss their assessment of others. The other person may use this information to block or undermine the leader's plans.

When leaders mistrust, they conceal and distort relevant information. They withhold facts, disguise ideas, and suppress conclusions. They hide opinions and feelings that would increase their exposure to others. As a result, they provide others with incomplete, untimely information and draw an inaccurate picture of underlying problems.

Influence

Influence refers to the sources of information and how that information alters behavior. Leaders show trust when they permit others to affect their decisions. When leaders accept the counsel of other people such as superiors, subordinates, or peers, they increase their exposure to harm in several ways. They may be seen as weak because they consulted others. They may be misled because some of their counselors are misinformed or have poor ideas. They may be demoted or fired because competitive or vindictive advisers deliberately misdirect them.

When leaders mistrust, they resist others' attempts to influence their decisions. They suspect the other person's goals, reject his views, and deflect his suggestions. They deny, or ignore, the other person's evaluation of results. Low-trust leaders reject the influence of those they mistrust but want others to accept their views and follow their influence. It's like saying, "I don't trust you, but you can trust me."

Control

Control, meaning the regulation and limitation of another person's behavior, is the most difficult element to estimate because it depends on what others will do in the future when the leaders are not present. Leaders show trust when they depend on others. They increase their exposure when they delegate tasks such as gathering information or analyzing problems. They increase their vulnerability and decrease their control when they let others make decisions or implement plans. The other person may gather incorrect information, misdiagnose a problem, or make a poor decision. They may snarl implementation and undermine the leader's program. As a result, the leader's reputation may be damaged and the leader may be demoted, transferred, or forced to resign.

When leaders mistrust, they minimize their dependence on others. They believe that other people will not perform their tasks or honor the spirit of their agreements. Leaders try to impose controls on those they mistrust. For example, President Ronald Reagan repeatedly said, during arms control negotiations with the Soviet Union, "Trust, but verify," which in diplomatic language meant, "I do not trust you, and I will agree to arms control only if the United States can independently verify your compliance." When leaders mistrust, they are alarmed when the other person attempts to evade controls. On the other hand, low-trust leaders strongly resist others' attempts to control their behavior.

A SPIRAL MODEL OF TRUST

Trust spirals in corkscrew fashion as leaders act out their trust through information, influence, and control and interpret others behavior in terms of these elements. Trust moves up or down the spiral depending on how leaders disclose information, exercise and receive mutual influence, and delegate and exercise control. In Figure 6-1 we show the elements—information, influence, and control—and the phases of the trust spiral: predisposing beliefs, short-cycle feedback, and equilibrium. In the following sections we describe these phases.

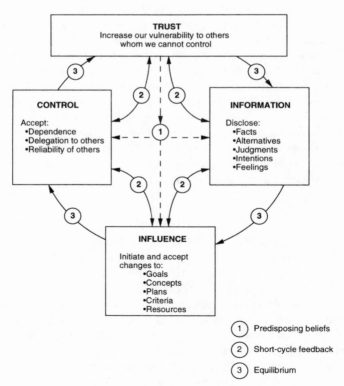

Figure 6-1 A Spiral Model of Trust

Predisposing Beliefs

Leaders rarely start work with others with a clean slate. Leaders enter meetings with predisposing beliefs about how trusting they should be and an estimate of how trustworthy other people are. These beliefs come from the leader's view of whether the other people have strong opposing interests, her past experiences with the other people, and what she has heard about the reputation of the other people. In the early stages of a meeting leaders regulate their behavior in accordance with their predisposing beliefs. They regulate how much information they reveal, how receptive they are to others interests and goals, and how much control they will try to exercise. Predisposing beliefs also affect how leaders interpret what other people say and do. If a leader trusts another person, and that person claims to lack certain information, the leader believes him. If the leader mistrusts him, the leader may be skeptical and hear the claim as an evasion intended to mislead.

Short-Cycle Feedback

As meetings proceed, people build a data bank, gathering impressions of others' trustworthiness. People think about how much relevant information other people have disclosed and how receptive others have been to their concerns, goals, methods for reaching those goals, and criteria for evaluating results. They wonder, how do I feel about depending on other people? How much can I delegate to them? How reliable do I think they will be? These impressions are short-cycle feedback; they confirm or disconfirm one's predisposing beliefs. If an other person gives comprehensive, timely information and responds receptively to influence by adjusting goals, methods, and criteria, for example, our trust increases. If he expresses commitment to fulfilling his part of what is to be done, that adds to our trust. When people increase their belief in another person's trustworthiness, they simultaneously increase their willingness to trust them.

Equilibrium

After a while, the short-cycle feedback becomes repetitive and the level of trust reaches a plateau, or equilibrium, usually by the middle of the meeting. Trust settles into a narrow band of low, medium, or high trust for the rest of the meeting.

When people trust each other, the three phases flow in a beneficial spiral. With a predisposing belief that they can be trusting, they reveal timely, accurate, relevant, comprehensive information from the outset. They accept influence from the other person. They commit to fulfill what they say. They accept dependence because they believe that each person will abide by the agreement and will not abuse anyone else's exposure. The other person behaves similarly. Both provide short-cycle feedback suggesting that they are trustworthy. The process continues to spiral up until it reaches a plateau for that meeting.

People can get caught in a downward spiral, however, when they start with a lack of trust. They conceal information because they mistrust and because they don't think that the other person is trustworthy. They block and resist influence and try to impose controls so that they don't have to depend on the other person. The other person's mistrusting responses give short-cycle feedback that further decreases trust. The erosion of trust continues to spiral down until both participants reach a plateau of greater mistrust than existed at the start of the meeting.

The spiral model does not say that trust is a substitute for knowledge and thinking. It does claim that trust modulates how well leaders access and use knowledge and thinking. We emphasize that leaders must have the knowledge and the competence to identify and solve problems. Throughout this discussion of trust we are assuming that leaders are knowledgeable, experienced, creative problem solvers. The spiral model describes the influence of trust on how well leaders are able to access the knowledge and the skills that people have in order to solve problems.

THE TRUST CYCLE

Like two people pedaling a bicycle built for two, people who trust each other synchronize and help each other. The trust cycle (Fig. 6-2) describes how two trusting people work together constructively. (The numbers in the following description are keyed to the numbers in Fig. 6-2.) When the leader trusts (1), he reveals information, accepts influence, and minimally controls the other person(2).

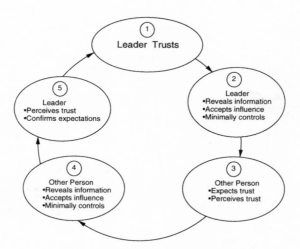

Figure 6-2 The Trust Cycle

The other trusting person, expecting trust, perceives the leader's initial behavior as trusting and concludes that she was right to expect the leader to be trustworthy (3). She therefore feels justified in showing trust and reveals information, accepts influence, and exercises self-control (4). The leader seeing the other's responses as trusting, feels confidence in his initial expectation that the other person would be trustworthy (5). He then feels justified in demonstrating more trust than he did at the beginning (1).

The two people continue to cycle around the loop, behaving with more and more trust, until they arrive at a plateau of higher trust. Each will increase his or her vulnerability and minimize his or her control of the other. The open flow of information and mutual influence will greatly increase their problem-solving effectiveness. After several cycles, each will have greater confidence in his or her initial trusting beliefs. With reliable information and shared influence motivating them, they will increase their commitment to each other and feel greater satisfaction with their work and their relationship.

Imagine what would happen, however, if two people on a bicycle built for two mistrusted each other. Their pretense, faking, and fear of being exploited would wreck the bicycle and bring them to a standstill while they bickered over who was to blame. When this happens in the U.S. Congress, we call it gridlock. The trust process, unfortunately, can operate destructively when two people mistrust each other (Fig. 6-3). In the mistrust cycle, leaders withhold information, resist influence, impose controls, and blame the other for problems. Their mistrusting behavior confirms the mistrusting expectations and intentions of the other person, and the two of them quickly cycle around the loop and rapidly increase their mutual mistrust.

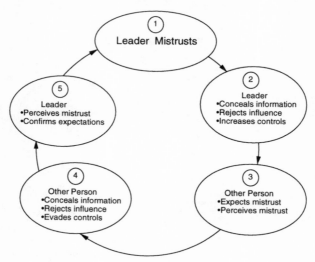

Figure 6-3 The Mistrust Cycle

In a mistrust cycle, the leader, out of frustration and anger, usually demands compliance and threatens to penalize the other person for noncompliance. This further confirms and reinforces the other person's mistrust. If there is a deadline, the mistrusting leader imposes controls, and the other person tries to evade them. By the end of such a meeting, the level of mistrust will be noticeably higher than it was at the beginning.

THE EFFECTS OF TRUST

Trust frees people to be open, lifting relationships to new heights of achievement; mistrust shrivels people, destroying their relationship through frustration and rage. In problem-solving groups, like those in organizations, high trust increases openness and mutual acceptance. People accurately perceive the values and motives of others. They concentrate on the task at hand and do not distort what they hear. They recognize and use good ideas. In contrast, mistrust provokes rejection and defensiveness in problem-solving groups. People misperceive the values and motives of others and resist taking on a commitment to their task. They distort what they hear and have difficulty recognizing and using good ideas. The effects of mistrust, however, are subtle. They are camouflaged behind a curtain of social uncertainty.

Mistrust Creates Social Uncertainty

There is some objective uncertainty in almost every problem. Leaders, for example, rarely know a competitor's future prices or product line. Leaders can speculate about the causes of consumer demand for their firm's products, but often they do not know those causes with any certainty. It can be difficult to gather data about customers and the factors underlying their purchase decisions and then to extract from the data a reliable, meaningful set of causes.

Mistrust complicates the leader's decision making by concealing objective uncertainty behind a curtain of social uncertainty. When people mistrust, they withhold relevant information and distort their intentions. They conceal their judgements and do not reveal the alternative plans they are considering. They create a curtain of social uncertainty, separate from the problem, that conceals important issues, masks difficulties and increases the likelihood that leaders will misunderstand risks and delay correcting poor decisions.

The marketing manager and the manufacturing manager of one large paper manufacturing company had developed a relationship of mutual distrust over a period of several years because of a series of incidents involving new products. The marketing manager had made optimistic projections about the demand for several new paper products.

He had convinced higher management to pressure the manufacturing manager to divert capacity to the new products despite the manufacturing manager's objections that this would make it difficult to make enough of the products for which there was known demand. Manufacturing had to spend hundreds of thousands of dollars on these product variations and continually disrupt production schedules while it learned how to run the new products on the paper-making machines. Changing the setup of high-speed paper-making machines, some of which were as long as a city block, was in many ways an art. Production crews had to learn how to get the right mix of ingredients, textures, dyes, and sizing powders and the right settings of speed, pressure, and temperature for a series of feed tanks, moving screens, dryers, and high-speed rotating drums.

Most of the new product ventures were failures; only a few were moderate commercial successes. When the products failed, rather than cooperating with manufacturing to analyze the causes, the marketing manager blamed manufacturing for getting the products to market too late, not making a product of competitive quality, or producing the item at such a high cost that it had to be sold at an uncompetitive price. On the surface, these charges seemed plausible, but they were not particularly accurate. The marketing manager strongly resisted looking at his role in these failures. The manufacturing manager greatly resented the marketing manager's "slick comments and shifty moves." Each manager was competent in his specialty. Each masked his escalating mistrust in highly rational-sounding arguments in meetings with higher management.

One incident that was especially costly to manufacturing dramatically increased the level of mutual mistrust. After manufacturing had spent millions of dollars modifying its plant and hundreds of labor hours developing the know-how to make a special grade of tinted paper for office use, demand for the product dried up. The marketing manager again portrayed manufacturing as the culprit. Curious about what had happened, the manufacturing manager used informal contacts in the headquarters finance department to obtain data from industry sources and from the marketing department about industry-wide sales of this and similar products for the past several years. It turned out that marketing had figured out almost two years earlier that there was strong evidence that demand for the product had matured and would rapidly decline. The marketing manager had concealed and distorted this information. He had a need to project an image of infallibility; otherwise, he feared, he would lose prestige and get a smaller bonus. He was also concerned that if he asked to cut back or stop the project, he would lose credibility with senior management, and manufacturing would trust him even less in the future. He also felt that he could again cover the situation by shifting most of the blame to manufacturing.

In this situation, the objective uncertainty of demand was a serious problem in itself. The marketing manager's mistrust, however, had dropped a curtain of social uncertainty on the situation, preventing other leaders from detecting and reversing a poor decision that was interrupting production schedules and diverting funds and labor from other projects. The manufacturing manager was frustrated by the marketing manager's censorship of timely, relevant information and bitter that marketing had hidden its judgment that demand for the product was vanishing. He thought that the product was good; if he had known about the demand problem, he could have shifted the project to a smaller mill, saving more than a million dollars, avoiding countless production problems, and profitably producing the product at a lower volume. Mistrust had deprived him of information and influence. He never had a chance to create alternative production solutions.

Shortly after this incident, the marketing manager was told to leave the company. Like characters in a Greek tragedy, the leaders of marketing and manufacturing had acted out the inevitable calamity of their mistrust, which they had concealed from higher management. Mistrust had trapped them in a superficially harmonious relationship that made low-quality, financially disastrous decisions.

Trust Reduces Social Uncertainty

Trust lifts the curtain of social uncertainty. It allows people to feel free to disclose timely, relevant information and to contribute creative alternatives. They can then see opportunities and more accurately assess risks because they create little social uncertainty that might obscure the objective uncertainty. They have reliable information about the goals and intentions of others on whom they will have to depend. They can more easily define underlying problems and see effective solutions.

THE CONRAD STUDY

Some 400 executives from several Fortune 500 companies took part in a study based on a series of simulations involving the fictitious Conrad Electronics Company, a composite company that combined the characteristics and problems of several businesses.

The simulations were part of executive seminars held several times each year, with up to forty participants in each session; the study gathered data from a series of simulations that took place over a period of two years.

In the simulation, each executive was randomly assigned to one of four leadership roles in Conrad—the presidency and three functional vice presidencies.

Background

Conrad Electronics, a medium-sized company in the northeast United States, designs and manufactures electronic equipment, radio receivers, transmitters, and amplifiers, which it sells to the military, electronics manufacturers, and distributors who supply retailers. The company had been profitable for twenty years, with 65 percent of its annual sales on a cost-plus basis to the military and prime contractors. Then military purchases declined, technology began to change, and the company faced increasing competition.

Top management cut the work force 25 percent in an effort to reverse Conrad's financial losses. Capital investment for plant and equipment was cut 75 percent to bolster cash flow. The company broke even one year after these drastic steps had been taken. The board of directors then replaced the president and the vice presidents of manufacturing and industrial relations. Conrad's chief financial officer was promoted to president; two other insiders were moved up to the vice presidential positions. The vice president of marketing continued in his position.

The new leaders operated the company at a small profit—4 percent on net worth—for the next two years. Marketing was developing sales to civilian customers, but manufacturing was having difficulty meeting delivery promises. Manufacturing facilities were becoming increasingly obsolete each year. Work in process was high because the plant was poorly laid out in old, multistory buildings. There had been high labor turnover during the three years following the 25 percent reduction in the labor force, and many of the best engineering and production people had left to take jobs with competitors.

The new top leaders felt that they were beginning to get control of the situation. They agreed that the company had to modernize and expand its facilities if it was to succeed in the long run. Unknown to the vice presidents, the board of directors, in a special meeting with the president, had demanded improved profits in the next year. The board said that it would ask the president to resign if profits did not improve.

The president tentatively concluded that, under the circumstances, plant modernization and expansion were not feasible in the short run. It would take more than one year to locate a new site, construct buildings, move equipment and people, and arrange the necessary financing. Also, given the board's demand for higher profits, the board members probably would not approve a heavy capital investment program; if anything, planning, construction, and moving to a new site would reduce productivity and decrease short-term profits. The president had to meet with the vice presidents to announce his decision and formulate appropriate plans.

The Simulation

A handout on the history and the background of Conrad was given to all the executives in the seminar. The participants were randomly assigned to the roles of the president and the vice presidents of Conrad. Each "Conrad" executive was given an additional private, detailed written briefing with specific information about his or her position and concerns, as would be true in any company. Thus, the president had information about his vision of company goals, the company's financial situation, and the concerns of the board of directors that the vice presidents did not have. Similarly, the vice president for manufacturing had details about plant operations, production scheduling, labor problems, and equipment difficulties that the others did not have. The vice presidents for marketing and for industrial relations also had details, problems, and concerns not known to the others. All the executives playing a particular Conrad leader, however, had received identical financial and operating data. Thus, all Conrad "presidents" had the same briefing; all Conrad "manufacturing vice presidents" had the same briefing, and so on for the other two "vice presidents." After absorbing their private briefing, each group of four Conrad leaders convened in a separate room to conduct a meeting called by the president to deal with Conrad's situation. The other executives attending each seminar became non-participant observers who silently watched and listened to the simulated meetings.

Conrad's leaders faced critical, complex problems. Small improvements in the quality of their decisions and their motivation would have a great impact on results. The leaders had to develop a strategy that would increase short-term profits without undermining long-term growth. The president would need the vice presidents' support for short-term actions despite their disappointment over delays in plant modernization and expansion.

More than eighty different groups of executives simulated the president's meeting. In half the groups, however, participants were inclined to mistrust the other members as a result of their work together during the past two years. Participants in the other groups were inclined to trust one another. Here is what we found.

Low-Trust Outcomes

The leaders in low-trust groups strongly resisted examining the situation in any depth. Instead, they kept blaming the president or the board of directors for short-sightedness. The president, after much frustration, forcefully issued edicts backed by threats of dismissal. The vice presidents reluctantly acquiesced in examining a few limited proposals, such as discontinuing lower-profit items, emphasizing sales of higher-profit items, and substantially reducing the labor force again.

Their antagonism and half-hearted commitment typified the behavior of low-trust groups under stress. They were defensive. They blamed others. They were unable to see the situation in its entirety and were unwilling to accept any responsibility for their part in the dilemma. They also focused on the withheld goal of modernization and expansion and had great difficulty considering other aspects of the situation and inventing other options.

When two vice presidents found that they agreed on a point, they joined forces to attack whoever else in the group disagreed with them. These attacks polarized relationships and drove the leaders farther apart. Although some workable ideas were proposed, they were ignored or discarded for spurious reasons. The leaders concentrated on protecting their department and pursuing only its interests. They paid little attention to their interdependence. After the meetings, the majority of leaders were frustrated and said that they would seriously consider employment with another company.

High-Trust Outcomes

Leader behavior in the high-trust groups was very different from that in the low-trust groups. The high-trust leaders analyzed the situation responsibly and creatively. They discussed their disappointment with the delay in modernization and expansion but concluded that they had to face up to the new constraints and see how they could move ahead despite the delay. They created proposals that would require little capital in the short run and that would both substantially improve profitability and aid their long-run interests. These included leasing nearby vacant manufacturing space and sourcing more semifinished or finished products. They selected promising new products and planned to move them more rapidly from research into production. They agreed to revise their short-range and long-range plans and to discuss their revised strategy with the board.

Their behavior typified that of high-trust groups under stress. They dealt creatively with new constraints and at the same time assisted each other. They explored a range of goals, both near-term and long-term. They created and listened to many proposals, selected promising ones, and shaped them into workable courses of action. They were supportive. They were not polarized and stalemated by differences. They used their differences to search for solutions that dealt simultaneously with the concerns of several functional areas (e.g., marketing, manufacturing, finance). They balanced short-term constraints and long-term needs and interests. After their meeting, the majority of the leaders said that they would not consider employment with another company.

These results may sound unrealistic and overly optimistic. Actually, the leaders were practical and hard-nosed. They discussed the risks and the real possibility of failure. But they said the situation was not hopeless and were willing to dedicate themselves to surmounting the difficulties.

AWARENESS OF TRUST

The spiral model and the Conrad study show that high-trust groups, are more likely than low-trust groups, to communicate relevant ideas and feelings. They define problems more clearly and set more realistic, comprehensive goals. They search more extensively for alternatives. They have greater influence on solutions and feel more satisfied with their problem-solving efforts. They have greater motivation to implement their decisions, and they become a tighter-knit team. They have greater loyalty to the company and less desire to leave for other jobs. But other than vague notions that trust is better than mistrust, what is the likelihood that executives will associate these powerful effects with trust?

Low Awareness

One unexpected finding of the Conrad study was that executives are remarkably unaware of the specific effects of trust and mistrust. Consider what happened after the president's meetings ended.

In each seminar all the leaders and all the observers of all the Conrad groups came together in a plenary debriefing meeting. Neither the leaders nor the observers had been told that the groups had started with different initial levels of trust. Also, there had been no discussion of the definition of trust, the elements of trust, the spiral model, or the trust cycle that we presented earlier in this chapter. Each group described its decisions to the plenary meeting. Then the observers described how the leaders had behaved while making their decisions. All the executive attendees heard the differences in the creativity and the quality of the groups' decisions. They also heard about the differences in the behavior and the commitment of the groups. It became apparent from the reports that there were two different types of groups: one productive, cohesive, and committed, the other unproductive, riven with dissension, and uncommitted. The executives were then asked for their explanation of what had caused the differences.

The executives consistently said that the outcomes were the result of three factors: (1) the personalities of the individuals (who had in fact been assigned randomly to the different roles); (2) the president's leadership style, whether autocratic or democratic (which was entirely determined by the person who had been randomly assigned to the role); or (3) whether the president had stated the decision not to expand early or late in the meeting (which was determined by the randomly assigned president). Practically none of the several hundred executives mentioned the word "trust" as a possible cause of the differences in group productivity and commitment.

When executives were asked whether they thought that trust affects decisions, they said yes. Researchers call this a "prompted" response because the question directs the person's attention to a specific factor. But when the executives simulated meetings to resolve Conrad electronic's problems and were not prompted—that is were not specifically asked about trust—then they were astoundingly unaware of the effects of trust. The executives in this study were among the best educated and the most sophisticated to be found in corporate organizations. Yet they did not connect trust—that is, a belief about how they should regulate their vulnerability—with the significant differences in problem-solving effectiveness, decision quality, and commitment that they observed. Trust apparently was important as a broad, intellectual concept, but leaders were unable to see how it shaped their behavior when they made decisions. Trust was, for practical purposes, a mysterious, magical element of leadership. Such low awareness of the positive effects of trust and of the corrosive effects of mistrust should be of great concern to all people. It means that many leaders may be mobilizing only a small fraction of their organization's competence without understanding why.

SUMMARY

Trust affects both how leaders make decisions and the quality of their decisions. People who trust increase their vulnerability to other people whose behavior they do not control. People can be friendly and courteous, but that does not mean that they trust each other. People show trust by how they handle three closely linked factors: information, influence, and control. Trust regulates the disclosure of information—how open people are with relevant information, including their intentions and judgments; trust regulates mutual influence—how receptive people are to each other's goals and concerns; and trust regulates control—the intention to fulfill the spirit of a decision and the willingness to rely on another person to implement her part of the decision.

The spiral model of trust says that these three elements—information, influence, and control—feed into one another, causing trust to spiral up or down. In each meeting, trust goes through three phases: predisposing beliefs, short-cycle feedback, and equilibrium. The predisposing phase consists of initial beliefs and intentions to trust. In the second phase, feedback confirms or disconfirms the initial beliefs. In the third phase, trust or mistrust settles at a certain level for the rest of the meeting. The trust cycle suggests that when two people with similar levels of trust or mistrust get together, barring any changes, they go through a series of mutually reinforcing steps in the cycle, increasing their trust or destructively escalating their mistrust.

Mistrust causes people to censor, delay, and distort relevant information. Social uncertainty compounds ambiguity, masks difficulties, and deprives leaders of the opportunity to make high-quality decisions.

We described the application of the spiral model of trust in the Conrad case, a simulation of leadership of a company facing severe competitive problems. Half the executive groups started with a planned predisposition to trust the other half with a predisposition to mistrust. The decision process and the outcomes of the trusting groups were clearly superior to those of the mistrusting groups. The trusting groups exchanged relevant information and set realistic, comprehensive goals. They accepted mutual influence, generated creative alternatives, increased their cohesion as a team, and were highly committed to implementing their solutions. The contrast with mistrusting groups was stark and undeniable. Mistrusting groups resisted probing below the surface of their difficulties. Their members became polarized into fixed positions and attacked one another. When pressured with edicts and threats of dismissal, they formulated pedestrian solutions to placate their increasingly irate president. Occasionally, someone proposed a creative idea, but it was quickly attacked, and discarded as unworkable. By the end of their meeting, the mistrusting executives were uncommitted to their decisions and were interested in finding jobs with other companies. An unexpected finding of this exercise in trust was that, in the debriefing and review, executives had remarkably little awareness or understanding of the specific effects of trust and mistrust.

In the next chapter we continue to address leadership and trust. What factors predispose leaders to trust or mistrust? What predictions can we make about trust? Can we postulate laws of trust?

7

Determinants of Trust

Leaders sense that many factors determine trust. Some are deeply rooted in people's emotional and psychological histories; others are closer to the surface and thus more easily changed. People are often unaware of the underlying factors that determine their approach to trust. In this chapter we discuss two durable foundation factors: personality and training. We explore how early experiences with dependence shape leaders' attitudes toward trust and examine how specialized training can combine with personality to affect a leader's trust. We then discuss several additional, more accessible determinants of trust in daily relationships: competence, openness, supportiveness, reward systems, and intentions.

DURABLE FACTORS

Personality and training, like breathing or blinking our eyes, are so much a part of us that people have difficulty seeing how they affect trust. Leaders, however, need to understand the connection.

Personality

Personality is an underlying factor that inclines a leader to be trusting or mistrusting. It is rooted in early experiences and in attitudes that develop before a person even thinks about leadership, before the person even learns to speak. Infants acquire a sense of trust from their day-to-day experiences, unmediated by words. Attitudes toward trust continue to develop through childhood and school years, when people have language to express feelings about their dependence on others—parents, relatives, and sometimes strangers—to meet their needs.

Some leaders have had childhoods of fulfilling, reliable dependence. Their parents and extended family were there when they were needed. In hindsight, as adults, these leaders see their parents as almost heroic figures, struggling against adversity but nevertheless providing the openness and stability that allowed their children to develop feelings of trust, respect, and affection. The children carry into adulthood the lessons they learned about trust from their parents.

Lee Iacocca is widely regarded as having an open, direct leadership style. As CEO of Chrysler, he led the company from near-bankruptcy to profitable growth by delegating extensively and developing one of the best product design processes in the auto industry. He earned the trust of Chrysler's managers, workers, creditors, dealers, and customers. Iacocca felt comfortable trusting others, which enabled him to disclose information, accept advice from others, and delegate heavy responsibilities while exercising light control. Iacocca reveals the development of his personality and his formative experiences with trust in this description of his parents and his childhood: "My father and I were very close. I loved pleasing him, and he was always terrifically proud of my accomplishments. If I won a spelling contest at school, he was on top of the world. Later in life whenever I got a promotion, I'd call my father right away and he'd rush out to tell all his friends. In 1970, when I was named president of the Ford Motor Company, I don't know which of us was more excited."[1] Iacocca recalls that when he was growing up, his family "was so close it sometimes felt as if we were one person with four parts." He says that his parents "always made my sister, Delma, and me feel important and special. Nothing was too much work or too much trouble. My father might have been busy with a dozen other things, but he always had time for us. My mother went out of her way to cook the foods we loved—just to make us happy."[2] Iacocca describes the openness of expression in his family that became a natural part of his own personality: "My parents were very open with their feelings and their love—not only at home, but also in public. Most of my friends would never hug their fathers. I guess they were afraid of not appearing strong and independent. But I hugged and kissed my dad at every opportunity—nothing could have felt more natural."[3]

Iacocca was ten years old in 1934 when his family, like so many others, fell on hard times at the height of the Depression. He recalls the uplifting spirit of his father. "Whenever times were tough it was my father who kept our spirits up. No matter what happened, he was always there for us." His father would philosophize that "life has its ups and downs"; each person has to come to terms with some misery he believed, but adversity helps us understand and appreciate the good times and the joys of our accomplishments. Iaccocca remembers that his father "hated to see any of us unhappy and would always try to cheer us up. Whenever I was worried about anything he'd say: 'Tell me, Lido, what were you so upset about last month? Or last year? See—you don't even remember! So maybe whatever you're worried about today isn't really all that bad. Forget it, and move on to tomorrow. He never let any of us surrender to despair." Years later when Iacocca was trying to save Chrysler from bankruptcy he says that whenever he felt "ready to throw in the towel," he kept his sanity by recalling his father's comforting trust that things would work out and that "this too shall pass."[4] Iacocca's childhood and his later experiences with his parents provided a solid foundation for building trust and for feeling comfortable trusting others.

Many leaders' childhood introduction to trust was not as positive as Mr. Iacocca's. In some cases their dependency needs were fulfilled erratically or not at all. Some were separated from their parents and deposited with relatives or sent to boarding school. Some were shuttled back and forth between warring parents who used them as pawns in their conflicts. Many of these children felt abandoned. As adults they may resist depending on others because of a deep-seated, inaccessible fear that other people will prove to be unreliable. As leaders, they develop tremendous self-reliance. They try to do and control as much as they can and become impatient with people who appear to be slow or who are not immediately available when summoned.

Some leaders have been deliberately trained by their parents or other adults to mistrust others. They have been taught to withhold information, keep their own counsel, and never seek help. Some adults intentionally betray a child's trust to drive home the lesson that "you can't trust anyone." Leaders with a childhood of unfulfilled dependence understandably attempt to limit their vulnerability. They try to control relationships in order to minimize their dependence on others. Leaders need to understand their fundamental orientation with regard to trust. In stressful, ambiguous situations, the ability to trust, or any limits on it, often becomes the major determinant of behavior.

Training

Like personality, training gives leaders a particular slant on the world. Each specialty subtly implants its own orientation toward trust. For example, law instills skepticism and mistrust of others as a starting assumption. Lawyers must deal with clients' natural desire to tell only what supports their position and to forget, omit, or distort information to the contrary. The adversary method used in U.S. jurisprudence also encourages lawyers to withhold information from their opponents and to reveal only what they are legally required to disclose. In short, they are oriented to trust neither their client nor their opposing attorney.

Engineering and the sciences, in contrast, orient people to trust what others say. The scientific community depends on the accurate reporting of results, whether they confirm or contradict one's subjective preferences. Scientists are trained to reserve judgment until they can replicate what others report. If subsequent studies do not confirm the claims, scientists attribute the differences to faulty control of conditions in the original research. They rarely mistrust the integrity of the original investigators. A scientist who distorts data or results is readily detected and loses the respect of her colleagues.

It is important that leaders understand how their particular training has oriented them with regard to trust. Each business specialty instills a different orientation. Professionals in accounting and finance, for example, may be particularly distrustful because they know how financial statements can report selectively and distort actual conditions.

Harold Geneen joined ITT as president in 1959 and during the next eighteen years "took a loosely knit $759 million confederation of companies and made it the largest, most rigidly controlled conglomerate in America."[5] Geneen's childhood and adolescent experiences with distant, unsupportive parents in a failed marriage was almost the polar opposite of Iacocca's experience.[6] Geneen's parents were married in England but emigrated to the United States shortly after he was born. In the United States, Geneen's father tried various small business ventures to support his wife and infant child. Geneen did not see much of his father, did not really know him, and had no meaningful ties to him. When Geneen was five his parents separated, and from the age of seven on Geneen lived at boarding school and at summer camps. He was a short, slight, almost frail child; while at the Suffolk School in Connecticut, which emphasized athletics and sports, Geneen, one of the youngest and least athletic students, was an isolated tag-along. His mother, a traveling singer and actress, was away on the road during most holidays, and Geneen, left to fend for himself, had to rely on the compassion of the schoolmaster and of his schoolmate's families to care for him on weekends and holidays. All of this provided the ingredients for a distrusting, lonely childhood. An associate who in the past had been close to Geneen felt that "the separation scarred, [and] the man's notorious mistrust even of intimates derived from the boy's sense of betrayal, a father who decamped; a mother who returned his adoration, yet functionally abandoned him to schoolmasters and camp counselors."[7] When Geneen graduated from the Suffolk School, he expected to go to day college, but there was no money. His father had stopped financial support, perhaps because his business was doing poorly. Geneen was severely disappointed: "It was such a tender point that neither he [Geneen] nor his mother would ever discuss Samuel [Geneen's father]."[8] Geneen went to work as a page for the New York Stock Exchange.

The training that shaped Geneen's view of trust and leadership began two years later when he started night classes at the New York University School of Commerce, where he specialized in accounting. With a load of five classes a week, it took six years for Geneen to graduate. He then got a job with Lybrand, Ross, which years later became Coopers & Lybrand, a major national accounting firm. For eight years, Geneen reviewed and audited the financial records of client companies. He saw how the figures revealed, with cold objectivity, the inner workings of each company and where its management had gone wrong. If the ratios were off, indicating some fault in operations, he wanted to tell the managers how to run their business.[9] He concluded that if one managed the ratios properly, one could manage the business. In his opinion, most managers did not know how to manage a firm to achieve financial goals. His experience in his subsequent jobs sharpened his accounting and analytic skills while confirming his mistrust of the competence of most managers.

During and after World War II, Geneen worked for Amertorp, a new subsidiary of the American Can Company set up to manufacture torpedoes. There he designed and installed general accounting, property accounting, and cost analysis and control systems for the company's two plants, which were operating at such a hectic pace that taking physical inventories was impossible. In his next job, as comptroller of Bell & Howell, a camera equipment company, he worked with the company's brilliant, new young president, Charles Percy. Geneen walked into an accounting wasteland and transformed it. Percy's predecessor had run the company as a one-man show, often making whimsical spending decisions. Accounting was rudimentary and after the fact. Geneen became a bulldog, relentlessly pursuing improvements in cost control before, rather than after, managers made decisions. He installed budgeting and forecasting systems that were prototypes of the leadership control he would perfect by the time he got to ITT. Marketing had to forecast sales; manufacturing had to forecast costs and capital investment needs, justifying each item; engineering had to estimate costs to develop new products and predict development schedules. All departments had to live within their budgets. Profit plans were developed, and the breakeven point for each product was calculated. His analysis convinced management that by lowering the price of a popular camera model they could spur an increase in sales that would lower manufacturing costs and increase revenues and profits. All of this thinking seems obvious today, but then it was a revolutionary use of accounting. Geneen's single-minded drive to install cost controls and to live with a financial compass began to arouse resentment and distrust. One product development engineer, recalling the period, said that Geneen's focus on financial controls inhibited product development during the critical postwar boom. To Geneen, budgets took top priority and trust was irrelevant; he built a reputation as "an authentic, stem-winding, ring-tailed bastard."[10]

Geneen next became comptroller of J & L Steel, where he again worked his magic of introducing budgets, controlling mill operating costs, measuring individual product profitability, and setting market share targets in a company with many skeptical managers who were devotedly resistant to modernized financial controls and analysis. His detractors nicknamed him "Little Tojo," and years after he left J & L there was still an enduring residue of mistrust and resentment. Geneen's next position was executive vice president of Raytheon, a military contractor with excellent scientists and muddled management. Raytheon's sales had climbed to $175 million, but Geneen felt that the company was being run with the management and staff of a $20 million company. Geneen was at Raytheon for only three years, but in that time he installed his program of leadership through tight, financial controls and low trust: detailed budgets with managers accountable for meeting forecasts; unit controllers reporting directly to the corporate controller instead of the unit manager; exhaustive monthly managers' reports. He sharpened his monthly managerial review meetings into inquisitions, publicly intimidating and humiliating defaulting managers before their peers. Trust was pummeled, shredded, and tossed out. Geneen's financial control system and his institutionalized mistrust lashed managers until they met his ratio goals. In two and a half years, Raytheon's sales grew from $175 million to $375 million, and its after-tax profits increased from $1.25 million to $9.4 million. The financial world, which was unconcerned with trust and the dysfunctional effects of Geneen's leadership, was impressed.[11]

Geneen became president and CEO of ITT in 1959, and for the next eighteen years its managers lived in a tornado, seeking safety in storm cellars or cast out by the whirlwind. At ITT, Geneen assumed full control. He installed his systems and people without resistance from above. He perfected his financial leadership regimen and imposed it on a long string of disparate acquisitions that ranged from Levitt, the mass builder of low-cost homes, to Continental Bakeries, the bakers of Wonder bread and Hostess Twinkies and cupcakes.

Geneen's leadership regimen had two critical pieces. One was the gathering of financial and operating information, down to the smallest detail, by people who were seen as an extension of Geneen's tight control and mistrust. They fed his remarkable talent for ingesting and processing huge amounts of information. The controller of every ITT division reported directly to the headquarters controller, who reported to and thought like Geneen. Division controllers were responsible for reporting to headquarters all the facts about all aspects of each division's business. Their job was to guarantee that the division manager concealed nothing from Geneen's searching monthly review. Geneen supplemented his intelligence gathering with additional sources. Product line managers stationed in headquarters roamed freely through the divisions. They had no operating responsibility but provided additional eyes and ears; they could go directly to Geneen to discuss their concerns about the internal operation of any division. Geneen also used a variety of external consultants, internal consultants, and multiple task forces to study the same problem, with each ignorant of the other's existence.

The second part of Geneen's leadership regimen was the budgeting, planning, and cost control system that was acted out in monthly meetings to review financial and operational results. The meeting for the U.S. subsidiaries took place in ITT's headquarters in New York, and another was held in ITT's Brussels headquarters for the European companies. Each meeting was "a weird spectacle with more than a hint of Dr. Strangelove."[12] For four days each month 120 people, including the top leaders of ITT subsidiaries from all over Europe, assembled around a huge horseshoe-shaped table in a hushed, darkened, specially constructed conference room. Sitting at the middle of the table were the senior vice presidents and Geneen. One of the division leaders or controllers would give facts about figures projected on the screen. Periodically Geneen, an "owlish figure" peering out of the subdued light would ask a question: "Why has a target not been reached? Why is inventory too high?" The manager would try to defend himself tensely and briefly. "The meetings, whether in Brussels or New York, are the central ordeal of the ITT discipline, the test that its men are attuned to the system. If there is a surprise, a task force is immediately appointed, perhaps two or three task forces unaware of each other, to find out the reason, to supply a solution."[13] There was a palpable feeling of dread hidden under civilized denial. "For a newly joined manager—and especially from a company newly acquired by ITT—the ordeal can be terrifying; there are stories of one man fainting and of another rushing out to get blind drunk for two days. For the hardened ITT man, it is no more than a routine test of sangfroid. 'You have to be prepared,' said one of them, 'to have your balls screwed off in public and then joke afterward as if nothing happened.'"[14] Mistrust and constant fear of the executioner's ax were pervasive, but no one was allowed to admit it.

Geneen ruled ITT with extraordinary financial acumen and control but little trust. His tenure illustrates leadership based on knowledge and power but low trust. Such leaders become, as we said in Chapter 1, distant, task-oriented martinets. In this case, Geneen became, to those who worked for him, the consummate financial technocrat. He paid extremely high salaries to executives who could perform to numbers and armor themselves against distrust and humiliation. When Geneen stepped aside as CEO in 1978, he had amassed acquisitions that had turned ITT into a gigantic conglomerate with revenues of $17 billion, 250 diverse profit centers, and 375,000 employees.

Geneen had built an intricate financial system that he administered with ruthless efficiency. In the process, leadership trust, commitment, and creativity had suffered. Geneen's training in accounting and his early experience installing financial systems in the face of what he saw as managerial ignorance and resistance had combined with a personality that made mistrust almost a natural part of his leadership style. One might speculate that mistrust was so deeply rooted that he considered it essential to his survival and to his competence as a leader. Trust was not an objective, impersonal variable that he could measure and fit into his control of financial performance. Because of his mistrust, he kept people alert, attentive, and at bay. People may have become defensive, self-protective, and uncreative, but he could be comfortable with such relationships, and he was willing to accept the costs. Geneen's goal was to build the greatest money-making organization in the world. As time went by, however, "the coherence and satisfying human purpose of [ITT] became less clear."[15] A thoughtful admirer says that "what ultimately kept Geneen from his goal was a want of soul. The sadness of Harold Geneen's story is not that he missed his goal but that such gifts served so narrow a purpose."[16]

Geneen's legacy of tight financial controls, while brilliant in concept and execution, was an inadequate leadership foundation to sustain ITT. Rand Araskog, Geneen's successor, downsized ITT, divesting many of its poorly performing acquisitions. Geneen's philosophy—that financial discipline could resurrect any business—no longer held sway. The culture of mistrust was renounced and dismantled; division leaders were given greater freedom and autonomy. By 1986, ITT's revenues had declined to $7.6 billion, less than half of what they had been at Geneen's peak. Araskog and his top managers struggled to make financial and operational sense out of the patchwork of businesses Geneen had stitched together but left without a sustainable core of trusting leaders and a unifying culture. In contrast, Iacocca's trusting style, which he acquired from his supportive parents and from his training in industrial management, rejuvenated Chrysler as a world-class organization. Iacocca left Chrysler with a cultural legacy of trust that supported a new, creative product design organization and the efficient production of high-quality cars. That legacy of trust earned high commitment and loyalty from workers, dealers, suppliers, and creditors. Iacocca's successors benefited from his legacy of trust and were able to continue growing Chrysler's revenues and profits to achieve the highest levels in its history.

ACCESSIBLE FACTORS

Trust depends on several factors in addition to personality and training. These include competence, openness, supportiveness, reward systems, and intentions.

Competence

People employ a locksmith to fix a lock, a cobbler to repair shoes, and a pilot to fly a plane. In each case, their willingness to trust the other person depends on their estimate of the person's competence to perform the task at hand. Although leaders may have a high personal inclination to trust their people, they are not going to leave their fate in the hands of someone who is incompetent or who has yet to prove their competence. Trust is task-specific—that is, leaders may trust someone with one task but not with a different task. Leaders of an advertising agency, for example, might trust neophytes to do statistical analysis of marketing research data, but not trust them to design a critical and expensive national marketing program for a major client.

Leaders continually assess their subordinates' competence to perform different tasks and adjust their level of trust accordingly. When a leader has a low estimate of another person's competence, friendship and harmony will not reduce the resulting mistrust. The leader must help that subordinate improve her competence to a level where the leader can trust her. Until the subordinate's competence improves, leaders will limit their vulnerability by restricting the subordinate's assignments and responsibilities. If leaders do not improve their subordinate's competence, their mistrust eventually will require that they reassign or replace the subordinate.

Competence is a necessary component of trustworthiness, but competence alone does not earn trust. It is, however, a critical beginning. We now look at other factors.

Openness

Openness is a gateway to trust. When people are open, they give and get rapid and direct disclosure of relevant information. This doesn't mean that they are offensive or obnoxious. They can be sensitive to the feelings of others and still be open with relevant information. Openness is especially important when the other person has low competence for the task at hand. Even though a person may lack competence, he may win the leader's trust if he is open about his need for greater competence. This allows the leaders to assess the risks of letting the person continue with the task and to take steps to limit those risks, perhaps by training the person while others fill in for his deficiency while he is learning. People who are open about their competence are often their own harshest critics and usually underestimate their own skills. When leaders express confidence in such people, as one executive said, "they can grow into giants."

Poor leaders erroneously believe that openness means social charm and poise—a gift for comfortable conversation. They think that if they are amiable and well mannered, people will trust them. They cultivate casual conversation and friendliness, freely express their views on current political and social issues, and discuss their family concerns. In business problem-solving meetings, however, they withhold or distort relevant information. Effective leaders, in contrast, are aware that social harmony and political smoothness are not substitutes for openness. People's willingness to trust leaders depends on how open those leaders are with relevant information. When leaders conceal or censor relevant information, they mislead others while maintaining advantage and control for themselves. People can distinguish between superficial and true openness, and eventually they catch on to the leader's propensity to withhold or manipulate relevant information. They mistrust such leaders.

A leader in a university-affiliated teaching hospital was working with several coleaders and staff specialists on a task force to redesign a complex health-services delivery system. He was amiable and competent in his medical specialty, but he stalled the task force for more than three months by not providing information he had promised to get. In addition, he did not implement his agreement with the task force to discuss change options with his subordinates and to seek their suggestions. Instead, unknown to the task force, the leader, with his subordinates' help, wrote a position paper on why his unit's activities should not be changed and requesting that his unit be staffed with more people.

He then met secretly with higher management and voiced his demands. He threatened to resign if these demands were not met. Higher management was unwilling to deal with his ultimatum. It was concerned about the difficulty of finding an equally prestigious medical specialist to replace him, and it wanted to avoid damaging general morale by escalating the conflict. Without any discussion with the task force, higher management directed the task-force chairman to include in the final plan the leader's demands.

The members of the task force were infuriated by this deceptive behavior. Their mistrust of the leader and of higher management skyrocketed. The task force closed down communication with the errant leader and with higher management. It continued to plan a revised system and set up experimental areas where it tested options on a small scale. The task force was then informally reconstituted without the errant leader and with a member of higher management. Although the new task force periodically communicated with the specialist, it provided minimal information about its plans for change. It devoted great energy to protecting itself from another end run. Eventually, higher management approved and implemented a plan that changed equipment and procedures in a major part of the hospital. The changes improved patient services, increasing patient referrals by 40 percent and revenues by 20 percent. The errant leader's unit, however, became only a small element in the larger plan. Its activities were changed slightly to conform to the new system. The leader complained about the new system, but his facade of openness had by now been widely seen through. Although he was extremely competent in his medical specialty, his lack of openness had diminished his trustworthiness. His peers and superiors were courteous, but they did not take his complaints seriously. They saw them as devices by which he hoped once again to secure undeserved advantage and resources for his unit. He and his unit were excluded from, or the last to hear about, future changes.

Supportiveness

Supportiveness has diverse effects. We discussed one of these—its power to stimulate knowledge and creativity—when we described the case of 3M and the creation of Post-it notes in Chapter 4. Supportiveness also affects trust—a person's willingness to risk increasing his vulnerability.

Effective leaders understand and employ three components of supportiveness that build trust: acceptance, tolerance for disagreement, and constructive use of people's openness. People trust leaders who accept them as they are. Effective leaders accept people's right to their concerns, opinions, and feelings. Effective leaders implicitly say, "Your views are valuable, even though we may disagree." The second component of supportiveness is a high tolerance for disagreement. Effective leaders can disagree with someone without personal attack or discourtesy and ridiculing, humiliating, or embarrassing the person. Instead, they can disagree and yet elevate the other person's sense of self-worth. The third component of supportiveness consists of the constructive use of a person's vulnerability rather than its exploitation. People increase their vulnerability by disclosing previously unknown facts about their situation and by revealing their analyses, opinions, and judgments and their concerns, intentions, and feelings. Poor leaders pretend agreement while concealing their opposition and then later exploit what they have learned. Effective leaders do not pretend agreement; instead, they use supportiveness to build creatively on a person's exposure to solve problems and help them learn.

The director of operations of a midwestern bank began giving poor performance ratings to a woman supervisor who had a ten-year record of above-average performance. The director explained to his superior, the vice president of administration, that the supervisor had become a source of friction and was distracting her coworkers from their work. At the next review, the director gave the supervisor another poor rating and told the vice president that he wanted to fire her. The vice president was puzzled by this development. He knew the supervisor slightly and had heard that she was a competent and enthusiastic worker.

The vice president met informally with the supervisor and then with her coworkers several times. Gradually he learned that the supervisor had periodically questioned the director of operations in the presence of others about the bank's slow move into computers. The director, who seemed irritated, gave her vague answers and seemed embarrassed by her relentless pursuit of the subject.

The vice president discussed the situation at length with the supervisor and with the director. The supervisor readily admitted that she knew little about computers, but she felt strongly that they were the wave of future technology in banking. The vice president asked the supervisor if she would be interested in learning about computers. She said yes but doubted that she would get the chance.

The vice president spent some time thinking about how to deal with the director's demand that the supervisor be disciplined or fired. He was impressed with the supervisor's vision, even though it was based on little practical knowledge. He understood the director's concern about his image, but at the same time he wanted to support the supervisor's interest and determination. In discussions with the director, he proposed that they encourage the supervisor by offering her an opportunity to learn about computers, suggesting that until she discovered the boundaries of her own limitations, she would continue to chide the organization about computer technology. Also, her public commitment would probably motivate her to learn. Her growth could be an example for others and might help the bank's efforts to install computer technology in operations.

The supervisor agreed to take aptitude tests that would be used to determine what to do next. The tests showed that she had a high aptitude for programming and skills related to information systems. The vice president then sponsored her attendance at computer courses offered by manufacturers and local colleges. During the next ten years, she relentlessly moved the bank into computer systems and kept it at the frontier of technology. The up-to-date information systems she installed were a major contribution to the bank's superior customer service. Under her jurisdiction, the bank also established a highly profitable service bureau that processed data for smaller banks. The service bureau contributed up to 15 percent of the bank's earnings. Ultimately, she rose to the position of director of information systems. She became a leader, and a legend, among bank data processing professionals in her region. Only a handful of people knew how close she had come to being fired.

In this case the vice president's supportiveness demonstrated his trust and earned the trust of the director and the supervisor. He accepted their differences and listened carefully to both of them. He was not disturbed by their disagreement but joined with them in a search for new opportunities. He did not blame either person. Instead, by creatively using their exposure rather than exploiting it, he supported their growth and learning. He earned their trust, and they and the bank reaped the benefits.

Reward Systems

Effective leaders understand that a company's reward system can encourage trust or mistrust. A collaborative, integrative, win-win reward system encourages trust. In a win-win reward system, one person's gain is a gain for the other person as well, and one person's loss is also a loss for the other. Effective leaders encourage trust by emphasizing the integrative aspects of reward systems. If the research division in a drug company develops a successful new product, for example, all departments benefit. Leaders who use win-win reward systems stress the importance of sharing information across marketing, manufacturing, and research so that research will develop timely, high-need, high-value products. They further emphasize collaborative rewards by linking bonuses to the overall profitability of the firm. This creates an incentive for each person to help others do well, because if one department does well, it is a gain for everyone. If marketing gains a major customer, all departments gain some benefit; if manufacturing produces high-quality products, reduces waste, and increases customer satisfaction, all departments benefit. In the collaborative, win-win reward system, with its shared gains and losses, people are rationally better off trusting each other. Trust helps them improve their mutual gain and reduce their mutual loss.

A competitive, distributive, or win-lose reward system encourages mistrust. In a win-lose system, one person's gain comes at another person's expense. If two salespeople from the same firm sell to the same customer and are paid a commission on their individual sales, for example, the one who closes the sale to the customer gets a commission and the other gets nothing. A competitive reward system practically forces people to mistrust each other; trusting others by disclosing relevant information and giving them the opportunity to reach the goal ahead of one works against one's self-interest. To trust an opponent in a competitive reward situation is to be a professional victim. It is in each person's interest to take advantage of and to use for her benefit whatever a trusting adversary reveals.

Poor leaders do not understand, or prefer to deny, that competitive reward systems encourage mistrust. They put people in competitive reward systems and then demand that they trust each other by sharing information and influence. People usually resolve this dilemma by mistrusting each other.

Mixed Reward Systems

Most leaders work in a mixed reward system—one that is partly collaborative and partly competitive. The leader's attitude and emphasis determine which way the balance of trust will tip. In a classic budget competition, leaders of marketing and manufacturing request operating funds from a fixed operating budget and capital funds from a fixed capital budget. They appear to be competing with each other in a win-lose reward system in which each additional dollar allocated to marketing leaves one dollar less for manufacturing, and vice versa. At the same time, the departments are in a collaborative reward system because they both benefit when marketing's activities lead to higher sales or manufacturing's activities lead to decreased production costs. In a mixed reward system, effective leaders understand that the fundamental question is: What is the best allocation of resources, or funds, across all departments, given the company's strategy and competitive environment? Effective leaders tip the balance toward trust. They answer the question by emphasizing collaboration and setting priorities that best implement the company's overall strategy. Poor leaders tip the balance toward mistrust. They emphasize the budget competition, losing sight of the firm's overall strategy.

Senior management of a financial services company had a choice as to whether to emphasize the competitive or the collaborative aspects of the company's mixed reward system. The leaders decided that they could best improve performance by emphasizing internal competition rather than interdepartmental cooperation. The firm's overall strategy, however, was supposed to emphasize building relationships with customers, encouraging them to purchase multiple products from the company's different departments. The firm's overall strategy depended on interdepartmental cooperation, but the top leaders' operating philosophy was competitive, stressing "every tub on its own bottom." Department leaders competed strongly, almost viciously, for budget dollars and staff resources. They were open only enough to ensure the uninterrupted operation of their own departments. Cooperation in seeking mutually beneficial opportunities was practically nonexistent; leaders would not collaborate for their common benefit, even though the company was losing market share.

Senior leaders in this company used the mixed reward system to pursue a policy of survival by ordeal. They let priorities emerge from the internal conflict among department leaders. Employees described the organization as a collection of fiefdoms ruled by jealous, warring barons. The loss of market share continued. The company closed many of its overseas offices and ultimately withdrew from several lines of business. Although the firm had a mixed reward system, leaders had tipped the balance toward competition. Several key departmental leaders left the firm for senior positions with other companies. The firm's lackluster performance, despite the stress on internal competition, made it an acquisition target for external competitors. Emphasizing the competitive side of a mixed reward system had increased mistrust, hobbling the organization while competitors continued to gain market share.

Intentions

People's beliefs about a leader's intentions have a powerful influence on trust. People trust leaders whom they believe have good intentions, even if the leader stumbles occasionally, and mistrust leaders whom they believe have harmful intentions, even though the leader rarely makes a mistake. If, for example, people believe that a leader has positive intentions, they will overlook her mistrusting behavior; if she withholds information or fails to fulfill an agreement, they will treat it as a temporary lapse attributable to stress or oversight. They do not change their beliefs about the leader's good intentions until they have suffered a significant disappointment. On the other hand, if people believe that a leader's intentions go against their best interests—if, for example, she intends to downsize their department, reduce their budget, or diminish their power—but she attempts to conceal this intention, they will be suspicious of her future actions. Even if she is open and supportive, people will be skeptical, they will interpret her behavior as a ploy to lower their defenses. When people believe the leader has harmful intentions, they interpret the leader's trusting behavior as clever deception. Poor leaders do not understand that if people believe the leader has harmful intentions, they will distort even trusting behavior into evidence of harmful intentions.

SUMMARY

Personality and training, two underlying, durable factors, are fundamental to a leader's attitude toward trust. If leaders are to improve their effectiveness, they need to understand how these factors affect their behavior. Personality, shaped by childhood dependence on parents and on other important figures, can incorporate fundamental trust and openness, as in the case of Iacocca. On the other hand, training in critical analysis can combine with a personality shaped by parental abandonment, to instill in the adult leader mistrust, skepticism, and a high need to control, as in Geneen's situation.

Several other accessible factors, in addition to personality and training, determine trust in daily relationships. Competence is the first factor. If a person cannot do the job at hand, it makes little sense for a leader to trust that person and risk almost certain failure. Effective leaders therefore coach and train subordinates to increase their competence. Leaders then increase their trust to the degree that the subordinate demonstrates increased competence. Openness is the second factor. Effective leaders are open about relevant information. Poor leaders conceal or distort relevant information, exploiting the openness of others.

Supportiveness—the ability to explore differences constructively—is a third factor in building trust. Effective leaders can hear and analyze differences without humiliating or attacking others. The reward system that people perceive is a fourth determinant of trust. If leaders install an integrative reward system, it becomes rational for people to trust each other because they will all benefit. A competitive reward system in contrast, encourages mistrust because under it a person can benefit by taking advantage of another's trust.

A fifth factor is the perception of intentions. If people believe that a leader has beneficial intentions, they will trust that leader and help him by collaborating to correct errors and minimize delays. If people believe that a leader has harmful intentions, however, they will mistrust the leader and see the leader's behavior as confirming those bad intentions, thereby reinforcing their mistrust.

Trust systems contain regularities that we call laws of trust. In Chapter 8 we discuss these laws and the steps effective leaders take to build trust.

8

Laws of Trust

Weather systems exhibit patterns of behavior that are sufficiently predictable to allow scientists to forecast the weather. Meteorologists know, for example, that high-pressure weather systems displace low-pressure systems and that wind speed and the amount of turbulence depend on the pressure and temperature gradient along the boundary between two weather systems. As with weather systems, there are reliable patterns of behavior in trust systems that lead to predictable outcomes. The laws of trust say that a particular outcome is likely if leaders do not change the level of trust, and reliable predictions can be made about how trust affects behavior. In this chapter we describe several of these laws of trust. One of the most important laws states that mistrust drives out trust. Other laws state that trust increases cohesion, mistrusting groups self-destruct, trust stimulates productivity, mistrust depresses productivity, and rapid growth masks mistrust. We also discuss the steps leaders can take to deal with the complex and challenging process of increasing trust. These include installing integrative reward systems, initiating reciprocal increases in trust, and analyzing relationships.

LAWS OF TRUST

In this section we discuss the implications of trust and mistrust, in terms of several laws or principles. We use the example of the leaders in the university-affiliated hospital described in Chapter 7 to illustrate some of these laws.

Mistrust Drives Out Trust

Gresham's law of money says that bad money drives good money out of circulation. There is a similar law of trust that states that mistrust drives out trust. People who are trusting demonstrate their trust by increasing their exposure to others, disclosing relevant information and expressing their true judgments and intentions. However, people who mistrust do not reciprocate. They conceal information and take advantage of the trusting person's exposure. To defend against repeated exploitation when faced with mistrust, trusting people are driven to mistrust. They too learn to withhold information and disguise their judgments. They decrease their vulnerability by isolating themselves from those they mistrust; if possible, they try to control them.

In the case we discussed in Chapter 7 concerning a hospital task force, a leader exploited information obtained from the task force to shield his department and to obtain additional resources from senior management while the task force was still in an early stage of its work. Holding the task force at bay by appearing to be trustworthy, he stalled its progress by failing to give the task force information he had promised and by neglecting to hold agreed-upon discussions with the people in his unit. In addition, unbeknownst to the task force, he pursued his hidden agenda, pressuring higher management to capitulate to his demands by threatening to resign and then cajoling higher management into imposing his demands on the task force. He had taken advantage of task force information and judgments and concealed his negotiations with higher management. When higher management imposed his demands, the task force felt that its trust and exposure had been abused. Its members perceived his behavior as mistrusting. The task force was in turn driven to mistrusting behavior in its relations with the leader and with higher management. To protect itself, it limited the flow of information to the leader and deflected his attempts to influence the work of the task force. Communication with higher management was reduced to the bare essentials on a "need-to-know" basis. One highly trusted member of higher management was recruited to the task force to keep it informed of higher management's intentions and actions, and the leader was isolated and mistrusted. The task force's trust in the leader and in the organization had been driven out by mistrust.

Trust Increases Cohesion

Trust holds people together, deepening their belief that all will do their utmost to fulfill their responsibilities. Trust means that people have confidence that they can rely on each other. If one person needs help or falters, that person knows that the others will be there to fill in. A trusting group is close-knit, its members sticking together through good and bad times. When facing adversity, members exert extraordinary effort to help achieve the group's goals and to protect each other against external attack. They find an equitable way to share reductions in resources or income. Sharing misfortune equally further increases their trust and cohesion. Effective leaders know that a trusting group has a spirit—a motivational cohesion, a dedication to group members, a deep, unswerving mutual commitment—that lifts productivity and creativity above the levels found in mistrusting groups.

Mistrusting Groups Self-Destruct

Related to the law of cohesion is its corollary: Mistrusting groups self-destruct. When members mistrust each other, they repel and separate. Members of mistrusting groups turn against each other. They pursue their own interests. Each seeks what is best for themselves. Members of mistrusting groups are highly suspicious of each other's intentions; each is constantly on the lookout for attack or exploitation from the others. Even when their jobs make them interdependent or higher management insists that they work together, members of a mistrusting group have no internal bond of mutual commitment and dedication to hold them together. They do not believe that they can rely on each other. To reduce the energy they squander on defending themselves, members try to isolate those they mistrust. The few members who trust each other meet separately, making decisions and agreements before meeting with the full group. If possible, they expel those they mistrust from the group. Members of a mistrusting group restrict communication with those they mistrust. They avoid or endlessly postpone meetings and, between meetings, do their best to circumvent the group. Members dislike meetings of a mistrusting group because the sessions are charades of concealment and deception. The antagonism is so great that the group teeters on the brink of self-destruction.

The members of the hospital task force who trusted each other increased their cohesion. At the same they reduced communication with and separated from the leader they mistrusted. In essence, they continued their work in a trusting subgroup and deliberately allowed the former full group to wither by not convening meetings.

Trust Stimulates Productivity

Trust stimulates productivity because it gives people confidence that they can depend on each other to define and achieve appropriate goals. When people trust others, they emphasize their common interests and take the steps necessary to cooperate. They disclose relevant information and develop plans together to reach their goals. When they face obstacles to productivity, trust lets them move ahead, confident that they will find a way to overcome the obstacles. If a person cannot deal with an obstacle alone, she knows that others stand ready to help. Trust lets people look on differences as a natural part of working together. They treat differences with respect, finding ways to resolve them in favor of their common interests. Trust stimulates people to think of productivity in broad terms, including the quantity produced, the efficiency of production, the quality of products, and their value to end users. Trust also encourages people to think of productivity in terms of the satisfaction they get from being productive, the joy of working together, and the exhilaration of being creative.

Trust encourages people to value two different forms of creativity—doing well the things they know how to do (creativity in the sense of craftsmanship and high levels of skill) and finding original, elegant theories and solutions to problems (creativity in the sense of the artful and original development and combination of ideas). When people trust their leader, they can use their imaginations to explore unusual assumptions and concepts. They can play with knowledge. They feel free to discover nuances, consider multiple meanings, examine juxtapositions, and probe paradoxes. Trust enlarges their thinking, revealing a wide range of concepts and possibilities that stimulate productivity.

Mistrust Depresses Productivity

The corollary to the law of productivity is that mistrust depresses productivity. When people mistrust, they do not believe they can depend on each other. They conceal and secretly pursue their own interests. When they face obstacles, they avoid calling on others, fearing that those they mistrust will take advantage of their predicament. Mistrust makes people suspicious of others' attempts to influence them; people feel that views different from their own should be suppressed or eliminated. Mistrust focuses attention on the differences in interests, making it difficult for people to visualize common interests, let alone cooperate to pursue them. When people mistrust, they work with incomplete information and distorted interpretations; they make decisions with an inaccurate picture of reality and an inadequate awareness of risks. As a result, productivity suffers. (Recall the case of the paper company that wasted millions of dollars when a mistrusting marketing manager concealed and distorted information about the declining demand for a new paper product.)

Mistrust obstructs creativity by polarizing thinking. When people mistrust, they tend to think in extremes. They exaggerate, stating issues in black and white. In effect, they say that if you do not think as I do, then you can't be trusted. Polarized thinking eliminates nuances and eradicates multiple meanings. By obliterating searching questions, it subverts comprehensive thinking. As a result, there is little creativity in people's efforts to improve productivity. Mistrust directs creativity into unproductive channels such as defensiveness and revenge. When people mistrust, they use their creative energy to defend against abuses of their vulnerability. They may conceal or distort information and then create excuses to explain why the information was not available or was misinterpreted. They also creatively retaliate against those whom they mistrust; for example, when they know that the other person urgently needs their assistance, they contrive to be busy and creatively explain why their other tasks must take priority. Again, as a result, mistrust diminishes productivity.

Rapid Growth Masks Mistrust

When sales grow rapidly, leaders push members of the organization to sustain that growth. As profits increase rapidly, leaders seek expedient solutions to problems. Growth gives leaders opportunities for rapid promotion, and for increased power and responsibility. In the heady atmosphere that prevails, leaders concentrate on demonstrating to top management that they are ready for promotion. They plan to stay in their positions for only a short time and expect to move to new jobs before they have to confront the effects of mistrust in their current positions. They solve problems with quick fixes that elude immediate detection by higher management and leave the problems arising from mistrust to their successors. Unfortunately for those successors, the lingering effects of mistrust become apparent when growth slows.

John Beryl, a young manager, was promoted to lead Granco (names disguised), a relatively small Canadian subsidiary of a large U.S. company. Granco specialized in home electronics, small appliances, and entertainment products and employed about 700 people. Bob Hopper, who preceded Beryl as Granco's leader, had been promoted to lead a larger industrial products division in a different city after increasing Granco's sales 25 percent a year for two years. Top management told Beryl that he was fortunate to inherit the fruits of the company's sales growth under Hopper. Beryl's briefing by Hopper occurred during a half-hour limousine ride to the airport as Hopper left to catch a plane to his new assignment. In so many words, Hopper said, "You're on your own. Good luck. Don't call me because I'll be busy with my new job." Hopper had arranged to depart just before the peak season of the year, which normally accounted for 50 percent of annual sales. During the next three months Beryl discovered that he had been handed a nightmare resulting from mistrust.

Inventories had been built to meet a forecast of an additional 25 percent increase in sales. Actual sales, however, were less than one third of the projection for the peak sales period. Beryl found that he had inherited a mistrusting, warring group of department managers presiding over a disintegrating organization. Hopper had pushed sales growth while cutting into essential marketing, product development, and manufacturing activities. Subordinates who had pointed out that his decisions were undermining Granco's long-term performance were fired or isolated. Hopper's imposition of unquestioning conformity to decisions that were clearly milking the business spread mistrust which he fanned by playing one subordinate against another. Beryl discovered that competitors' products and manufacturing technology were more advanced than Granco's and that Granco's business was in serious jeopardy. Granco was left with millions of dollars of obsolete inventory. Beryl found that, because of infighting, marketing research had been slashed and new product design had been gutted. Much of the factory's equipment was obsolete. Granco was a major employer in its small city, and the factory manager, a long-time resident, had loaded the factory with cronies and was running it overtime to produce a high-cost, bloated inventory. Several managers were angry that Hopper had not told them about the search for a new leader. Some deeply resented Beryl and were bitter that they had not even been considered for the position. By focusing on Granco's rapid sales growth, Hopper had masked mistrust, effectively concealing from higher management the erosion of Granco's organization and strategic position.

Over the next two years Beryl replaced several department managers to build a new, more trusting team. Together they reduced the labor force to about 450 people, and through their openness about the facts in the situation managed to develop a workable level of trust with the union after a year of bitter negotiations. By the second year, Granco's managers were a more trusting, cohesive group. Granco was profitable and better positioned to prosper, albeit at a lower, more realistic, and more sustainable rate of growth. When Beryl was asked whether he had discussed his predecessor's legacy with top management, he said: "I was not in a position to do that. Hopper was a fair-haired boy who had a reputation for rapid sales growth. I was a newcomer without credibility. Why would higher management trust me when I had yet to prove myself? They would probably see my complaints as sour grapes or as a sign that I wasn't tough enough. Anyway, they would say, it's your problem. You're Granco's leader; fix it." Rapid growth had masked mistrust, allowing one leader to move ahead with a promotion while leaving his successor an organization about to self-destruct because of mistrust.

INCREASING TRUST

As they try to increase trust among their employees, effective leaders deal with a paradox: People who are mistrustful must nonetheless feel a minimal amount of trust in order to be able to work on improving their ability to trust. In this section we discuss three complementary approaches to increasing trust: integrative reward systems, reciprocal increases in trust, and relationship analysis.

Integrative Reward Systems

It makes little sense for leaders to try to increase trust when the reward system in the organization is based totally on competition—that is, a win-lose setup. Because a competitive reward system forces people to focus only on their own interests, it fosters mistrust. In a purely competitive market, people may accept mistrust between organizations in the belief that competition will increase overall economic efficiency and innovation. But, within an organization, competition and its resulting mistrust are extremely destructive. Effective leaders carefully weigh the cost of internal competition between departments against its potential benefits.

Poor leaders rationalize the benefits of internal competition and its concomitant mistrust by saying that the costs—withholding information, resisting collaboration, feigning fulfillment of agreements—are offset by the larger sales that internal competition generates. For many years IBM's leaders rewarded competition among its large, mid-sized, and small systems divisions. Management's rationale was that the internal competition helped IBM, because the customer was still buying an IBM product, whether the system was large, medium, or small. Internal mistrust driven by the competitive reward structure, however, made it extremely difficult for IBM's leaders to confront the sea change in the market place. Customers were increasingly confused and annoyed by contradictory system proposals and cost projections from IBM's competing divisions, and variations in the performance claims and costs of the different systems increased customers' mistrust. As customer sophistication grew rapidly, a growing number of smart customers capitalized on the explosion in information technology, designing their own systems and buying smaller, less costly, non-IBM products. A system of competitive rewards had increased mistrust among IBM divisions and between IBM and its customers, hindering IBM's response to major changes in customers, technology, and external competition.

Effective leaders increase trust by shifting the reward system toward integrative, or at least mixed, rewards. This change is necessary because an internal competitive reward system continually undermines a leader's other efforts to increase trust. Louis Gerstner, who was recruited to become CEO of IBM in the early 1990s, had to grapple with the competitive reward system when he was brought in to turn IBM around. He shifted IBM's marketing structure to reward an integrated approach to selling to the company's customers. Marketers and system designers continued to focus on specific industries, as they had in the past. But in Gerstner's altered reward structure, specialists in the different system sizes—large, medium, and small—were combined into an integrated marketing and design team that presented one overall best configuration of systems to the customer. The change moved marketing toward an integrative reward system and was a key step in increasing internal trust.

For purposes of our discussion, we shall assume that leaders have installed an integrative, or at least a mixed, reward system. Leaders can also build trust through reciprocal increases in trust and relationship analysis, which are the topics of the next sections.

Reciprocal Increases in Trust

Effective leaders increase their trust or exposure slowly, signalling that they seek similar responses from other people. A major shift from mistrust to high trust rarely occurs quickly. People must develop sufficient confidence that they will not be exploited before they trust. Effective leaders increase trust in small increments that allow people eventually to reach and cross that confidence threshold. People who mistrust need time and continual reconfirmation to accept the idea that there truly has been a change in the level of trust. Initially, they may misinterpret trusting behavior, seeing it as a ploy by a duplicitous leader trying to catch them off guard. They often reject or exploit the leader's extra vulnerability, rather than offer a matching increase in their own trust. By offering trust in only small increments, leaders limit the penalty or loss to which they are liable if their trust is exploited. They also prepare for continual tests of their sincerity and their dedication to increasing trust. Poor leaders unrealistically expect an immediate, high-trust response to their first effort. When their early signals are rejected or exploited, they feel intensely angry and seek revenge.

Effective leaders, after demonstrating their trust, seek a similar response from the other person before proceeding further. They understand that the other person will evaluate the relationship to determine if she should reciprocate and will try to test the leader's commitment to increasing trust. If a mistrustful person decides to reciprocate, she will need time to demonstrate a small, acceptable increase in her trust, since she too is concerned that her increased trust might be exploited by the leader.

Effective leaders use the joint planning and implementation of change to build trust through reciprocated increases in trust. Jointly planning and implementing a successful change is one of the most effective ways to use graduated, reciprocal increases in trust. If leaders and their people learn to trust each other by planning change together and then enjoy the fruits of a successful change, they will develop greater confidence in each other's competence and reliability. Poor leaders and those who mistrust them use change as an opportunity to exploit and punish each other. They use change to increase their mistrust.

Relationship Analysis

Effective leaders periodically review how they can increase trust to improve their relationships and their productivity. They analyze the way they work with other people, examining the flow of information, identifying sources of competence and reliability, and planning how they can improve their relationships. Effective leaders have the skill to do this review constructively. Poor leaders avoid it or do it destructively.

Actually, relationship analysis goes on informally all the time. Leaders and their subordinates continually think about what each is doing that helps or hinders their productivity and their levels of trust. Effective leaders simply organize relationship analysis so that they and their subordinates can more systematically learn to work together better and to supplement routine periodic reviews of performance.

Relationship analysis depends on three factors—receptivity, preparation, and skill. Receptivity depends on voluntarism—that is a voluntary decision to analyze a relationship. This decision grows out of a need to improve trust and a preexisting level of trust sufficient to allow the participants to be non-defensive. A person who feels coerced, whether a leader or a subordinate, will try to avoid the analysis or keep it superficial.

Preparation for relationship analysis is greatly helped if the leader and the other person have a common understanding of the meaning of trust, the spiral model, and the effects of mistrust. In addition to reading about trust, it is helpful if leaders and their subordinates separately attend a leadership or human relations workshop that deals with trust. These workshops often use nonwork-related exercises to help people probe their understanding and feelings about trust. In one such exercise, the trust walk, one person is blindfolded and has to rely on another person to guide him through all activities for several hours. Mealtime during the trust walk is usually a trying but informative experience. After a while, the partners reverse roles. The dramatic shift in dependency brings to awareness many feelings about vulnerability and the fear of exploitation. At the end of the exercise, the participants spend time, in pairs and then in a larger group, reviewing their experiences. They discuss what happened, how they felt, and what they learned about trust. There are many other trust exercises, some of which are physical (e.g., requiring a group of people to help one another scale a ten-foot-high wall or cross a pond without getting wet). All of these exercises extend and deepen participants' awareness and understanding of trust.

Preparation for relationship analysis includes developing an image of how each person sees the relationship. This is done by having both people think about the following questions: What do you do well in your job? What do you do that encourages the other person to trust you? What does the other person do well in her job? What does she do that encourages you to trust her? Some additional questions probe difficulties and mistrust: What does the other person do that makes it difficult for you to do your job? What does she do that increases your mistrust? What do you do that makes it difficult for the other person to do her job? What do you do that increases her mistrust of you? Still other questions deal with improving the relationship, and increasing trust: What could you do to improve the other person's productivity? What could you do to increase her trust? What could she do to improve your productivity? What could she do to increase your trust? Many people find it helpful to discuss their responses confidentially with a third-party facilitator in a sort of dry-run rehearsal before meeting with the other person. Having a rehearsal reduces defensiveness and develops skill in discussing the relationship.

Skill in conducting constructive discussions that often extend over several meetings, is the third factor in relationship analysis. People understandably want to avoid antagonizing each other and worsening their relationship. Unskilled leaders usually keep their discussions on a superficial level or become defensive and belligerent. It is helpful, at least initially and occasionally even later in the process, to have a skilled facilitator moderate the relationship discussion. Leaders can learn the following skills from facilitators: how to make it easier for the parties to talk; how to pace analysis so that people have a chance to absorb what they hear; how to introduce ground rules about constructive behavior; and how to deal with defensiveness. With these skills, leaders can better conduct future analyses of their relationships themselves. Facilitators often meet separately with each person to discuss issues that are hindering the development of trust. They help people examine what might be done to improve the relationship and to increase the level of trust. Such confidential discussions with a facilitator reduce tension and enable people to rehearse the skills they will need for a constructive meeting.

Ultimately, relationship analysis links business problems to trust. The process looks at goals, intentions, and the flow of information. People discuss their own receptivity to influence and evaluate how reliably they fulfill agreements. They examine their perceptions of each other's competence, and trace the use and the effects of controls. They evaluate how well the organization's reward system encourages integrative behavior. They may discuss their own tendencies to trust or occasions when they did not trust.

Nick Rogers, director of engineering of Chromat (names disguised), the research and development subsidiary of a large chemical company, had incurred the mistrust of his subordinates without realizing how this was depressing productivity. When Rogers came across something that displeased him—a purchase of equipment, a use of budgeted funds, an approach to an engineering problem—he would write a scathing memo and send copies to all his subordinates and project leaders. These were known in the company as Roger Missiles; some engineers called them random missiles, or RMs. People spent days talking about RMs and how best to evade them. Before taking the slightest creative action, Rogers's subordinates would discuss in great detail how to conceal the action from Rogers or, if he discovered it, how to describe it so that it appeared uncontroversial.

As part of top management's effort to improve productivity in Chromat, several levels of leaders were invited to workshops in leadership. After Rogers and his subordinates had been to the workshops, several subordinates asked to meet with him individually to discuss how to improve working relationships in the engineering department. In their relationship analysis discussions, they spoke about the destructive effects of Rogers's memos. Rogers responded that those "memos were the only way to get people to do something correctly and have a record of what they should do." The engineers explained that the memos greatly limited their flexibility and creativity and that circulating copies to people other than those directly concerned was embarrassing. Through the discussions, Rogers began to realize that people in his department were closing down the flow of information to him. The more memos he wrote, the more they closed it down and the more they mistrusted him. They had also begun to mistrust each other. Subordinates would threaten each other, half in jest but half seriously, saying, "wait till you see the next RM after Rogers hears about what you want to do." After each RM, subordinates would try to identify who had leaked the information to Rogers.

After much discussion about how to improve relationships and trust, Rogers and his subordinates agreed to take several actions. When Rogers wanted to write a memo, he would instead go directly to the person concerned and discuss the matter with him. If he planned to write a memo that would affect several people, he would meet with them and discuss the issues. They would submit a draft memo for his approval, which he could revise as he saw fit. He would meet with all his subordinates bimonthly to review priorities, new developments, and progress on projects. Within six months after these relationship analysis discussions, there were no more RMs. Rogers said that occasionally he would still whip off a memo, but he would put it in his desk drawer. After he had calmed down, he would walk down the hall to discuss the matter with his subordinate. Minor relationship issues were handled as part of daily work discussions. Periodically, when Rogers or one of his subordinates wanted a longer discussion of relationships and trust, they would set aside time, often having lunch together at a relaxed location away from the office. Rogers and his subordinates reported that after a year the relationship discussions had led to a remarkable increase in trust and productivity in the department. At cocktail receptions Rogers's subordinates would regale each other and Rogers with bizarre stories of how they had tried to defuse RMs in the past. They could talk about the era of mistrust with the humor of hindsight—and with great relief that it was over.

Relationship analysis will not work if people are unreceptive, unprepared, or unskilled. Some subordinates would like to change their leader's behavior to increase the level of trust but believe that the leader is unreceptive to relationship analysis. These subordinates often do not recognize that trust is a two-way relationship. They need to examine their own receptivity. How ready are they to hear their leader's reasons for mistrusting them? Often subordinates want to lecture the leader expecting that this would enable the leader to change. Lecturing, however, is as unproductive with leaders as it is with adolescents.

Poor leaders prefer to see themselves as trusting and trustworthy, but that is rarely how others see them. Effective leaders are supportive and minimally defensive. They have the skills to conduct a periodic relationship analysis, maintaining and improving the trust that drives commitment and productivity. Poor leaders see relationship analysis as embarrassing and believe that it increases mistrust. Their attitude is that it's better to let sleeping dogs lie. Effective leaders, however, use relationship analysis as an opportunity to learn and to improve trust. Their vision is to soar on trust, liberating creativity and increasing cohesion and productivity.

SUMMARY

There are regularities in trust systems that we call laws of trust. First, mistrust drives out trust. To protect themselves from people who mistrust, trusting people shift to mistrust. They reduce the flow of information, resist attempts to influence them, and increase their control of those they mistrust. Second, trust increases cohesion. People who trust know that they can depend on each other. They bond, cooperate, and support each other in a crisis. The corollary law is that mistrusting groups self-destruct. They fragment and splinter, and their members try to get work done by making decisions outside the group away from those they mistrust. Third, trust stimulates productivity by giving people confidence that they can define appropriate goals and work together to achieve them. Trust enables people to solve problems creatively and to find original methods for improving their productivity. The corollary is that mistrust depresses productivity. Suspicion and unreliability suppress relevant information and inhibit cooperation. Mistrust polarizes thinking, diverting creativity into defensiveness rather than productivity. Fourth, rapid growth masks mistrust. Leaders in rapidly growing companies move to other jobs so quickly that they can leave a legacy of mistrust for their successor without being detected. Growth in output and financial measures can conceal the shaky underpinnings of mistrust. When growth slows, leaders stay in their jobs longer, and it is difficult to conceal mistrust in glowing reports of growth and to shift the effects of mistrust to a successor.

There are three complementary steps for building trust. The first is to introduce and emphasize integrative reward systems that encourage people to trust because they get a better payoff by trusting than by mistrusting. The second step is to initiate reciprocal increases in trust through the leader's behavior—increasing his openness, building the competence of his people, increasing his supportiveness, and clarifying his intentions. This step requires patience and caution. Leaders need to be prepared to offer many small overtures until the other person develops enough trust to cross her individual threshold of confidence. People shift from mistrust to trust gradually and need continual reconfirmation along the way. The third step is relationship analysis. This is best done as a voluntary review. Before meeting, the participants prepare by exploring in private their answers to a series of questions about their relationship. Leaders need discussion skills to pace the meeting and to keep the tone constructive rather than defensive. It can be helpful to rehearse with a skilled facilitator and perhaps to have one present during the meeting.

We have discussed knowledge and trust, two of the essential ingredients of contemporary leadership. In Part III we will examine the traditional ingredient of leadership—power. What are the leader's sources of power? How has the dispersion of knowledge, and the growing importance of trust, affected the leader's exercise of power?

III

POWER

The less we use our power, the greater it will be.

Thomas Jefferson

9

Legitimate and Decision Process Power

Economic tides rise and fall, cross-currents of change ripple through organizations, but effective leaders know how to use power to navigate through the shoals of competition and set a course for opportunities. Power is the ability to influence people. It is the ability to get someone to do or not to do something, to persuade or dissuade. Leadership and power are almost synonymous. One might well ask if leadership can exist without the ability to affect the actions of others—that is, without power.

Legitimate power is still the anchor of leadership. It is decision power—the right people give to leaders to make choices, set a direction, and resolve conflicts. In this chapter we discuss legitimate power, its scope, and its link to a position in an organization. We also discuss decision process power—the leader's right to determine how a decision will be made—and analyze the effective leader's use of four fundamental decision modes—commanding, consulting, concurring, and consigning.

LEGITIMATE POWER

Although legitimate power is sometimes obscured, leaders rely on it as their fundamental source of power. Teamwork and empowerment greatly contribute to performance, but legitimate, formal power persists as the core of leadership. Legitimate power is defined as the lawful right to make a decision and to expect compliance. "Lawful" simply means that, by social convention, people have agreed that the occupant of a position shall have the right to make certain decisions. Legitimate power means that the leader can expect compliance from people in lower positions.

Organizations function because most of the time people cooperate and work together, adjusting to one another to get jobs done. So long as people cooperate, effective leaders simply use legitimate power to ratify decisions. But people often have limited, self-interested views of corporate goals. They do not see the challenges facing the entire organization or understand that departments have to depend on one another. They need leadership to define proper goals and to mobilize resources to reach those goals, as well as to resolve conflicts about selecting goals and the methods to be used in achieving them. American culture extols independence, competition, and self-sufficiency, and some people lack the motivation or the skills to build consensus. Even when they have the necessary skills, there are times when fundamental, irresolvable differences prevent agreement. Leaders need legitimate power to resolve such conflicts and to hold the organization together while they sort out the situation. Leaders use legitimate power to ensure that the organization moves ahead with a coordinated plan to achieve a common goal.

General Electric acquired the NBC television network as part of its acquisition of RCA in 1985.[1] Grant Tinker, the president of NBC, had moved the network from third place to first place in viewer ratings. This was a significant accomplishment because networks make their money from advertising revenues from their prime-time hit shows, and by 1986 NBC had ten of the top twenty-five network shows. Tinker, who knew the entertainment industry well, had been given a free hand by RCA, which was active primarily in the technology industry. He, in turn, led with a loose, supportive management style. Having turned the network around, Tinker decided to leave NBC to return to Hollywood to produce new entertainment ventures. Even before the GE acquisition, he had told the chairman of RCA of his intention but had not announced it publicly. After the acquisition, Jack Welch, the CEO of GE, became the CEO of NBC. Unable to persuade Tinker to stay, Welch appointed Robert Wright to succeed Tinker as president of NBC. Wright, a lawyer and a skilled deal maker, had risen to CEO of GE Capital, which, as GE's fastest growing business, had profits of $500 million in 1985.

As president of NBC, Wright acquired the legitimate power to set goals, design strategy, and make budget allocations. When Wright arrived, NBC executives were riding the crest of a wave of profitability and hubris. Under Tinker's loose rein, they had made NBC the most profitable of the three networks, and they basked in their vision of a munificent world. Wright and Welch, however, had a less optimistic view of the future. They envisioned a steady decline in the size of network television audiences in the coming years and an increasingly competitive environment. The size of NBC's audience determines its advertising revenues; an increase of one point in a prime-time program's Nielsen rating can add $100 million a year to revenues. But network audiences were shrinking. Ninety-two percent of U.S. homes watched one of the three networks in 1976. By 1984, that figure had dropped to 75 percent (and plunged to 62 percent by 1991.) The industry was undergoing a structural change. There already were twelve national programming services, including Home Box Office, Showtime, and MTV. Ten of the twelve were earning more than the rival ABC network. On the basis of this trend, Wright predicted that an increasing proportion of U.S. households would shift to viewing non network competitors.

Wright felt that he had to prepare NBC for tough competition and lean days. He had to get costs under control. He foresaw difficult times ahead while other NBC executives were listening to the mellow sounds of their current profitability. Wright saw NBC as a company that should meet the standards of profitability and growth set for other GE divisions. He treated NBC as a business with divisions and products rather than as a creative endeavor that was not to be troubled by financial discipline. He discovered that the NBC news and sports divisions were losing substantial amounts of money and that the network was living off its entertainment division and its five wholly owned television stations (the TV stations alone generated four of every ten dollars of NBC's profits and accounted for half of NBC's market value).

Wright was particularly appalled by costs and attitudes in the news division. News was budgeted to spend $275 million in 1986 and planned to lose $80 million—or close to $100 million if general overhead was included. These "planned" losses were estimated to rise to $130 million in later years. At the time, Ted Turner at CNN was broadcasting news twenty-four hours a day at a cost of $100 million and was making a profit of almost $60 million. Wright, who was aware of CNN's profitability, felt that NBC News had to change its ways. He directed Larry Grossman, the president of the news division, to submit a budget for the next year that would reduce expenses 5 percent below those of the current year.

Grossman resisted Wright's decision. Grossman believed that News was a critical, creative contributor to the network's programming. The news division, he argued, distinguished NBC from its competitors. He asserted the network journalists' sacred belief that newscasting was a public trust and argued that the division's losses should be supported by earnings from entertainment programs such as NBC's highly profitable *Bill Cosby Show*. He repeatedly tried to convince Wright and

Welch to accept the view that an effective news division would have to lose substantial amounts of money, but they were not convinced. For several months Grossman resisted submitting a reduced budget. At one time he presented a budget with an 8 percent increase in expenditures. Grossman argued that even to go through the exercise of preparing a hypothetical budget with a 5 percent cost reduction would demoralize the news staff. Grossman's persistent failure to comply was seen as insubordination, an unwillingness to accept Wright's legitimate power. As president, Wright could have reduced Grossman's responsibilities, demoted him, or fired him.

Wright surmised from their discussions and from information about accounting practices in the news division that Grossman might not even know what expenses were being incurred by different components of NBC News. The news division's goal seemed to be to scoop the other networks, regardless of cost. News management believed that the more money spent on news coverage, the better the coverage had to be. They thought that even a nonjournalist like Wright could understand that expenditures and news quality rose and fell together. In their view, if NBC was to have the best news coverage, it would have to spend the most.

Eventually, Wright persuaded Grossman to use external consultants to survey the activities and the costs of the news division and to help prepare a reduced budget. Grossman agreed, apparently thinking that he could convince the consultants that the cost of the news division was more than justified by its contribution to quality public programming. Perhaps he also thought that if he was eventually forced to reduce expenses, he could retain the loyalty of his staff by blaming the consultants and claiming that the reductions were the result of an edict from higher management.

The consultants, with Grossman's participation, found that between 1977 and 1987 the number of stories aired annually on the network's national news broadcast had fallen from 2,500 to 1,500—a 40 percent decline—while the average cost per story had increased from $12,400 to $63,000. The average nightly newscast was devoting 10 percent less time to news in 1986 than it had in 1977. For a cost of $95 million the nightly news was delivering less than it had delivered for $30 million ten years earlier. Breaking stories, which cost an average of $63,000 to cover, were being covered to prevent the network from being scooped, with almost no thought as to whether the reports would actually be used. As many as thirteen crews were being sent to cover each story even though film from only four might actually be used. Although half of the nightly newscast consisted of prechosen, nonbreaking stories, half or more of these prepared, or feature, stories were not being aired. Of NBC's ninety correspondents, the top twenty were on the air nearly half the time and the bottom forty were on the air less than 10 percent of the time. The need to be ready for "crisis coverage" was given as the reason for maintaining a large stable of correspondents. But during crises, such as the 1986 Challenger shuttle explosion and the 1985 Achille Lauro hijacking, ten correspondents monopolized 90 percent of the airtime. The report suggested that the news division, which employed 1,261 people, was overstaffed. Managers needed training in cost control, hiring and supervising staff, and the art of management.

Wright concluded that he should replace Grossman, but because several other top NBC managers had recently left, he decided not to act immediately. After a search for an external successor, Grossman was replaced by Michael Gartner in July 1988. Ultimately, with the aid of the consultants' analysis, expenses were lowered and the news staff, as well as other NBC staff, was reduced by 30 percent. By 1991 the news budget was $70 million less than it had been in 1988. NBC News losses had been contained at $50 million, which Wright considered an acceptable and sustainable level. Despite declining audiences, NBC earned $750 million in 1989 and continued to be profitable in the following years. By 1995, NBC was still enjoying robust profit growth, thanks to good ratings. Wright's directive style was not popular, especially when compared to the looser style of his predecessor, Tinker. Wright made some mistakes in judgment, and news people vilified him as a Philistine who did not appreciate the special contribution of journalism. His tenure, however, illustrates the effective use of legitimate power by a leader to deal with difficult problems. Such leaders pay a price in decreased popularity, but if they do not use their legitimate power to lead when necessary, the organization itself may fail, in which case popularity becomes meaningless. Wright used his legitimate power as president to deal with a looming external threat that incumbent NBC executives could not or would not confront.

Scope of Power

The legitimate power given to leaders to make decisions and impose discipline is still evolving. Chronicles of the British navy report that as recently as the nineteenth century, minor misbehavior aboard a ship—being slow to respond, showing disrespect to an officer, cursing—was punishable by flogging. If the crew attempted to replace the lawfully appointed captain, no matter how cruel he might have been, they were committing a capital offense punishable by death. Although a leader's near-absolute power to make and enforce decisions is still the core of legitimate power, in recent years organizations have circumscribed that power with policies, reviews, moral strictures, and legal precedents, and a leader's right to inflict severe punishment for insubordination has been greatly reduced. The legitimate power to make and enforce decisions, however, continues to anoint leaders with great ability to benefit or harm others.

Ultimately, leadership still revolves around legitimate, or formal, power—the right to make and enforce a decision. As leaders move to the top levels of an organization, their legitimate power becomes so great that they can make or destroy subordinates. Leaders' decisions about the strategy their organization should follow can elevate or devastate the lives of thousands of people; General Motors and IBM, for example, reduced their workforces by tens of thousands of people during the 1980s because of the strategic decisions their leaders had made. The top leaders of large organizations today have as much power, if not more, over the long-term welfare of people as the British sea captains of the nineteenth century. Effective leaders appreciate the potential benefits and the destructive effects of their legitimate power and use it judiciously.

Position and Power

Legitimate power resides in one's position or job within the organization; the organization grants the temporary right to exercise legitimate power to the person appointed to the job. Power does not move with a leader when she leaves a job; it passes to the new incumbent. A threat to a leader's position becomes a threat to legitimate power and to the carefully woven social fabric that gives direction and order to daily life. It threatens the stability of organizations and, in some cases, society. Leaders and their subordinates, therefore, need to manage wisely their differences lest they give rise to insubordination, which threatens legitimate position power and endangers organizational stability.

When North Carolina Senator Jesse Helms quipped that President Bill Clinton was so unpopular on military bases in North Carolina that he'd "better have a bodyguard" if he visited the state, the remark created a furor among Helms's congressional colleagues and the public.[2] Many people demanded that Helms retract the statement and apologize. Helms, who by seniority was in line to become the chairman of the Senate Foreign Relations Committee, seemed not to understand that he had challenged the foundation of legitimate position power in U.S. society. His statement was an implied threat to the legitimate power inherent in the position of the presidency; the issue was never Helms's right to disagree with President Clinton's policies but the lack of respect for his position.

Helms's remark suggested that the lawfully granted power of the presidency might be subverted by assassination and was seen as akin to a statement by a senior officer obtusely encouraging malcontents to mutiny aboard ship. It provoked great dismay because a senator was offhandedly threatening the fundamental order and political stability of U.S. society. In addition, it is a fundamental principle of U.S. society that citizens have superior, legitimate position power over the armed forces. Suggesting that military personnel might attack a president raised the terrifying specter of military usurpation of civilian power. Although Helms protested that he was not serious, he failed to understand that his remark had attacked the position power of the presidency. He had tacitly invited the overthrow of the legitimate power of one of the most respected positions in the U.S. political system. Helms seemed unaware of the vast difference between threatening the legitimate power of an incumbent's appointed position and disagreeing with his policies. A leader or subordinate who dabbles in mutiny threatens the fabric that holds an organization together and can expect swift and strong retaliation.

Effective leaders understand their legitimate power and exercise great discretion in using it. In the following section we discuss decision process power, a key component of legitimate power.

DECISION PROCESS POWER

Effective leaders orchestrate their decision process. They carefully choose a decision process, knowing that the process they choose will affect the quality of the decision and its implementation. They decide whether the decision process will involve a solo, a duet, a trio, a quartet, or a twelve-piece band. They decide what part each person will play and when. It is the leader's legitimate power to decide who, when, and how people will be involved in making a decision.

Leaders can use one or a combination of four basic decision processes that differ in the amount of participation the leader grants to others and in the extent to which the leader shares his legitimate power (see Fig. 9-1). Commanding, the first process, is a solo decision mode—the leader alone makes the decision, permitting no participation by others and sharing none of his legitimate power. In consultation, the second process, the leader permits limited participation by

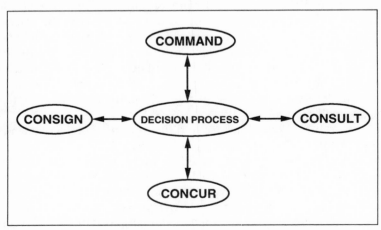

Figure 9-1 Decision Process Modes

disclosing his problem to subordinates and staff and seeking their views and advice. The leader moderately and indirectly shares his legitimate power to the degree that he accepts their advice and lets it influence his decision. In concurrence, the third process, the leader and his people will not act until they jointly agree on the definition of the problem and the solution. In this process the leader grants his people major participation in the deliberations about the problem and makes them partners who share his legitimate power. In consignment, the fourth process, the leader transfers his legitimate power to make the decision by delegating it to another person and thus grants maximum participation. The leader, however, retains the right to oversee the decision of his deputy and to rescind the consignment. Effective leaders create flexible combinations of these four modes to best fit the situation and the people, whereas poor leaders use one mode regardless of the situation and the people. We now take a closer look at each mode.

Commanding

Commanding is a simple, clear-cut decision process. It is a directive, take-charge, fast-moving mode. The leader makes a decision and initiates action. The down side of this process is that nothing happens until the leader makes a decision. Under what circumstances does command work? First, subordinates need to believe that the leader should make the decision. If they do not, they will find reasons to stall and not act. Second, since the leader is not consulting others, she needs to have sufficient knowledge and problem-solving skills to make a high-quality decision. Third, if it is to be acceptable to the leader's subordinates, the decision should be legal, ethical, and consistent with the organization's goals.

When effective leaders use the pure command mode, they understand its underlying assumptions—that the leader knows the situation well enough to identify and properly define the right problem or opportunity, has all the relevant information, and can think of high-quality solutions; can define the right evaluation criteria and apply them objectively to choose the best solution, and can communicate the decision so that the people will understand what is to be done and will do it.

Because these conditions are so difficult to meet, effective leaders use pure command selectively and judiciously. Prior to giving a command, they usually consult their subordinates to gather information and develop insight into the problem. They also use concurrence to develop understanding and trust. By using these other modes, they lay a foundation for command if they have to use it. When effective leaders are remote from a rapidly changing situation and poorly informed about local details, they know that it makes little sense to issue commands. People on the scene, who have firsthand knowledge, are better able to exercise judgment. In such cases, effective leaders seek competent people and consign decision making to them. Effective leaders also understand that their legitimate power sometimes requires them to command, if only to "sign off" on a decision so that others can act. Subordinates need a leader's authorization when she has not consigned authority; they need a leader's concurrence when they do not feel sufficiently prepared to accept a consignment.

Poor leaders misuse command, giving it a bad reputation. They do so because they believe that leading means commanding. They have that one decision process for all situations and people and do not understand the assumptions underlying command. When they should be consulting, concurring, or consigning, they command. Even when poor leaders consult, they are often so ineffective that they are seen as commanding. As a result, they obtain limited information and have little insight into complex situations. With these handicaps, poor leaders make low-quality decisions that gain little acceptance. In contrast, effective leaders make selective, carefully timed use of command. They use other decision processes to gather and disseminate knowledge. They prepare people for commands; when they do command, they are ratifying the understanding and decisions that people have helped to shape through consultation, concurrence, and consignment. Subordinates of effective leaders do not feel that commands are heavy-handed. Rather, they see them as directives that neatly summarize the discussions and conclusions they have reached together.

Consultation

Consultation, like an adjustable camera lens, enables leaders to clarify different aspects of a complex situation. Effective leaders are effective consultants. When they need information, they consult by giving people a picture of their concern and its context. They disclose their tentative view of a problem or opportunity. They do not force their preconceived solution on others.

A marketing manager concerned about declining sales in her company's southeast region wanted sales data to see if they verified her impression about the company's performance. She thought that she might have to reduce the sales force in the region and possibly close some branch offices. She decided to consult her marketing research manager. She framed the issue as follows: "I'm concerned about sales in the southeast, and I'm thinking about what to do about the salesforce there. As a starter, let's review the data on southeast sales for the past several years, and let's look at other information that you think we should consider." In this case the leader was using moderately broad consultation—a wide-angle lens that opened the field of the decision process. The marketing research manager could suggest looking at other data such as turnover in the sales force, products and volume sold by different sales people in the region, the compensation system, the penetration of major customer groups, sales in comparable territories, and the sales of competitors.

Effective leaders use broad, searching consultation when looking for a high-quality decision in a complex situation. They consult by bringing together a group with a cross-section of relevant specialities and posing open-ended questions. Continuing with the marketing situation we have described, the marketing manager could have convened a group composed of managers from sales, marketing research, product development, manufacturing, and accounting. She might have framed the issue very broadly: "Recommend a range of options for what to do about sales in the southeast, and how to implement those options." Broad consultation opens all the elements of problem solving—defining the problem and gathering information; creating options and developing and applying criteria to choose a solution; beginning implementation and communicating the decision. Effective leaders use broad consultation to cope with rapidly changing, complex situations. Broad consultation brings together widely dispersed knowledge and increases trust between leaders and those they consult.

Poor leaders consult narrowly by asking only for specific facts. In effect, they say, "Give me nothing more than the facts I ask for." Poor leaders assume that they know the situation and have properly defined the problem. They assume that they can generate superior solution options and that they know what criteria should be used to evaluate those options. When they consult, they ask only for the missing facts they believe they need. By not giving other people background or context, they close the decision process.

Consider the marketing situation we have discussed. A poor leader would make a decision based on insufficient information and limited perspective. She would want sales data that confirm her decision. She would ask specifically for data on sales in the southeast region for the past five years, without providing context about her concern or explaining why she wanted the data. Poor leaders overuse narrow consultation, which is a close cousin to the command mode. They say, in so many words, "I will tell you what information I want so that you can confirm my decision." This is not to say that leaders should never use narrow consultation. In a stable, simple environment, when leaders can be sure that they truly understand the situation, narrow consultation is sufficient and is often all that subordinates expect. Broad consultation complicates a simple situation and exasperate subordinates. Poor leaders, however, force many complex situations into narrow consultation, not realizing that it should be reserved only for the most routine, repetitive cases.

Effective leaders have the self-confidence to manage the paradox of consulting widely even though they have the legitimate power to command. They consult others to assemble the knowledge necessary for high-quality decisions and to develop trust that will be required to implement those decisions. Poor leaders fear that consulting others will undermine their legitimate power to command and lack the self-confidence to risk consulting. They pretend to know, rather than consult and reveal that they have a need to know. They would rather make a poor decision that demonstrates their legitimate power to command than consult others. Poor leaders, by misusing consultation, suppress the knowledge they need for high-quality decisions. (Consultation is so critical to the effective use of legitimate power that we discuss it in greater detail in Chapter 11).

Concurrence

Concurrence is like playing in a jazz combo. Players blend a routine melody with improvisation to achieve a creative, coordinated outcome. Leaders and their subordinates listen to the rhythm of their analysis and build on one another's contributions. Concurrence is dynamic group decision making in which effective leaders implicitly say, "We have the competence and the trust to work on this together. If there is an urgent need to act and we cannot agree, it is understood that, although I will make a decision, it will have the benefit of our open discussion." Effective leaders and their subordinates use concurrence to define a problem and gather information jointly. They jointly generate and evaluate solution options. Effective leaders use concurrence when subordinates know the situation as well as or better than they do or when subordinates will have great discretion in how they implement a decision. Concurrence ensures that subordinates will influence decisions that should incorporate their first-hand knowledge and increases mutual commitment and trust.

Effective leaders move adeptly between consulting and concurrence. They work in a zone where the two overlap. When they consult subordinates, they implicitly seek concurrence. They rarely act without substantial agreement and trust. Subordinates realize that leaders, having legitimate power, can change the decision process as they see fit; when time is limited and people cannot reach concurrence, leaders have a right to command and make a decision. Effective leaders, however, carefully prepare subordinates before they go from concurrence to command by reviewing the costs of delay with their subordinates. When action is critical and people cannot reach concurrence, subordinates expect leaders to take the best of their deliberations and resolve the conflict.

Poor leaders misuse concurrence. They have low tolerance for dissent, and they try subtly to coerce subordinates into agreeing with their decisions. Poor leaders exercise command under the guise of concurrence. When people persist in disagreeing, poor leaders sulk, attack, or impulsively command. Subordinates, unprepared for their leader's sudden shift from concurrence to command, learn to conceal their disagreements and come to understand that concurrence means agreeing with the leader. Poor leaders evoke mistrust when they pretend to use concurrence but impulsively impose orders without adequate discussion and preparation. Poor leaders would do better not to dabble with concurrence. At least they would not waste time, frustrating subordinates by putting them through a charade of concurrence.

Consignment

Consignment means giving over to the care of another person, entrusting him to perform in one's stead. It involves guiding and overseeing the decisions a deputy makes and ensuring that the power entrusted is used competently and responsibly. In consignment the leader can oversee decisions loosely or tightly, consigning with a silk thread that allows subordinates to move freely or with a thick rope that closely controls each move. Depending on how competently and responsibly the subordinate uses her consigned power, the leader makes adjustments to the power he transfers; he can increase, redefine, or rescind all or part of the legitimate authority he consigns.

Leaders need to be aware that the terms delegation and empowerment often arouse in subordinates two subtle but common misperceptions of consignment. In the common misperception of delegation, subordinates minimize the oversight component of consignment, expecting the leader to leave them on their own and immediately give them complete discretion to make decisions. When using consignment, however, the leader needs to monitor decisions continually to ensure that they are consistent with the organization's goals and strategy. In the misperception of empowerment, the newest term in the lexicon of leadership, subordinates stress the power transfer component of consignment but overlook the concomitant increase in their responsibility and gloss over their role as representatives of the leader.

Many subordinates fail to realize that consignment is not an irrevocable transfer of power, so they are severely disappointed when the leader changes the distribution of power. When effective leaders consign, they clarify the new distribution of responsibility and the representation role that goes with sharing power. They also point out that, as with any consignment, they can modify the transfer of power as people and circumstances change.

Effective leaders increase their use of consignment as a business grows because they cannot know or do all that needs to be done. They consign decisions to lower levels of the organization and move decisions as close as possible to the point where people have the information and the competence to make the best decisions. Poor leaders hold onto decisions beyond their knowledge and capacity to act. They do not know how to consign and instead remain mired in day-to-day work, failing to see the threats and opportunities on the horizon.

Effective leaders have mastered the three components of consignment—guidance, development, and review. First, they provide guidance. They set and explain the organization's goals to subordinates and focus attention on what they hope to achieve by delegating an assignment. They explain the strategy—the broad methods by which those goals may be achieved and discuss the resources subordinates will have and the limits, such as funding, equipment, and personnel, within which they will have to operate. Second, effective leaders continually develop subordinates to take on greater and greater consignment of responsibility. They assign subordinates projects of increasing scope and challenge. Third, effective leaders periodically review with subordinates the performance of assignments. They coach by monitoring progress and discussing problems as they occur. When an assignment is completed, effective leaders go through post mortem analyses with subordinates in which the subordinates examine what they have learned and consider how those insights might be applied in the future.

When Chrysler creates a new automobile model or redesigns an old one, its leaders use consignment.[3] Robert Eaton, Chrysler's CEO, working with his senior managers, forms a project team that may include as many as 700 people from engineering, design, manufacturing, marketing, and finance. A vice president, or "godfather," supervises the project, and leaders below the level of vice president direct the actual work. Eaton and up to twelve of Chrysler's senior managers provide guidance at the start of the project. They meet with all the team leaders to discuss a vision for the vehicle and concur on broad goals for design, performance, fuel economy, and cost. Senior management and the project leaders work out semidetailed objectives. Their mutual understanding becomes an implicit contract. The team is then turned loose to organize itself and do the job. Members can go back to senior management if they have a major problem. In Eaton's experience, all design teams have been able to resolve their problems within the guidelines of the original understanding and goals.

The practice of consigning design started at Chrysler in the 1980s under Lee Iacocca, then Chrysler's CEO, and Bob Lutz, the company's president. By the mid-1990s, management had learned how to use consignment so effectively that, starting with only a concept, Chrysler was able to create a car for as little as $1.3 billion, much less than its U.S. competitors spent. Speed to market was another payoff. Chrysler used to take five years to go from concept to production of a car. That dropped to two and a half years by 1994 besting most Japanese carmakers. In 1994 Chrysler had record sales of $52.2 billion and record earnings of $3.7 billion, by 1995 industry analysts were saying that Chrysler had the newest products and the best cost structure of the three U.S. auto companies.

Before becoming Chrysler's CEO, Eaton had spent twenty-nine years with General Motors, the last four running its European operations. While at GM, he said, he didn't go a week without being involved in a product decision. Although there was talk of consignment, GM bosses still tightly controlled the decision-making process. At GM everybody tried to put together self-directed groups, but Eaton felt that they were never as successful as those he worked with at Chrysler. Chrysler's groups succeeded, he thought, because the company truly consigned responsibility. There was no hierarchy or committees to second-guess the project team's work. Decisions were being made by people down in the organization who knew much more about the issues than the senior managers.

Chrysler's leaders had learned to consign with a silk thread. Over a period of more than ten years they had developed managers with the skills to make consignment work on a grand scale, using self-contained, self-organizing, multidisciplinary teams. Eaton strongly believed that consigning the design process allowed the final vehicle to become the team's product, not management's. With consignment, people worked much harder, took greater pride in their work, and made sure that the project was a success. Every vehicle designed by the consignment process since Eaton came to Chrysler in 1992 has been completed below its cost-per-car target and its total investment target.

SUMMARY

Power is the ability to influence others so that they do or do not do something. Legitimate power, the right of leaders to make decisions and expect compliance, is inherent in a position. Leaders can use the legitimate power of their positions so long as they are incumbents. The scope of senior leaders' legitimate power permits them to greatly benefit or harm large numbers of people. Insubordination, by threatening the social foundation of legitimate position power, evokes swift, strong retaliation.

Leaders have legitimate power to determine the process by which decisions will be made. They use four fundamental modes—commanding, consultation, concurrence, and consignment—that move from minimum to maximum use of participation and power sharing. Command, the mode most frequently associated with power and the one most overused by poor leaders, is often misunderstood and misused. Effective leaders use the full repertoire of modes, knowing when and how to consult and concur to solve problems and increase trust. The success of consignment, a process with maximum participation and power sharing, depends on the leader's guidance, development of subordinates, and review of performance.

Chapter 10 discusses agenda power, staffing, and review of performance and considers two elements of triadic leadership—knowledge and trust—as sources of the third element, power.

10

Agenda, Staffing, and Review Power

Leaders have a wide range of legitimate powers in addition to decision process power. This chapter discusses other key powers—agenda, staffing, and review power. To use these powers wisely, leaders also need knowledge. Although knowledge has been discussed in Part I of this book as one of the triadic leadership forces, in this chapter we discuss knowledge as power—that is, as a source of influence. We have also discussed trust as a triadic force, but here we discuss it as power—that is, as an influence on what people are willing to do.

AGENDA POWER

Agenda power is navigation power. It is a leader's right to determine where the organization will go—to define goals—and how it will get there—to design strategies to achieve those goals. Effective leaders select appropriate targets and determine how best to reach them. They also develop systems that sense and track how well the organization is performing.

Effective leaders have high on their agendas the continuing accurate assessment of their environment. The opportunities and threats they see in the environment become the context of their agenda. Using that context of opportunities and threats, they work with their subordinates to set wise and challenging goals. They formulate strategy, positioning the organization to prosper in its future environment. They design a suitable organization structure and plan the actions that will reach the organization's goals. They install systems to monitor progress and guide corrective actions. They staff the organization—that is, they select, motivate, and nurture the people who will transform the plans into results. (Staffing is such a vital agenda item that we discuss it separately in a later section.)

When the environment changes slowly, a leader's agenda power is scarcely noticeable. Maintaining current operations and incrementally improving strategy require only small, absorbable changes in agenda. So long as people can operate routinely, adapting to small changes, the leader's agenda power is inconspicuous. When leaders see a major shift in the environment and substantially change the firm's agenda, however, people become acutely aware of the leader's agenda power.

Compaq's Strategic Change

Compaq Computer Corporation, formed in 1982, grew from scratch to sales of $3.6 billion and profits of $432 million by 1990.[1] Compaq designed, produced, and marketed PCs and PC systems to business organizations. Its leaders viewed IBM as both their benchmark and their major competitor. IBM's reputation for high-quality mainframes had a halo effect, making IBM's PC's the market standard for business users. IBM PCs were the safe choice for information system managers. Compaq's leaders' goal was to position their PCs as an alternative to those of IBM. Their strategy was to price their IBM-compatible PCs at the same high level as IBM's machines but to offer more features and higher quality than IBM. The strategy was extremely successful.

By the late 1980's, however, information system managers, small-business owners, and home users had learned enough about computers to feel comfortable buying low-priced PC clones. These less expensive PCs performed as well as the higher-priced Compaq and IBM PCs and offered greater value to consumers with limited budgets. Compaq and IBM were holding a price umbrella over a growing group of clone makers such as Dell, AST Research, Gateway, and Packard-Bell. The clone makers were rapidly gaining market share in a burgeoning global market. Even large businesses were buying clones. In 1991, Compaq incurred the first quarterly loss in its history. Clearly, competition was heating up.

Rod Canion, Compaq's CEO, insisted that Compaq's declining market share was the temporary fallout of a downturn in general business conditions. His agenda was to continue Compaq's high-price strategy and its limited focus on business customers. He did not see the phenomenal growth of the clone makers as a threat. However, Benjamin Rosen, the company's Chairman, and Compaq's board of directors saw the situation differently. They decided that the firm's agenda should be changed. They appointed Eckhard Pfeiffer CEO in 1991, to replace Canion, who had been a cofounder of the company.

Working with the board of directors and with Compaq's senior leaders, Pfeiffer used the full range of decision processes—consultation, concurrence, consignment, and command—applying his legitimate power to transform Compaq's agenda. Compaq's new goal was to compete head to head with the clone makers. Together, Pfeiffer and his team revolutionized the company's marketing, product design, and manufacturing strategy. Working with the leaders of marketing, Pfeiffer set a goal of matching the low prices offered by the most aggressive, low-priced, mail-order clone makers, such as Dell and AST. He enlarged Compaq's target markets to include small and mid-sized businesses and home users, in addition to Compaq's traditional customer, the large business user. He expanded marketing distribution channels to include outlets that sold to small businesses and to consumers. The number of outlets increased from 2,000 to almost 10,000. The advertising budget was increased 60 percent to $90 million. Retail point-of-sale displays were added. One Compaq executive who had previously marketed only to large businesses was incredulous when he learned that simply wrapping a colorful piece of cardboard that explained the model's features—a "monitor hood"—across the face of the monitor increased sales 11 percent.

Pfeiffer, working with the leaders of engineering, also changed the product design agenda. Compaq's products would continue to be high quality, but they would not be overengineered as in the past. Instead of making as many as fourteen redesigns of a circuit board for a new model, engineering cut the number of redesigns to three. Circuit board costs were cut more than 50 percent, from an average cost of $450 to $200 a board. The engineering staff was reduced 20 percent, from 1,200 to fewer than 1,000. Compaq introduced forty-five new models, enlarging its line from thirty to seventy-five models. Less than a year after Pfeiffer became CEO, Compaq had several models for each market segment.

Pfeiffer, with the leaders of manufacturing, changed the manufacturing agenda. He set a goal of radical cost reduction to support the new, low-price strategy. Instead of assembling all components, Compaq began to buy subassemblies from contractors. Competitive bidding among suppliers replaced prices negotiated with a single supplier. Compaq's plants were operated for three shifts a day instead of one. Manufacturing processes were streamlined. Computer testing—"burn-in"—was reduced from ninety-six hours to two hours. Manufacturing installed a flexible assembly process that reduced the time needed to make a computer and shifted production to building to order instead of trying to predict future sales and stockpiling huge inventories.

Pfeiffer's new agenda cut manufacturing costs more than 50 percent. Compaq was able to produce 3 million computers for a total cost that was less than it had previously spent to produce 1.5 million computers. Compaq increased its share of the world market from 3.5 percent in 1990 to 10 percent in 1994, making it the global leader in PC sales. Pfeiffer's leadership in formulating and communicating a revolutionary new agenda of goals, strategy, organization, and systems had increased Compaq's market share and achieved new heights of profitability. He had catapulted Compaq into a leading competitive position.

STAFFING POWER

Staffing consists of selecting, developing, and motivating the people who will help the leader plan and implement decisions. Effective leaders surround themselves with effective people. As an organization grows, leaders know that their dependence on others will grow and they will need to rely on intermediaries, surrogates, and deputies. The leader's staffing decisions are therefore crucial to the organization and are a top agenda item. Effective leaders select strong people—people who have proven leadership ability or high potential for leadership. These people provide the wisdom and the foresight for high-quality decisions and the energy and the dedication to implement decisions effectively.

Effective leaders search for staff by visualizing the future challenges of a position. They then define the characteristics a candidate should have to cope with those future challenges. Last, they assess each candidate for the desired qualities. Effective leaders have great skill in assessing candidates. They can cut through surface appearances and see a person's key characteristics. They focus on the strengths essential to a position and can unerringly sense if a candidate has those qualities.

Walton's Staffing Skill

Sam Walton, the legendary founder of Wal-Mart, had extraordinary staffing ability.[2] Walton saw his function as picking good people and giving them maximum authority and responsibility. One manager said that Sam would take people with hardly any experience and give them six months with Wal-Mart; if he thought they showed potential, he'd make them assistant managers. They would help open new stores and be next in line to manage their own stores. "In my opinion," the manager said, "most of them weren't anywhere near ready to run stores, but Sam proved me wrong."[3] Another manager said that Walton was "very sharp" at reading people—their personalities and their integrity. In the early days, when the company was small, one bad manager could have sunk the company. But Walton didn't make any mistakes. He unerringly selected people he could go forward with.[4] His knack for staffing enabled Wal-Mart to open as many as fifty stores a year, when other companies were struggling to open five or six. By the end of 1993, Wal-Mart had more than 2,500 stores, a twenty-year average return on equity of 35 percent, and compound average sales growth of 34 percent. Walton's astute use of staffing power made this possible.

Top-Level Staffing

The pool of candidates who can lead an entire organization is quite small. When a company must choose a CEO, president, or division manager to lead it through a radically changing environment, the selection process demands careful thought and analysis. Top-level leaders like Walton and Iacocca and boards of directors face extremely difficult decisions. The future environment and its challenges are often unclear and open to different interpretations. There can be many different strategies for coping. Hiring the best requires carefully assessing each candidate's views of the future and considering how she thinks the organization should cope. Leaders probe a candidate's thinking, as well as her character, integrity, and leadership style. Although top-level staffing decisions are infrequent, effective leaders know that staffing may be their most important exercise of power. Top-level staffing decisions have an enormous impact on the organization's performance and often determine its survival or demise.

The staffing decisions that were critical to the strategic change at Compaq are a case in point. Benjamin M. Rosen, chairman of Compaq's board of directors, was a key figure—some would say an unsung hero—in the Compaq saga. After reviewing the changing environment and Compaq's declining market position, Rosen persuaded Compaq's board of directors to make a major staffing decision—to name Pfeiffer as CEO to replace Rod Canion.[5] Compaq's three fold increase in market share, and stock price, indicated that Rosen, and the board, had made an astute staffing decision.

REVIEW POWER

Leaders use review power to keep the organization on a steady course, despite choppy economic conditions and changing competitive currents. Review sizes up performance and corrects undesirable deviations through a continuous process of measurement, evaluation, feedback, and correction. In the review process, leaders modify individual performance and fine-tune the organization's operations and strategy as it works toward its goals. Effective leaders use review to prevent meandering into unattractive markets and distraction by random events. They also use it to avoid neglecting customers and competitors.

Effective leaders make review a valuable learning experience. Review by effective leaders helps subordinates learn how to set goals, appraise performance, and plan corrective action. By using review power sensitively, effective leaders show subordinates how to review their own performance and constructively review the performance of others. Poor leaders, however, misuse their formal review power to intimidate and punish their subordinates. The subordinate's goal then becomes avoiding detection and punishment, rather than furthering the organization's interests.

Individual, Operational, and Strategic Review

Effective leaders conduct three different types of review—individual, operational, and strategic. Review of individual performance is the most common. It considers a person's accomplishments, growth, and working relationships with others and is usually done quarterly or less frequently. It sets goals for the next review period and spells out how the person will meet those goals. Leaders also conduct on-the-spot reviews as they work with others on a task. Reviews conducted close to an event, when details are still fresh in everyone's mind, are the most useful for learning. Poor leaders avoid or rush through individual reviews because they feel uncomfortable doing them. They fear that discussions about how a subordinate could improve will be taken negatively and demotivate the subordinate. The poor leader wants subordinates to improve, yet fails to tell them what or how to improve. Effective leaders and effective subordinates accept that they may feel defensive during a review. They have learned, however, to manage their defensiveness so that together they can conduct a constructive review.

In operational reviews, leaders examine current work flow, equipment, and methods to see how they may be improved. This review continuously improves operations by correcting inefficiencies and errors. Leaders look for best practices and spread them through the organization. Sam Walton made constructive review of operations a hallmark of his leadership of Wal-Mart. From the beginning, Walton's store managers reported a "best-selling item" in their store as part of their weekly reports on store sales. If he didn't get a best-selling item report, Walton would show up at the store and study the merchandise himself. This was his way of teaching managers to review their merchandise and their customers and to look for what was selling all the time.[6] Walton would bring all his managers together once a week for a companywide critique. They would review what they had bought, plan promotions, and plan what they would buy. Walton said, "We wanted everybody to know what was going on and everybody to be aware of the mistakes we made. When somebody made a bad mistake—whether it was myself or anybody else—we talked about it, admitted it, tried to figure out how to correct it, and then moved on to the next day's work."[7] These meetings worked so well that they became a part of the company's culture of constructive review. Hundreds of people—managers of all levels and associates—still attend the weekly meetings, which are part planning, part communication, part fun, and always unpredictable. The meetings review the good news, as well as the company's weaknesses. It looks at both problems and suggestions for correcting them. David Glass, who succeeded Sam Walton as CEO, believed that the constant review of merchandising and its support functions had been the key to Wal-Mart's dramatic increase in sales per square foot and to its double-digit growth in annual sales for more than thirty years, and the key to its status as the largest retailer in the world.[8]

Leaders review operations to simplify work and improve productivity. Frederick Taylor and Frank and Lillian Gilbreth, among others, in the early 1900s formulated a process for simplifying work that has been rediscovered and popularized as "reengineering." Effective leaders simplify work by closely examining and questioning current methods, exploring options for improvement, and stimulating a willingness to change. Simplification starts with a detailed study and description of what people are doing now. This provides the baseline for improvement. Then leaders ask Why: What is the function of each step in the process, and what is its contribution? Can it be eliminated? Can it be combined with other steps? Can it be simplified? What would be the best way to do this if people were starting anew, without the constraints of existing equipment and the burden of existing methods? What would people do differently? What can be learned from other businesses that are doing this type of work? Leaders of a manufacturer of machinery, for example, wanted to manage better the large inventory of spare parts they kept in several warehouses around the world. They studied the warehousing, shipping, and cataloging practices of large mail-order distributors of clothing and footwear, such as L.L. Bean. From what they learned, they were able to simplify their ordering, billing, and warehousing practices and substantially lower their inventory, while at the same time providing better service to their customers.

In strategic reviews, the third type of review, leaders appraise how well the organization's strategy fits its environment and its competition. Reviewing strategy, a critical use of formal power, can drastically change the organization's direction, as it did at Compaq. The strategic review and the subsequent strategic change propelled Compaq's profits to a new record of $865 million in 1994. Compaq's leaders had reviewed strategy, operations, and individual performance and had fit them together into a superbly coordinated response.

Review rounds out and adjusts the leader's use of formal power. Review monitors and corrects decision processes, the organization's agenda, and the staffing process. Leader have formal powers enabling them to greatly affect the organizations success, and the well being of individuals. But in addition to formal power, effective leaders understand the role of knowledge as power, and trust as power.

KNOWLEDGE AS POWER

Expertise

Knowledge acts as a source of power when one person knows so much about a problem or subject that people willingly accept his influence. Expertise is a source of power different and separate from formal power. Even if a person lacks formal authority, people will seek and defer to his knowledge in certain circumstances; people let physicians prescribe remedies for their ailments, lawyers write their contracts, and accountants prepare their tax returns. These are common examples of experts who have knowledge but not formal authority. People grant expert power to individuals who do not have legitimate position power because they believe that they will make a better decision with the expert's knowledge than without it.

Top management leaders increasingly rely on others for the knowledge they need to make high-quality decisions. Expert specialized knowledge is distributed throughout organizations, and it is becoming increasingly common for leaders with formal power to have little expertise and for experts to have little formal power. Engineers, marketers, production specialists, and financial specialists know more than their formal leaders in many situations. Effective leaders with formal power integrate knowledge into their decision processes and their agendas. A battle-seasoned infantryman who had to contend with a new, inexperienced lieutenant picturesquely explained to the officer the difference between legitimate power and knowledge power, and the need to synthesize them: "You can tell me what to do, but I ain't gonna do it if you don't know what you're doing, because I can get killed doing it. Now if the sergeant was to tell us to do something, I wouldn't think twice about doing it, because he knows what we ought to do. So you and him better put your heads together."

Effective leaders know how to call on knowledge through teamwork, which we will talk about in the concluding Chapter. Leaders understand and properly evaluate knowledge in which they are not expert, especially when formulating strategy; they need to understand, and appraise, the strategic options experts propose, because these will greatly affect the organization's success.

Compaq and Pentium Chips

By the early 1990s, managing new product introductions had become critical to success in the PC industry. New models were proliferating at a dizzying pace, and the uniqueness of any new product lasted less than six months. In this hyperactive market a small flaw in a new product decision could lead to a major loss. If a PC model didn't have the right features, was mispriced, or was late, it quickly glutted dealers' shelves and had to be sold at vastly reduced prices, and many components in the manufacturing pipeline quickly became obsolete and unusable.

Because of Compaq's rapid growth and the enlargement of its product line, the company's leaders formed a business operations unit, composed of expert analysts, to study the company's production and marketing. As one of its activities, the unit used complex simulation software to study the introduction of new products. The simulation was extremely detailed, taking into account such things as consumer interest in different features, fluctuation of demand with changes in price, the impact of competitors' models, and the trend affecting component costs. Using the knowledge obtained from these simulation studies, the business operations unit had a major impact on one critical top-management decision in 1994. Intel's new Pentium chip had become available, and Dell Computer and Gateway 2000 were selling models with the new chip. Compaq's historic strategy had been to incorporate new technology into its new PCs as soon as possible. But this time its leaders decided to do something different. The simulation model had predicted that most corporate buyers would not want Pentiums until 1995. If Compaq moved up the introduction of the Pentium to 1994, it would erode sales of existing models without gaining much from the new models. Overall, it would be worse off. Michael Parides, director of business operations, knew all this, but he had to convince the formal leadership system. He took the simulation results to the senior vice president of the desk-top division, to financial executives, to the company's top strategists, and finally to the CEO, Eckhard Pfeiffer. Pfeiffer listened intently and approved holding back the release of the new Pentium models until spring 1995. The power of the knowledge provided by the simulation and the top leaders' willingness to use it proved to be a boon for the company. Compaq's earnings rose 61 percent in the last quarter of 1994, and profits rose by another $50 million by the second quarter of 1995. When users discovered a defect in the first batches of Pentium chips, Compaq reaped an additional windfall—it was spared the problem of replacing flawed chips. Following the recommendation of the business operations unit to delay introducing models with new Pentium chips demonstrated the awesome potential of knowledge power. But, as Parides said, in doing so, "We bet against everything the company believed."[9]

Vision

Vision is the ability to see the future and to understand its meaning. It is also the ability to see what can be done now to adapt to that distant future. Vision foresees a future ideal condition that others cannot see and suggests the ability to convince others to believe in and strive for that ideal. Vision comes from insight, the ability to see below the surface of events and to understand their meaning. It comes from imagination, which goes beyond what is observed to conceive new connections and new possibilities. A vision communicates a destination. It communicates the attractive features, the goodness, the promise of that distant goal and outlines a path, a broad set of principles for reaching that distant goal.

Vision is an uncommon form of knowledge. It goes beyond the simple, direct link between an action and its immediate result. Vision is a concept of long-term relationships; it floats in imagination. Effective leaders continually communicate and interpret their visions to inspire others with a sense of prophetic urgency. Vision addresses the core of an organization's being, its sense of why it exists and what it should do. To be used effectively, vision, which is fundamentally knowledge, needs the support of legitimate power. A leader who has both legitimate power and vision combines in one person two potent sources of power.

Ben Rosen, the chairman of Compaq, whom we mentioned earlier, illustrates a rare confluence of vision and legitimate power. When the PC market was beginning to take off in the early 1980s, he had the vision to see an opportunity to compete against IBM. His vision convinced investors to finance the formation of Compaq, which he cofounded with Rod Canion in 1982. For the next nine years he conveyed his vision to senior management, as Compaq grew into a global organization with revenues of $4 billion. In 1991 Rosen foresaw that to survive in what had become an intensely competitive industry, Compaq would have to change its strategy. In his new vision for the company, it would become a price-competitive mass marketer and a low-cost producer, continually introducing a wide range of new, technically attractive models. He was so deeply committed to that vision that he was able to persuade the board of directors to replace Rod Canion, the cofounder, who wanted to stay with the initial vision of Compaq as a high-priced, limited marketer that selectively introduced premium products. With a new CEO, Eckhard Pfeiffer, in place, Compaq's revenues rose to $11 billion and captured a dominant share of the PC market. Rosen's vision had prevailed, enabling Compaq to continue its explosive growth. Rosen had melded legitimate power and vision.

Process Knowledge

Process knowledge is knowing how to do things—how to access the knowledge distributed in an organization, how to build trust, how to convert knowledge into effective action, how to command, consult, and consign. We have already discussed process knowledge (e.g., finding knowledge, using knowledge, and learning) and will return to it in Chapter 11, which takes a detailed look at consulting. Effective leaders synthesize their legitimate power with the power of knowledge in its various forms—expertise, vision, and process.

TRUST AS POWER

Trust

Trust is a potent source of power that is different from legitimate power. Trust is something people grant informally. When people trust another person, they accept the other person's influence—they grant the other person power. People voluntarily risk their fate by following those they trust. They eagerly cooperate, altering their behavior without hesitation—the very thing that leaders with formal power who are mistrusted struggle to achieve by issuing commands. People readily disclose relevant information and creative options to leaders they trust. They also accept responsibility and diligently control their behavior to reach goals shared by people they trust. Trust is a critical source of power that motivates people to collaborate and to overcome great obstacles. Poor leaders who are mistrusted often face insurmountable resistance despite their having formal power. Effective leaders are trusted, so they gain access to the distributed knowledge in organizations. Trust is a crucial supplement to legitimate power if leaders want commitment, rather than antagonistic obedience.

Trust should not be confused with ability to communicate or charm. Many effective leaders with formal power are not exceptional speakers or talented showpeople. They get their message across because people trust them. They are honest, and they have integrity. They disclose relevant information, and they share influence. They use two-way communication; they listen more than they talk. They live up to the spirit of their agreements and give credit to other's accomplishments. They may not be dazzling speakers, but their intentions, knowledge, and behavior are trustworthy. Harry Truman, the former U.S. president, won the nation's trust to a degree that very few presidents have enjoyed. He was not a great communicator, unlike his predecessor, Franklin Delano Roosevelt, who was a mesmerizing speaker. Truman spoke simply and directly and acted with unfailing integrity. He negotiated the end of World War II and set the foundation for the peace and prosperity that followed. Although he worked less than most public figures to ingratiate himself with people, he succeeded better at it because he was utterly honest with and about himself.[10] He won the nation's support and gratitude and was elected in one of the greatest upset victories in politics because people trusted him. People want leaders they trust to succeed, so they do what has to be done to make those leaders effective. They give the power of their trust.

Charisma

Personal attractiveness that mesmerizes us is called charisma. It is a special, almost magical, talent possessed by a few exceptional leaders. Charismatics are gifted at winning our trust. They communicate so persuasively that people base their trust largely on the leader's style. If the charismatic is indeed trustworthy, it can be inspiring to work with him. Trust, however, not charm, is the underlying source of a charismatic's influence. Charisma is nice, but not many leaders have it. Effective leaders, however, can and do build trust, whether or not they are charismatic. Trust, as we have explained, depends on behavior—disclosing information, sharing influence, and exercising self-control. Charismatics can readily mislead people and misuse their trust. Because charisma inspires people to feel great faith, the fall is steep and the desire for vengeance great if believers discover that they have been deceived. Effective leaders know that charisma is not a substitute for trust. Effective leaders build trust.

SUMMARY

Legitimate power consists of the leader's right to select the decision process, determine the organization's agenda, staff the organization, and review performance. We discussed the decision process in Chapter 9. Agenda power, the first topic of this chapter, gives leaders the right to determine where the organization will go and how it will get there. It consists of selecting goals and formulating strategy; designing the organization's structure and information systems; installing control systems; and setting priorities. Compaq's revolutionary change in strategy was used to illustrate agenda power.

Staffing power comprises selecting, developing, and motivating people who will help plan and implement decisions. Effective leaders have great skill in assessing and motivating people. They surround themselves with effective people because they know that they will have to depend on them to do the organization's work. We described Sam Walton's great talent for selecting store managers to illustrate the value of staffing power.

Review power consists of assessing progress and correcting undesirable deviations. It covers individual performance, operations, and strategy. Effective leaders make review a learning experience. They clarify goals and show how to use the reporting system constructively. They demonstrate how to find creative corrections to unacceptable deviations and use reviews sensitively rather than as vehicles to intimidate or punish subordinates. We described Walton's weekly staff meetings as one form of creative review.

Knowledge is a source of power that differs from legitimate power. Knowledge can be expertise, vision, or process skill. In organizations with distributed knowledge, leaders need to integrate knowledge—expertise, vision, and process skill—with their legitimate power if they are to make high quality decisions. We described Compaq's use of knowledge generated by expert analysts to delay the introduction of new Pentium chip computers and discussed Ben Rosen, Compaq's chairman, and his remarkable melding of legitimate power and strategic vision. Trust is another source of power that differs from legitimate power. Trust gives leaders access to knowledge and creativity and increases people's commitment and willingness to exercise self-control to reach a common goal. Charisma is valuable, but not a substitute for trust. Effective leaders use knowledge and trust as sources of power to supplement their formal power.

In Chapter 11 we discuss consulting—a decision process vital to leaders working with distributed knowledge. Effective leaders have mastered the consulting process and skillfully employ it to use power sensitively, gain access to knowledge, and build trust.

11

The Power of Leaders as Consultants

Leaders use consultation much as a photographer uses a wide-angle or zoom lens—to change range and focus, to get a clear image of a fuzzy situation. Leaders consult to find the knowledge they and their subordinates need to understand their complex, changing environment, to diagnose ambiguous problems, and to generate creative solutions. Using consultation, leaders gain the insight to make high-quality decisions. By acting as consultants rather than as commanders, effective leaders use power tactfully, helping people develop perspective and insight. They are also competent clients, seeking the perspective and counsel of their subordinates when shaping decisions.

Consultation, a form of legitimate power, sets aside the barriers of formal authority and allows leaders to explore the knowledge and to promote the trust they need to solve problems. It also increases participation, circumvents the wall of power differences, releases knowledge and increases trust, making it the preferred leadership mode in highly adaptive organizations. When used by effective leaders, consultation is a potent and extremely sensitive exercise of power. Poor leaders, on the other hand, believe that power should be exercised through command, or some variation of command, in which the leader directs and controls dependent followers.

Power has two dimensions: influence and control. To poor leaders, influence is the directive, authoritarian use of power and control refers to actions that maintain or increase the dependence of follow-ers. As the Chinese philosopher Lao-tzu said of this type of leader: "When the task is done, the people say the leader did it."

Consultation as a form of power, although frequently used in U.S. culture, is widely misunderstood. By consultation we mean exerting influence through an exchange of views about problems and solutions as part of a search for knowledge. The leader-consultant and the client share control, with the ultimate goal being to reduce, rather than increase, the client's dependence. Some people call this participation, but we believe that term is too inclusive and too vague. Consultation is a more precise concept of how leaders may use power. As Lao-tzu said of the consulta-tive leader: "When the task is done, the people say we did it."

This chapter begins with a review of the need for consulting and examines why leaders need to be both consultants and clients. Next, we describe a method for improving consulting skills and present a model of consulting that includes two levels: content and process. We discuss the phases and the leadership skills of the two levels. We con-clude the chapter by looking at the problematic areas that leaders need to master as consultants and clients.

NEED FOR CONSULTING

Given today's complex organizations and rapidly changing markets, it makes greater and greater sense for leaders to counsel and consult people before taking action. Effective leaders make wise decisions and obtain commitment by using consultation. They consider prior con-sultation a necessity rather than an option. Many conditions drive leaders toward consultation. Although we discussed some of them in Chapter 1, they are worth reviewing here.

Knowledge is distributed throughout the organization, where it resides in an educated workforce that often knows more operating details and better methods of analysis than its leaders. Leaders need to act as clients who know how to consult other people to gain access to their knowledge, creativity, and motivation. When leaders attempt to command people to reveal knowledge or contribute creativity, the demand often arouses resentment and blocks access to what the lead-ers seek. With the increasing dispersion of knowledge, effective lead-ers need to learn to be competent clients.

At the same time, subordinates need the counsel of their leaders. As organizations compete in volatile markets, people need access to their leaders' judgment and creative insight, their wisdom and vision. When asked for counsel however, poor leaders respond with decisive commands. They do not realize that they are increasing their subordi-nates' dependence and rigid compliance. Adaptive organizations, however, need effective leader-consultants who develop subordinates by providing perspective and counsel.

Leaders also need to be consultant-clients to keep their organization afloat in a sea of uncertainty. Technological innovations, shortened product cycles, and new marketing methods are radically changing markets. Global competitors are vaulting across traditional industry boundaries. In publishing and entertainment, for example, the boundaries that formerly divided the print media, audiotapes, compact disks, computers, television, telecommunication, and electronic networks are vanishing. Leaders need to be consultant-clients to anticipate and understand the volatile changes in their environment.

The rise of mutual-influence practices also drives leaders toward consultation. Leaders have been encouraged to increase participation and to share power through such activities as joint goal setting, mutual appraisal, team building, total quality management, and reengineering. These practices depend to some degree on the leader's ability to consult. If leaders are good consultant-clients, these practices will work; if not, they will fail. Diversity has also increased the need for leader-consultants. Companies now routinely market to and employ people from many different cultures. Globalization has made cultural diversity an everyday event. When working with people from different cultures, being a consultant-client is more effective than issuing commands or prematurely consigning to unfamiliar people.

Many leaders think of consultants as outside specialists hired to perform a specialized service as part of a limited project. Not many leaders think of themselves as consultant-clients in their relationships with other people—superiors and subordinates, staff and coworkers, headquarters and field, customers and suppliers. It may seem obvious that leaders ought to see themselves as consultant-clients. Some leaders say they do, but beyond agreeing that this makes sense, few understand and accept what consultation means. Effective leaders, however, are extremely good consultants and clients and continually refine their consultant-client knowledge and skills.

A MODEL OF THE CONSULTING RELATIONSHIP

A surprising number of leaders approach consultation like gladiators. They swing an idea like a sword, intent on decapitating their opponent. If their opponent parries and counterthrusts, they have a worthy adversary. If not, they thrust again, seeking their opponent's capitulation or demise. Consider the marketing manager described in Chapter 9 who was concerned about declining sales in the southeast region. As a gladiator-consultant she would thrust by saying, "I'm going to close two branches and lay off twenty-seven people in the southeast region." Then she would wait to see how the marketing research director reacted. Did he capitulate and immediately agree, or did he parry, citing reasons to adopt another tactic, and fight back with counterproposals? Gladiator leaders dispatch capitulators. They use consultation as intellectual combat, believing that forceful challenge is the best way to probe what people know and to stimulate their creativity.

Other leaders consult like ferrets, endlessly burrowing for information and counsel and postponing decisions. They relentlessly consult, pursuing others who after a while scurry away, concealing themselves intellectually. Ferret-consultants continually need more meetings. They endlessly search for a snippet of information or insight that will give them sufficient comfort to make a decision.

An alternative to the gladiator and the ferret images is a model that examines the levels and phases of consultation. Figure 11-1 portrays the consulting relationship as having two levels: a content or subject level and a process or method level. Each level consists of three phases, which are discussed below.[1]

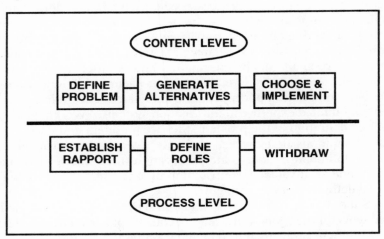

Figure 11-1 The Consulting Relationship

CONTENT LEVEL

Most leaders are comfortable with the content level of the consultation model, which focuses on diagnosing a situation and defining and solving a problem. But there is much they can learn about the three phases of this level—defining the problem, generating solution options, and choosing and implementing—that will improve their consultation skills.

The three phases overlap and rarely flow in a linear sequence. Many leaders know this, but because they want quick, decisive action they dislike ambiguities. They get impatient when consultation recycles through the three phases, refining the diagnosis and clarifying assumptions. Many leaders demand that problem solving march crisply from problem definition to solution to implementation. When leaders demand linear problem solving for complex, ambiguous problems and intimidate subordinates who do not deliver it, their consulting relationship will founder on this point alone. Leaders need to be wary of linear problem solving. As a rule, when simple problems amenable to linear problem solving reach higher levels of management, they have been seriously oversimplified or else should have been solved by lower-level subordinates without the involvement of upper-level leaders.

Define the Problem

Subordinates consult leaders and leaders consult their subordinates to find the right problem and define it properly. The initial definition of a problem often is neither the best definition nor the final definition. Recall the case of the bank vice president whose operations manager defined his problem as "a trouble-making supervisor who should be fired for lowering morale by publicly questioning the bank's information system strategy" (see Chapter 7). Acting as a leader-consultant, the vice president sought information and counsel from others. He then helped to creatively redefine the problem as follows: "How can the bank open an opportunity for a motivated, energetic supervisor who has limited expertise in information systems?" Working with this revised definition of the problem, the vice president and his staff generated solutions that enabled the supervisor to transform the bank into a dominant regional data-processing center. The leader-consultant made an invaluable contribution by examining and probing the initial definition of the problem.

Subordinates often view a situation narrowly because of the limited scope of their jobs and need the counsel of a leader-consultant to find the right problem and to define it properly. Superiors have a different problem. They are remote from operations and preoccupied with distant concerns. They tend to abstract situations, reducing them to financial measures, headcounts, and productivity ratios. To find the right problem, it may be necessary to act as clients, consulting subordinates to gain insight into the realities behind the abstractions.

Some leaders insist on imposing their initial definition of the problem on their subordinates. Subordinates who have this type of leader learn that if they ask for counsel, the leader will take over definition of the problem. As a result, some subordinates avoid asking for help so that they can retain control. Others deliberately ask for the leader's counsel so that they can transfer the problem to the leader. These subordinates have learned how to use consultation to delegate upward. Effective leader-consultants recognize the need to keep problem definition fluid. They are willing to consider alternative definitions, and are comfortable working with a tentative definition before arriving at a final definition. Rather than rush to solve the wrong problem, they are willing to revise a definition in the light of new data. Effective leader-consultants help themselves and others by carefully probing to find the right problem and then defining it properly.

Generate Solution Options

It is common sense that a decision can be no better than the best option people can devise. If leaders can come up with only a small set of poor options, they cannot make a good decision, they can only choose the best of a group of low-quality solutions. Poor leader-consultants, in the rush to make a decision, make restricted, uncreative searches for options. Effective leader-consultants, however, encourage creative search. They have mastered the consulting skills of working with others to generate a rich set of options. They know how to use brainstorming so that people separate the creation of options from the critical evaluation of options. They know how to use synectics, a process that encourages imaginative speculation by looking at problems from different points of view and by using innovative and unusual techniques, such as pretending that one is an animal in nature, a military commander, or a physician and trying to imagine how such a being would deal with the problem. Leader-consultants know how to use six-hat lateral thinking in which people assume different roles, becoming the "white hat" who focuses on facts and figures, the "red hat" who expresses feelings, hunches, and intuition, the "black hat" who plays devil's advocate, explaining why something will not work, the "yellow hat" who envisions opportunities and constructive possibilities, the "green hat" who grows new ideas, asks provocative questions, and looks for fertile connections across disparate fields, or the "blue hat" who conducts the discussion, thinks about procedures, and calls on a particular "hat" to fill in gaps in thinking.[2] Poor leader-consultants assume that, as counselors, they should take over the generation of solutions, and create superior options from their past personal experience. Effective leader-consultants concentrate on encouraging the clients to generate options, using the search methods we have described. Effective leader-consultants may contribute hints or trial balloons, but they use them primarily to stimulate clients to generate their own solutions.

Choose and Implement

Leaders choose and implement solutions every day, so they feel familiar with this phase of the content level. Effective leader-consultants, however, continually review in slow motion the steps and assumptions that other people often take for granted. First, they look at the key steps in choosing a solution. To choose a solution, people need to predict the consequences of each option. It is difficult to predict consequences when many important forces are beyond one's control, so people make assumptions. Leader-consultants work with clients to test these assumptions. For instance, recall the case of Cotran (described on page 32), the natural gas company that was planning to enter a new market and whose managers were assuming that their cost of gas would be equal to or less than the costs of their major competitor. The vice president asked his subordinates to review the basis for this assumption. They found that their major competitor actually had long-term, low-cost gas contracts. This review of assumptions led the company to reduce the aggressiveness of its market entry and to narrow its definition of target customers. (We discussed the process of testing assumptions in greater detail, in Chapters 2 and 3). After testing their assumptions, leader-consultants and their clients need to define the criteria for evaluating options and apply those criteria objectively. They need to assess the trade-offs each option makes across the different criteria and then rank the proposals. After they select an option, they should identify back up solutions that can be used to deal with various contingencies. Effective leader-consultants review each of these steps and their assumptions and carefully question clients to ensure that they have considered each step and understand the assumptions they are making; poor leader-consultants short-circuit the choice process and jump to a predetermined solution.

Implementation, the second element in this phase, is more than simply telling people what to do. Yet poor leader-consultants persist in behaving as if command were all there is to implementation. Effective leader-consultants know that implementation requires careful planning. They walk clients through the details—who will be involved in implementation, when, how, and why. They discuss how the client plans to communicate the decision and review the likely obstacles and resistance to implementation and how these will be managed. Effective leader-consultants examine systems for monitoring progress and the process for feeding back information about undesirable deviations. They look at who will take corrective action and how will they do it. Faulty implementation is a recurring problem for poor leaders because they overlook many of these fundamental questions. Effective leader-consultants have the skills to help clients move through these steps in choice and implementation.

Now we move to the process level of our model.

PROCESS LEVEL

Although we separate the process level from the content level, in reality, when leaders consult, they operate at both levels simultaneously. The two levels interact, but we separate them for the convenience of discussion. The process level depicted in Figure 11-1 has three phases: establishing rapport, defining roles, and withdrawing. The three phases have no sharp separating boundaries and often overlap. Some leader-consultants have difficulty with the idea of a process level. They are unaware of it or dismiss it as unnecessary and as a result have difficulty understanding why their consulting relationships fail.

Establish Rapport

It may sound strange that a leader-consultant needs to establish rapport with a subordinate, a superior, or a coworker with whom she has worked for some time. But each problem is different; circumstances change from one situation to another, and the stakes are different. Furthermore, people change. With each new problem, clients go through a ritual of figuring out how open they can be with a leader-consultant. Effective leader-consultants understand that they need to reestablish rapport each time they work on a new problem. Depending on the situation and the past relationship between the leader-consultant and the other person, establishing rapport may take only a few minutes or it may take an extended series of feeling-out meetings. Poor leader-consultants assume that rapport exists and want to drive to the heart of the problem immediately. They see only the content level and want to plunge into its first phase, defining the problem. They remain unaware of or ignore the process level.

Linda Prager, north-central regional manager of Savoy Pharmaceuticals (all names disguised) asked Gail Meenan, a headquarters marketing specialist, to review the region's marketing plans and methods. Meenan unwittingly offended Prager on the first visit by publicly criticizing the region's performance and implying that Prager was at fault. It was not politic for Prager to reject Meenan immediately. Prager and her staff spent almost a year fending off Meenan and compiling evidence to show headquarters that she was incompetent. Actually, Meenan was very competent but, having failed to get Prager to accept her recommendations, she was about to be recalled from the assignment. An external consultant to the regional leader suggested a meeting with the marketing specialist to review what could be learned from the study and how their relationship might have been improved. The external consultant acted as a third-party intermediary.

At the meeting Meenan expressed disappointment over her inability to influence the regional organization. Prager then reviewed the evolution of their relationship and gradually revealed the felt insult of the first day. The marketing specialist was astounded. She was completely unaware of the defensiveness her remarks had aroused. She had thought that her critical evaluation would show people that she was a marketing expert and that she would not "soft-pedal" adverse findings. With this incident out in the open, Prager was finally able to consider and use several of Meenan's recommendations. Prager redesigned the training program for salespeople and changed the bonus system. She focused on developing closer relationships with distributors by increasing the number of visits made by branch managers. She improved coordination between regional sales promotions and national advertising. These changes helped move the region from one of the worst-performing to one of the best-performing divisions in the company. Although delayed almost a year, the regional manager and the marketing specialist had finally established the rapport they needed for an effective consulting relationship.

Effective leader-consultants realize that establishing rapport is the gateway to defining and solving a problem. After rapport has been established, the parties can begin to investigate the problem productively. Without it, they skim the surface and skirt around the problem. When establishing rapport, the leader-consultant assesses how strongly the client feels a need for help. Is this situation seen as serious by the client? Is the client in great pain or distress, or is this situation a transient annoyance? How ready is the client for change? Have the client's previous efforts failed, or is the client at the early stage of simply floating a few initial ideas? How much can the parties trust each other? What does the client know about the leader-consultant's credentials and experience in dealing with this kind of situation? Does the leader-consultant have the competence to help this client with his problem? What are each party's goals for the consulting relationship? At this stage, what does each expect of the other? All of these considerations are part of establishing rapport. Effective leader-consultants realize that establishing and maintaining rapport with a client—whether subordinate, coworker, or superior—is an on going process that will continue throughout their work on the problem.

Define Roles

Effective leaders can play the various roles of a consultant individually or in combinations, like a master musician playing individual strings or chords on a guitar. Poor leader-consultants have a one-string, authoritarian concept of the roles of consultant and client. They stick to a "doctor-patient" view of consulting roles in which the client presents symptoms and the consultant diagnoses the situation and defines the problem. Poor leader-consultants assume that clients share the leader's one-string, authoritarian concept of the consulting relationship; effective leader-consultants understand and play a wide variety of rich roles that inspire creativity and go well beyond the limited doctor-patient model. We discuss these roles in the next sections.

Acceptor

In the acceptor role the leader-consultant confirms that it is all right for the client to have the difficulty he has. Many clients already feel defensive and incompetent because they have sought help and will clam up if the consultant condemns them for having a problem. The consultant, in the role of acceptor, communicates that the client need not condemn himself or immobilize himself with guilt and that the situation can be examined to see what might be done. The acceptor plays a critical role in establishing rapport and building trust. Many poor leader-consultants overlook the acceptor role, brushing it aside because they don't want to "mollycoddle" clients, or perform it incompetently. Jim Hopkins (names disguised), a middle-level manager of transaction processing (traditionally called "back-office operations") for Mitchel-Crombie, a large financial services company, attempted to consult his superior, Mike Stonefield, vice president of operations, about a problem. One employee had been transferred, and a second had suddenly fallen seriously ill. Months later it had been discovered that several large security transactions and transfers had been mishandled and that errors had occurred in the accounts of several important customers. Tracking down these errors and correcting them was a complex, labor-intensive process that was still going on, and some customers were threatening Hopkins with litigation. After hearing a brief summary of the situation, Stonefield interrupted and said to Hopkins, "How could you be so stupid as to foul this up the way you did? How could someone with your intelligence get into this mess? Now we have to get the legal department involved, and that's not going to look good on your record." Actually, Hopkins had already discussed the matter with the legal department. They understood his concern, and their study of the situation had found no evidence of fraud or deliberate concealment. They felt that the matter was not serious, although there might be some additional costs to straighten it out. They thought that the real issue was customer relations. Hopkins never got a chance to tell this to Stonefield. Hopkins clammed up and decided that he could not attempt to consult Stonefield about anything in the future. Stonefield prided himself on being a no-nonsense manager who was available to subordinates. His inability to take on the role of a competent acceptor, however, deprived him of the opportunity to use consultation as part of his decision making process.

Reflector

The reflector's function is to help clients hear what they are saying. In the role of reflector, leader-consultants listen actively, which means that they rephrase and summarize their client's description of the situation, including the client's feelings. When clients hear what they have been thinking in the words of another person, the situation becomes objectified and less personal and they can begin to distance themselves emotionally from the situation. The situation then appears more tractable and less overwhelming than it did when the client was thinking about it alone. By objectifying difficult situations, leader-consultants as reflectors helps clients deal with their inclination to delay, deny, or avoid dealing with problems.

Poor leader-consultants, when in the reflector role, talk at great length about their personal experiences, which they insist hold important lessons for the client. They move their own experiences to the center of the relationship, distracting the client. When clients try to return to their own concerns, the leader-consultant feels rejected and persists in exploring his experiences to demonstrate how relevant they really are to the client's problem. When salespeople at American Foods (names disguised), a large food-processing company, attempted to consult their branch manager, Ben Staley, about problems they were having with new purchasing agents in several customer companies, Staley, an old-timer who had come from another branch, insisted on describing his experiences in successfully selling to customers in his old branch. When his clients tried to explore how their situation might be different from the one he was describing, he pointed out that he had been the best salesman in his branch and then further elaborated on his experiences. After a few rounds of this treatment, salespeople stopped consulting Staley. Over coffee, they would embellish and joke about the events the branch manager had described when they had tried to consult him. Effective leader-consultants can confine themselves to the role of reflector. They do not feel compelled to impose their experiences on the client. They mirror and put in perspective for the client's benefit the content and the emotions the client has been trying to express.

Questioner

In the questioner role the leader-consultant questions the client primarily to enlarge the client's view of the situation: What is the context of the situation? What is its history? How long has it been going on? Who else is concerned about the situation? What are their concerns? How do you know? How serious is the situation, and what solutions have been tried in the past? What happened? Why do you think they did not succeed? What other solutions have been considered? Why were they not used? What would be your preferred solution at this time? Why? Who would support and who would not support your proposed solution? Why? What other factors would make implementing a solution difficult or easy?

The questioner's principal function is to increase the scope and the depth of the client's understanding of the situation. Questions help clients see and create new courses of action. They may seem intended to elicit information to help the leader-consultant, but this is a secondary aspect of the role. The primary purpose of questions is to help clients understand their situation, and what they can do to resolve it. As Sam Goldwyn, the canny Hollywood movie producer, used to say, "For your information, let me ask you a few questions."

Poor leader-consultants ask questions in a way that embarrasses and attacks clients. They appear to say, "Here is another thing you overlooked or did wrong." Clients greatly resent leader-consultants who play "gotcha" with them. Effective leader-consultants ask questions that help clients better understand their situation, assumptions, knowledge gaps, and feasible options. Effective leader-consultants do not ask questions to humiliate or intimidate clients or to formulate a solution which they intend to impose on the client.

Problem Definer

Leader-consultants can play different roles in defining the problem. They can act primarily as facilitators, limiting themselves to helping clients clarify their definition of a problem. They can go further, collaborating with clients to define the problem by examining some of the problem's content. Or they can become even more expert, getting deeply involved with the problem's substance and making the major inputs that define the problem.

The leader-consultant and the client need to clarify several points. What diagnostic models will they use? Models focus on different aspects of an organization. Will the leader-consultant and the client concentrate on organization structure? Business strategy? Work flow? Information systems? Quality of personnel? Performance feedback and appraisal? Reward systems? Some of these, or all of them? The diagnostic models they choose will determine what data they will gather. What methods of data gathering will they use? Interviews? Questionnaires? Observations? Documents? Who will gather the data? Who will summarize them? Who will interpret them? What about confidentially? Who will have access to the data and the results? Effective leader-consultants make critical use of their power when they help clients define a problem; they know that the definition of a problem will determine the client's focus and channel her future actions.

Solution Generator

Leader-consultants can also play different roles in generating solutions. They can act primarily as facilitators, limiting themselves to helping clients generate their own solutions. They can go beyond facilitating and collaborate with clients to generate solutions together. Or they can get deeply involved, becoming the main generator of solutions. Leader-consultants, and external consultants, who do not feel bound by the constraints or the culture of the business are particularly valuable in this role because they feel free to ask unusual questions that provoke consideration of unusual solutions.

Senior management of an electronics company that made citizen-band radios created a task force to determine in which cities the company should build new manufacturing capacity. One manager who was familiar with the business and its competitive outlook acted as a leader-consultant, asking, "Why are we in this business?" Initially the task force ridiculed the question because it seemed to challenge the wisdom of senior management's decision to expand production. In this company, one did not challenge an assignment handed down by senior management. After the initial reaction, the leader-consultant's question provoked a searching reexamination of the situation and of solution options. The task force determined that it was dealing with an unusual spike in demand that could not be sustained. Product life cycles were extremely short, and competitors were making and buying high-quality products at very low cost from Asian factories. The task force decided to recommend not expanding capacity because of the extremely high risk that a domestic plant would rapidly become obsolete. As a backup position, the task force also tentatively identified two cities as possible sites for a new plant. The task force then discussed its findings with senior management. Ultimately, the company's leaders decided to forgo the investment in new plant and instead bought more components and subassemblies from foreign sources. This unexpected solution lowered costs. Two years later, when demand plummeted, competitors who had expanded in the United States had to close large, unused plants, and some were driven into bankruptcy. The task force had generated a richer set of solution options than the obvious solution of selecting one U.S. city for expansion.

Through their behavior, leader-consultants demonstrate new norms that help clients generate superior creative solutions. Effective leader-consultants legitimize questioning assumptions about goals, methods, resources, and competitors, freeing clients to move outside the boundaries of their mental constraints. They encourage clients to explore and to create a rich set of possible solutions. Poor leader-consultants jump in and quickly give clients solutions. As followers of the doctor-patient model of consultation, they mistakenly believe that the leader-consultant's role is to solve the client's problem. Effective leader-consultants, sometimes with the aid of external consultants, push the boundaries of possible solutions and help clients find their own solutions.

Evaluator

Acting as evaluators, leader-consultants look for criteria for a good solution. What would a good solution do? What would it not do? How would people evaluate it? Leader-consultants and clients evaluate proposals by judging their predicted outcomes against preset criteria. What are the benefits, the costs, and the risks of each proposal? How will poor implementation affect the outcomes and the evaluation? As they do in the other roles we have discussed, leader-consultants can make different contributions to evaluation. They can concentrate on facilitating the client's own evaluation of solution options; they can jointly evaluate options with the client; or they can make most of the evaluation themselves.

Effective leader-consultants help clients learn how to define and apply evaluation criteria and improve their ability to do their own evaluations. One headquarters marketing executive described it this way: "At first, I used to tell my field managers what I thought they were doing wrong and what they should change. I found that they resented what I said, and they changed very little. Then I decided to discuss with them the criteria I was using to evaluate what marketing was doing. They often disagreed with me, but it encouraged them to think about criteria and how they might apply to different situations. The field managers didn't change all at once, but gradually they got to be very insightful in developing and applying criteria to decisions in their regions."

Withdraw

Withdrawal by a leader-consultant in a consulting relationship with subordinates, coworkers, or superiors may seem strange. Withdrawal, however, does not mean permanent separation for all future work. It simply means winding down and letting go of the client regarding the task or specific problem about which they have been consulting. In the withdrawal phase, effective leader-consultants prepare to wind down by helping the client continue with decisions or changes he has started. Sometimes this means reviewing the skills and the resources the client needs to move ahead on his own; sometimes it means devising measuring systems that the client can use to evaluate his own performance.

Productive consulting increases the trust and the mutual respect between consultant and client, enhancing their ability to work together on future problems. Through consultation, they have worked through a difficult situation. Winding down consultation on a successfully completed task should include an opportunity for people to express their mutual respect, appreciation, and joy. Effective leader-consultants know how to say, "Well done," and effective clients know how to say, "Thanks for your help." They can celebrate their accomplishment simply, with a handshake, or more elaborately, with a festive dinner. The celebration, whatever form it takes, completes the leader-consultant's withdrawal and leaves the parties with a sense of fulfillment.

PROBLEM AREAS IN THE CONSULTANT ROLE

Many leaders would like to use consultation more often, but they are trapped by a conventional model of formal authority that sees consultants as superiors and clients as subordinates. To be effective consultants, leaders need to manage three issues that come from the conventional model: defensiveness, inadequate process skills, and reluctance to withdraw.

Defensiveness

Many leader-consultants, concerned about preserving an image of formal authority, become defensive if they construe the client's behavior as a challenge to their power. These leader-consultants believe that when they are consulted, they should control the relationship, defining the problem, generating the options, and solving the problem. If the client questions the leader-consultant's definition of the problem or disagrees with the leader-consultant's solution, poor leaders feel that they are losing control of the relationship. Joan Griffin (names disguised) a headquarters marketing manager was consulted about sales of an established food product by Karen Harper, a recently appointed product manager. Griffin had concluded that the problem was how to get better shelf space for the product in retail stores. She suggested solutions such as having salespeople push the item with store managers and hiring local people to stock shelves with the product. Harper resisted Griffin's definition of the problem and her solution options. In subsequent meetings, Harper began talking about using coupon promotions, repricing the product, and changing the theme of a forthcoming advertising campaign. In exasperation, Griffin said, "How can you expect me to help if you keep changing the problem? If you intended to reject my advice, you shouldn't have asked for my help in the first place." Harper was completely surprised by the intensity of Griffin's remarks. Harper concluded that from then on she would have to be careful about saying anything that might diminish Griffin's sense of control. Poor leaders, when acting as consultants, quickly become defensive, misconstruing questions and legitimate differences as challenges to their power or competence. They need to manage their frustration and anger and learn to respond constructively when clients do not passively accept their definition of the problem or their proposed solution.

Process Skills

Process skills pose a problem for poor leader-consultants who focus exclusively on the content level. These leaders are unfamiliar with the process level and its three phases. They overlook the need to establish rapport in each consultation and assume that the client knows what to expect, is ready to accept advice, and trusts them. These leaders say, "There is no need to waste time on preliminaries; let's get right down to business." They want to define and solve the problem immediately. These leaders have little awareness of the different roles they can play as a consultant—acceptor, reflector, questioner, solution generator, and evaluator—and the skills these roles require. They ignore or distort the withdrawal phase, which we discuss in the next section. Effective leader-consultants, however, understand the process level and its skills.

Withdrawal

Poor leader-consultants have particular difficulty with the withdrawal phase. Some of them get impatient with subordinate-clients and pull away too quickly. Typically, these leaders say, "I've told her what to do; now it's up to her. I'm not going to waste my time holding her hand." Others become compulsive about ensuring that the client understands their counsel and will take proper action. They take over the client's responsibilities and will not let go. If the client is a subordinate, the client finds himself fending off the leader-consultant. Instead of working on the original problem, the client feels that he must recapture his authority and responsibility from an overbearing leader-consultant. Effective leader-consultants are able to discuss the withdrawal process with clients and work out a mutually satisfactory withdrawal.

CLIENT ROLE DILEMMAS

Many leaders know that they could benefit by consulting superiors, coworkers, and subordinates. These leaders can become effective clients if they learn to manage three issues: fear of loss of control, low tolerance for ambiguity, and discomfort with being a constructive client.

Fear of Loss of Control

Poor leaders who try to be clients sometimes think that this means giving up control of the relationship to the consultant. Working in hierarchical organizations, these leaders have been schooled to believe that they must appear to be in charge at all times. They believe that they need to project an image of strength and independence and worry that being seen as a client seeking counsel will detract from this image. Effective leaders come to grips with these feelings, enabling them to be competent clients. When effective leaders are consultants, they understand and are sensitive to how others may feel as clients. They have learned that being a client does not suggest a loss of control, that, to the contrary, it implies that one has the courage, wisdom, and risk-taking ability to confront and surmount difficulties.

Low Tolerance for Ambiguity

Poor leaders have little tolerance for the ambiguity that accompanies efforts to diagnose a problem and find a solution. They have difficulty being clients because problems rarely come tied in ribbons with clear, concise definitions. Diagnosing a problem and generating solutions are circular, time-consuming processes. Leader-consultants and clients have to probe below the presenting symptoms; if they do not, they probably will solve the wrong problem. In one case, middle-level leaders of the maintenance division of an oil refinery believed that in order to improve the unit's ability to complete jobs within estimated costs, foremen should immediately be trained in how to discipline malingering craft workers. Fortunately, higher management had sufficient tolerance for ambiguity to seek, in addition the counsel of the foremen. As clients, the leaders learned that most delays occurred because the refinery schedule was frequently changed after crews and materials had been assembled for a job and even after a job had been started. Maintenance crews then had to be reassigned and often had to wait for parts necessary to complete the new job. When they returned to their earlier jobs, parts had been cannibalized, and they again had to wait for replacement parts ordered through central purchasing. The problem was not discipline but refinery scheduling, over which the maintenance foreman had no control. When the refinery's leaders brought this to the attention of the people in charge of refinery scheduling, they revised their method of scheduling to give greater consideration to how changes would affect maintenance assignments. The changes enabled maintenance to improve its cost performance significantly. Tolerance for ambiguity had enabled the refinery's leaders to be effective clients, avoiding quick definition of and rapid action on the wrong problem.

Discomfort with Being a Constructive Client

Poor leaders visualize consultation as an extension of the formal authority of a superior over a subordinate. This view makes it difficult for them to be constructive clients. Effective leaders can think beyond the stereotype of the compliant, subordinate client, opening a realm of new possibilities in which the client can constructively shape the relationship. Constructive clients know how to guide the consulting relationship. They know the difference between the content and the process levels in consultation (Fig. 11-1), and they understand the phases in each level. They know where they are in the process and what is happening in each phase. They have the skills to guide their consultant constructively. They are aware of how well they and the consultant have established rapport. If their rapport is unsatisfactory, they can talk about their concerns about the consultant's competence, motivation, and expectations without attacking, or embarrassing, the consultant. Constructive clients know the different roles consultants can take, and they periodically review with the consultant how the roles will be distributed between them. They accept the ultimate responsibility for their problem and its solution and feel comfortable with a process that requires them to actively define and solve their problems. Being a constructive client requires having the courage and the skill to work with consultants as collaborators, rather than as adversaries.

SUMMARY

Effective leaders use consultation to acquire knowledge and build trust. Consultation sets aside formal power in favor of a focus on the exchange of information and the creation of ideas. Effective leaders, acting as consultants and clients, gain access to distributed knowledge and provide counsel and vision that their subordinates accept and use. They use consultation to understand the uncertainty in a global competitive world, to work effectively with people from diverse cultures, and to reap the benefits of mutual influence practices.

We discussed a model of consultation that has a content level and a process level. The content level consists of three phases—defining the problem, generating solution options, and choosing and implementing. Most leaders feel intellectually comfortable with the content level but need to master the skills of each phase. Defining the problem requires leaders to control their rush to action so that they can effectively counsel clients, helping them uncover information and insight, so that they define the right problem. Generating solution options depends on creating a rich set of good options from which to choose. The quality of options, in turn, depends on the extent to which the leader-consultant has encouraged a creative search through such methods as brainstorming, synectics, and lateral six-hat thinking. In the choose and implement phase, effective leader-consultants pay close attention to each component. They predict the consequences of each option, define evaluation criteria, apply the criteria to make a decision, develop contingency plans, and plan for implementing the selected option.

Effective leaders understand that the consulting process opens the gate to content. Our model described the three phases in the process level—establishing rapport, defining roles, and withdrawing. Even though leader-consultants may regularly work with clients as subordinates, coworkers, or superiors, they need to establish and maintain rapport for each new consultation task, developing trust and a shared understanding of the client's need for consultation and readiness for change, the options tried, the consultant's competence for this task, and their expectations. The second phase of the process level, defining roles, calls for fulfilling one or more of the roles available to the consultant—acceptor, reflector, questioner, problem definer, solution generator, and evaluator. The third phase of the process level, withdrawal, consists of efforts to develop the client's ability to act on her own and then winding down the consulting relationship.

Effective leader-consultants have learned to manage the issues attendant on being a consultant. They have learned to be nondefensive with clients who are not passive and compliant. They understand the process level of consultation and have mastered its different roles. They have learned to help clients stand on their own and to let go of their consulting role and celebrate withdrawal. Effective leaders have also learned to manage the potential problems that go with being a client. As clients, they do not make control the central issue in the relationship. They have developed a high tolerance for ambiguity, enabling them to find the right problem and then create a superior solution. They have learned to be constructive clients who know how to develop and guide a collaborative consulting relationship. Leaders know that consultation takes great skill and courage. They also know that it is a remarkably effective way to liberate distributed knowledge and build a trusting, adaptive organization.

In the next chapter we discuss teamwork and the integration of knowledge, trust, and power.

CONCLUSION

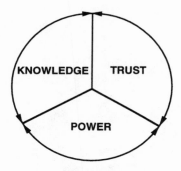

Triadic Leadership

Teamwork and
Triadic Integration

Effective leaders build productive, adaptive teams by integrating knowledge, trust, and power, guiding the teams toward common goals, employing their competence, and building mutual trust. They work with these teams in two modes—a production mode and a knowledge mode. Leaders use the production mode for well-structured, daily work and shift to a knowledge mode for ill-structured, nonroutine situations, such as developing strategy and contending with volatile market changes.

A football team plays a game in a production mode, under power-directive leadership. The coach calls the plays, and the quarterback directs the team, implementing the plays. Each player knows his role and trusts the others to perform their assignments. The coach select's the strategy; the players implement it, improvising only when a play goes awry. Between games, however, leaders shift the team to a lateral knowledge mode to improve performance and adaptability. Coaches and players review films of their last game and films of their next opponent, and share their knowledge of how to improve. They grunt, groan, whoop with joy, laugh, and make critical comments as they watch good and bad plays. Together, they revise the team's offensive and defensive strategy and plan the implementation of the revised plan. They then go to a hybrid knowledge-production mode, using what they have learned to improve player skills, practice team coordination, and sharpen play execution. Finally, the team returns to the production mode in its next game. Even during a game, leaders still use a lateral knowledge mode to improve the team's performance. The quarterback, for example, may call a time out and go to the side-line to discuss with the coaches how to deal with an unusual alignment of the defensive team or with a problem he sees in his own team. Thus, leaders skillfully use their power to blend a lateral knowledge mode and the production mode. The combination generates the knowledge and the trust that drives team productivity and adaptability.

This chapter examines the two basic types of situations leaders face—well-structured, routine situations and ill-structured, non routine situations. It discusses the characteristics of the production mode and the knowledge mode. It looks at the leader's need to match modes to situations and to integrate knowledge, trust, and power and offers an example drawn from the banking industry. The chapter discusses the relationship between the knowledge mode and task forces and looks at blending the production and knowledge modes and the operational realities of using a knowledge mode. It concludes with a discussion of the characteristics of triadic leaders.

DEFINING SITUATIONS

A situation can be well structured or ill structured. Some situations, of course, have characteristics of both, but we discuss the pure types to clarify the analysis. Well-structured situations have the characteristics of routine physical or low-level mental work, such as high-volume manufacturing. Producing thousands of Ford automobiles, Compaq personal computers, or packages of Oreo cookies calls for continually repeating the same operations with only minor variations. Preparing customers' bills from lists of items and prices is a well structured activity. Totaling purchases at the checkout counters of Safeway supermarkets, computing NYNEX monthly telephone bills, or compiling Visa credit card statements involves repeating similar operations over and over. Posting millions of check transactions to bank accounts each day is well-structured mental work; accounting for millions of monthly home-mortgage payments that reduce principal and pay interest is well structured. Even the esoteric task of pricing a thirty-year U.S. Treasury bond is well-structured; any literate person can calculate it by punching the bond's coupon rate, settlement date, maturity date, and transaction interest rate into a desktop computer.

Ill-structured situations have the characteristics of complex, non routine mental work. How do leaders determine which new products they should add to their product line in a volatile market? How do they price new products that never existed before, such as a new drug or a plastic that is a hundred times more heat resistant than any known material? How do they project the market and financial effects of a new product, such as an electronically published newspaper or a cash management account? Ill-structured situatations are uncertain and affected by outside forces not under our control. They are complex, with many causes. They occur infrequently and have unique features that make it difficult to identify the best options at the time a decision must be made. Feedback about results will come much later, sometimes years after the decision is made. Past experience, like the mind-sets of generals who are still fighting the battles of their last war, is an unreliable guide to expertise, making it hard to identify experts. Many people, however, can and do claim to be expert, because in ill-structured situations it is difficult to disprove their claim. We summarize the characteristics of ill-structured and well-structured situations in Table 1.

Table 1
Situation Characteristics

Element	Well-structured situations	Ill-structured situations
Future Events	Predictable Adequate precision	Unpredictable Inadequate precision
Other's Actions	Knowable Predictable	Unknowable Unpredictable
Goals	Few Consistent	Many Contradictory
Priorities	Few Stable	Many Variable
Causes	Simple Identifiable	Complex Shifting
Change Rate	Slow Continuous	Rapid Discontinuous
Repetition	High recurrence	Unique situations
Better Decisions	Identifiable at time of decision	Indeterminate at time of decision
Feedback of Results	Timely Attributable to actions	Delayed Many causes
Experts	Experience helps Identifiable	Experience unreliable Hard to identify

MODES OF ORGANIZATION

Effective leaders work with teams in both the production and the knowledge modes, studying the situation and then choosing the appropriate mode. There is a hybrid mode, but for analytic clarity we focus on the two pure types.

Production mode

The production mode standardizes procedures, routinizing work to achieve high productivity. It uses a hierarchy to control people, ensuring that they follow standard procedures, and divide jobs into small, easily learned tasks with clear boundaries. Leaders have little discretion in this mode, except to adjust for an absence of personnel, an equipment breakdown, or a shortage of materials. Leaders scrupulously observe the ladder of authority, crossing boundaries between units only with authorization. Leaders' decisions conform to a web of rules, standard procedures, and past practices. Influence is strictly determined by one's level in the hierarchy. The production mode coordinates people and equipment to maximize output. High-volume production systems such as General Motors's assembly plants, Kellogg's cereal plants, and McDonald's fast-food outlets use the production mode.

Knowledge Mode

Leaders using the knowledge mode find and solve problems by creating and synthesizing knowledge. Influence derives from contributing knowledge—concepts, ideas, questions, facts, and insights. Leaders move their formal power into the background, temporarily suspending it as the primary determinant of influence. They become facilitator-consultants, rather than directive-commanders. The knowledge mode flattens the organization into an all-connected network with

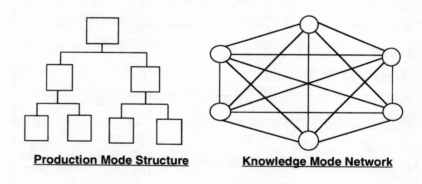

Production Mode Structure   **Knowledge Mode Network**

	Production Mode	**Knowledge Mode**
Purpose	Maximize output of a known product or service	Analyze and create knowledge to solve problems
Source of power or influence	Position in the hierarchy	Ability to identify and solve problems
Links to others	Few	Many
Levels of authority	Many	Few
Use of rules and procedures	High	Low
Division of labor	High	Low

Figure C-1 Mode Characteristics

new channels of communication unrestricted by formal organization boundaries. Leaders use differences in views of threats and opportunities, definitions of the problem, and possible solutions to stimulate creative search and learning. They remove narrow assignments, freeing imaginative individuals to contribute valuable concepts and insights. They install knowledge-mode norms of questioning and support the free flow of creative ideas over the production-mode norms of conformity and deference to formal authority. If leaders in the knowledge mode discover a well-structured task, they delegate it to a production-mode team where people know how to do it efficiently. We summarize the characteristics of the knowledge and the production modes in Figure C-1.

MATCHING MODES AND SITUATIONS

Effective leaders choose the mode that best matches the characteristics of the situation.[1] Production-mode teams produce more output faster in well-structured situations than do knowledge-mode teams doing the same task. When knowledge-mode teams can reorganize and change procedures, however, they shift to a production mode when they work on a well-structured task, standardizing procedures and giving people specialized, limited assignments, installing a hierarchy to coordinate work and resolve conflicts, and eliminating unnecessary channels of communication.

Knowledge-mode teams create better, more imaginative solutions faster in ill-structured situations than do production-mode teams working on the same task. Knowledge-mode leaders and teams also use and adapt unsolicited innovations. In Chapter 4, we described how 3M's leaders, using a knowledge mode, built a company that thrives on unsolicited innovations.

Production-mode teams working in ill-structured situations are burdened with norms, a division of labor, and narrow specialization that were designed for well-structured situations. Their rules, hierarchy, and limited communication restrict search and creativity. Production-mode leaders fear that changes will disrupt established procedures and lower productivity. As a result, they usually reject unsolicited innovations, thereby limiting their ability to deal effectively with ill-structured situations. When production-mode leaders unexpectedly face a market rocked by changes in consumer demand, new technology, or competitors' continuous improvements in product design and quality—as U.S. manufacturers were challenged by Japanese companies in the auto, electronics, and construction equipment industries—they may be unable to shift to a knowledge mode and cope successfully with the new, ill-structured environment. Instead, they may force their concept of the situation to fit their existing production strategy and organization structure. It is increasingly clear that leaders can no longer afford to pursue a production mode unsupplemented by a knowledge mode. If they do, their organizations will decline, and often fail, unless salvaged by a change in leadership. Before Lee Iacocca was hired, for example, Chrysler's leaders were so chained to a production mode that they continued to produce large, fuel-inefficient, low-quality cars long after consumer demand had led competitors to shift to smaller, fuel-efficient, high-quality cars. Chrysler's leaders' concept of the situation took the bizarre twist of continually increasing the production of cars they could not sell, theorizing that they would lower unit costs by distributing the overhead of their plants over a larger volume of (unsold) cars. Even with lower retail car prices, Chrysler found that consumer aversion to Chrysler products was so high that the company still had to sell huge inventories below cost. Chrysler's leaders were unable to switch out of their production mode to develop a new vision. When Iacocca arrived, he brought in new key managers, installed a lateral knowledge mode, and created a new strategy.

Effective leaders know that the production mode works best with well-structured situations (Table 2, Quadrant I) and the knowledge mode works best with ill-structured situations (Quadrant III). The other combinations—the knowledge mode with well-structured situations (Quadrant II) and the production mode with ill-structured situations (Quadrant IV)—are not well matched. Leaders use the production mode despite its shortcomings because

Table 2

SITUATION - MODE MATRIX

	Production Mode	**Knowledge Mode**
Well-structured Situations	**I** •High output •Fast •Few errors •High rejection of unsolicited innovations •Less satisfying	**II** •Lower output •Slower •More errors •Accepts unsolicited innovations •More satisfying
Ill-structured Situations	**IV** •Lower quality solutions •Low creativity •Lower output •Orderly, but not functional •Slower	**III** •High-quality solutions •High creativity •High output •Functional, but seems disorderly •Fast

it works so well in well-structured, repetitive production situations. Effective leaders know, however, that the production mode has limited adaptability and shift to a lateral knowledge mode when an ill-structured situation falls beyond the adaptability of the production mode. Effective leaders supplement the production mode with a knowledge mode to create strategies to cope with a changing environment.

A CASE STUDY: LEADING STRATEGIC CHANGE IN A MAJOR BANK

Fred Newman, vice president of international banking for Omnibank (all names have been disguised), was concerned about his department's future strategy. Omnibank was one of the top fifteen banks in the United States. The international banking department (IBD) faced strong competition in a changing but expanding global market. Several competitors had already established branches in major cities throughout Europe and Latin America, and compared to them Omnibank had a small number of overseas branches. Demand for international banking services was expected to grow as a result of the growth in world trade and the increases in U.S. investment overseas and in foreign investment within the United States. IBD was organized into five divisions—Europe and Canada, Latin America, Africa and the Middle East, Asia Pacific, and Government Lending (which specialized in U.S. government foreign aid and trade transactions). There was also a foreign exchange trading unit and two major processing centers, in New York and London. Canada's banking system was similar to the British system, and much of Omnibank's service to Canada also involved European countries, so to facilitate coordination, Canada had been made part of the European division. Omnibank's competitiors were extremely well entrenched in Canada, Africa, and the Middle East, and IBD maintained a small presence in these markets to serve its large U.S. and European clients.

Newman and the IBD division managers worked primarily in a production mode. Although there was glamour in international travel and some creativity in negotiating the structure and convenants of large loans, most situations—loan analysis, credit review, loan terms, loan servicing—were well structured. Newman and his subordinates were cooperative and deeply committed to their work. Leaders were busy managing their divisions and traveling, so they rarely met as a group. For several months, Newman attempted to discuss the department's strategy with his key subordinates, but found that they were too busy to dig into strategy issues in any depth; each leader would focus only on short-term administrative obstacles to his own division's productivity. Analyzing long-term strategy, an ill-structured situation, seemed beyond their problem-solving interest and capability. Despite the opportunity for growth, Newman sensed that IBD was having difficulty keeping up with its competitors.

Newman decided to discuss his concerns with an external consultant who had been working with another department in Omnibank. After introductory discussions, they agreed that the consultant would interview Newman, and his division leaders in order to make a preliminary assessment of the situation. The consultant's observations confirmed that the leaders were deeply entrenched in a production mode. Their daily work was extremely demanding and required many immediate decisions. The leaders said that loan negotiations were so time-sensitive that they had to be reachable by telephone twenty-four hours a day. Often they came to work at 4 A.M. to compensate for time differences around the globe. It was common practice to work ten to twelve hours and then leave on an international flight at midnight to meet with clients the next day in a foreign city. Newman and the consultant concluded that the leaders would have to break out of their intensive production mode and shift to a knowledge mode to analyze strategy. They would have to develop new norms to do knowledge-centered work. Newman and the consultant discussed the need for a lateral knowledge organization with the IBD leaders. They decided to hold an initial three-day off-site meeting, at which strategy and operating issues would be identified, discussed, analyzed, and, if possible resolved. The leaders were so production-driven that they insisted on scheduling the meeting on a weekend, from Friday evening after work to Sunday evening. They refused to be out of their offices on a normal business day.

Preliminary Information and Norm Development

Newman and his division leaders agreed that the consultant, as a neutral outsider, would interview each leader ten days before the off-site meeting. The interviews would be used to gather information and to answer questions about the meeting. The interviews covered the following points: each leader's understanding of the purpose of the off-site meeting; a brief description of the leader's job; how the job fit into the work of the department; what strategic issues or problems the leader thought the group should discuss at the off-site meeting; what outcomes would make the leader feel that the meeting had been worthwhile; what might make it difficult for leaders to discuss important issues openly; and what questions, if any, the leader had about the upcoming meeting.

The interviews introduced the leaders to the lateral knowledge mode and its norms. Leaders openly and creatively began exploring some ill-structured issues of strategy with the consultant. The interviews stimulated them to think about the strategic analysis process and how IBD made strategic decisions. They thought about their communication channels and about what they felt free to communicate. They described difficulties they might encounter while meeting off-site as a team, why those difficulties might arise, and what would be reasonable expectations for the lateral knowledge mode. These open, consultative, knowledge-mode norms differed from their day-to-day production norms. The next step was to continue using the knowledge mode with each other.

Orientation

To orient the leaders to the lateral knowledge mode, Newman and the consultant made several points and returned to them periodically to clarify the process and keep it focused on strategic issues. They would set limited, attainable goals and identify key issues, but with the understanding that in the short time available at the off-site meeting the group would not be able to discuss more than two or three priority issues in detail. There would be unanswered questions and unresolved issues remaining after the off-site meeting. Toward the end of the meeting the leaders would need to design a structure and a process for continuing work on the unresolved questions and issues. During the off-site meeting, which was only the introductory phase of the lateral knowledge mode, the team would need to plan for dealing with new, ill-structured situations that would arise in the future. The team would also need to plan what, how, and when it would tell others in the formal organization—subordinates, coworkers, superiors—about what the knowledge mode was doing. Communication could cover decisions, information about the knowledge mode and its agenda, and progress on specific issues.

Leading in the Knowledge Mode

The meeting convened off-site, with Newman, seven of his direct reports, three of their subordinates, the leader of Omnibank's London branch, who was a peer of Newman, and the consultant attending. The off-site meeting started with Newman and the consultant clarifying the norms of the lateral knowledge mode and its connection to the formal organization. They stated that this was Newman's meeting, not the consultant's. As in the formal organization, the group, or its individual members, could make recommendations, but Newman would have to approve any proposal before it could be implemented; in strategic analysis, any individual, regardless of his level in the production organization, can contribute valuable information and insights, often across formal boundaries. There would be a natural tendency within the group to self-censor rather than risk disagreeing with people who had greater formal authority. Efforts to protect one's turf or attacks on others would arouse defensiveness and inhibit communication and were discouraged. People would need to help each other get around these natural barriers to openness. It would be especially helpful if senior, higher level leaders would facilitate the expression and the constructive analysis of potentially controversial views. Since strategic issues are usually broad-based and ill structured, much of the discussion and many of the proposals would probably affect many different areas of the department.

Newman and the consultant continued the group orientation to knowledge-mode norms and connected the knowledge mode to the production mode. They pointed out that the group was in an early stage of exploring issues and strategy and was not in a position to make final decisions and take action. Initially, therefore, members should concentrate on identifying, clarifying, and understanding the full scope of strategic issues and on setting priorities. It should hold off on proposing solutions and evaluating them; this step would come later, after the group had a clear picture of the issues and options. As consultants to each other, each person could facilitate the knowledge mode by asking questions and suggesting procedures that would help identify, analyze, and solve problems. The power differences inherent in the formal production-mode organization would recede as the group worked in the knowledge mode. Power differences would still exist, however, and the group would need to consider them toward the end of the meeting when it would recommend decisions and implementation plans to the production organization.

Developing Knowledge-Mode Norms

The meeting then moved to a report by the consultant that summarized the issues the leaders had said they wanted to discuss. At first, as the discussion proceeded, people behaved as if in the usual production mode. Leaders assumed that when they spoke, everyone understood and accepted their statements. Some leaders, accustomed to taking action, immediately proposed a solution even before a problem had been clearly defined and cut off or interrupted others in the middle of a sentence. This was a dynamic, results-driven group that expected incisive questions and immediate answers. It was difficult to develop and complete a thought. Leaders evaluated and immediately discarded ideas without discussion. Several leaders and subordinates hung back, saying nothing. The active leaders ignored them, proceeding as if silence meant complete agreement with all that had been said. The consultant, acting as a facilitator, continually made process comments, shifting the group from its authoritarian production norms toward knowledge norms. He brought the discussion back to leaders whose views had been cut off or not heard and asked leaders to summarize what they had heard, checking their understanding against what others had said.

With Newman's and the consultant's guidance, the leaders gradually discovered major differences in their views of issues in banking and of IBD's problems in particular. They had vastly different projections for growth in demand for IBD's services and different explanations for that growth. They differed significantly on the types of services and products for which demand would grow. They disagreed about who their key competitors were and about the effectiveness of their competitors' strategies. They differed on when loan analysis or servicing should be done in New York, London or in a branch and on how these services should be done for different types of clients and loan sizes. The differences stimulated deep, probing discussions. Newman and the consultant continually asked questions to determine how many of the leaders understood and accepted the description of a problem before solutions were proposed and discussed. Status differences gradually faded as all the leaders began to contribute important information and insights. Newman and his senior division leaders could see that the knowledge-mode norms were opening communication and improving their problem-solving process. At the end of the first day, when one person slipped back into production norms, team members, rather than Newman or the consultant, asked questions and made process comments that returned the group to its lateral knowledge mode.

A New Norm

The leaders developed and adopted a special norm for their lateral knowledge mode: Incomplete ideas were welcomed, even if they were not thoroughly reasoned and defendable. One leader called these ideas shards, pieces of a puzzle, waiting to be assembled into a complete thought or strategy. Another called them phrases in the process of writing a poem. Newman and his team concurred in this norm, which they said significantly departed from their behavior in the formal organization. They felt that the norm stimulated the search and creativity that their production-mode norms had systematically suppressed. They said, however, that recommendations would still have to be supported by thorough reasoning and documentation in the formal organization. The team had clarified and understood an important difference between working in the lateral knowledge mode and working in the primary production mode. Leaders did not attempt to displace the production mode with the knowledge mode. Rather, they began to see that the lateral knowledge mode could supplement and parallel the production organization.

On the last day of the off-site meeting, Newman and the team decided to continue their knowledge mode back at work. They planned "lateral knowledge time" for open discussion, free questioning, and creative brainstorming. They agreed to use their flat, multichannel network to continue working on strategy and other ill-structured situations in parallel with the day-to-day, hierarchical production organization.

The Knowledge Mode in the Formal Organization

Newman and the other participants in the off-site meeting met as a team, working in the knowledge mode, one morning a week for the next several months. They had concluded, at the off-site meeting, that working on strategy was so important to IBD's future that each member would rearrange his or her travel schedule if necessary to attend the weekly meeting. The manager of Omnibank's London branch was the only one who did not attend these follow-up sessions. As leader of a very large overseas branch, he had many other responsibilities unrelated to IBD. It was agreed that Newman would call and give him a summary of each meeting and that they would discuss any points the team raised about processing transactions through the London branch. When necessary, the London branch manager would send his operations manager or another representative to IBD's meetings. The IBD knowledge-mode team continued analyzing and defining the ill-structured issues of their strategic situation: What would be the pattern of growth in different regions of the globe? Who were their competitors in their major markets? What were Omnibank's strengths and weaknesses? Should Omnibank have different strategies and organizations in different markets? What customers should IBD target and what products should it offer? How would limits on human and financial resources affect IBD's ability to grow?

Newman and his team developed their knowledge-mode skills in their weekly meetings. As they began to see how globally interdependent they were, they came closer together, realizing that they had to work as a team if they were to provide the coordinated services that clients around the globe expected. Newman and his team prepared a strategic analysis plan, identifying key unresolved issues and creating task forces to work on them. Three task forces were formed: One for Europe and the Middle East, one for Latin America, and one for Asia-Pacific. Each was to analyze demand, competition, resources, and Omnibank's strategic options in its region. A fourth task force studied ways to improve processing, global telecommunications, and coordination between the New York and the London processing centers.

Newman and his team periodically reviewed the progress of the task forces and continued to work on other, secondary issues. After several months, they had resolved most of their secondary issues, so they shifted to meeting one or two evenings a month, with a three-day off-site meeting at four-month intervals. They discussed the details of the task force reports, critically reviewed proposals, and planned their next steps. The full team and the task forces, using knowledge-mode norms, went through several iterations of strategic analysis during the year. They projected their business environment and analyzed it for threats and opportunities; scanned their organization for strengths and weaknesses; assessed how well their current strategy would achieve their future goals; generated alternative strategies to deal with the threats and opportunities and to use resources better than their current strategy; evaluated their alternative strategies and designed and selected a composite strategy that best balanced the various risks and opportunities; and planned the systems, staffing, and structure needed to implement and monitor their selected strategy (see the Strategy Wheel, Fig. C-2). Gradually Newman and the team formulated a comprehensive international banking strategy.

Figure C-2 Strategy Wheel

Results of the Knowledge Mode

The original stimulus for the lateral knowledge mode was Newman's need to develop a strategy for international banking in a changing global environment. The strategic decisions made with the lateral knowledge mode were especially impressive in view of subsequent political and economic developments around the globe. Newman and his team concluded that although the European market was large, strongly entrenched competitors had made heavy investments in Europe and competition there was intense. Rather than squander resources and incur long delays trying to go head-to-head against large, well-established competitors, Newman and his team formulated a strategy of affiliating with strong foreign banks in France, Germany, Belgium, and Scandinavia, supported by a few carefully located offices.

This permitted IBD quickly to provide clients with extensive services and expertise on a par with those of its competitors, but with only a modest investment.

Newman and his team formulated a different expansion strategy for Latin America and for the Far East. They concluded from their analysis that demand in these regions would grow very rapidly, at a higher rate than in Europe. They also concluded that competition in these areas was thin and not as well established as in Europe. They decided to expand IBD's existing relationships in Brazil and Colombia, opened a combination of branches and offices in Argentina, Chile, and Venezuela, and opened offices in Hong Kong, Singapore, and Japan to tap the expected increase in U.S. trade in those areas.

Newman and his team developed plans to implement their new strategy. New affiliations with foreign banks were staffed, and branches and offices were opened in several foreign cities. A long-term plan for hiring and developing personnel around the world was instituted. Leaders and operating staff were systematically rotated through assignments in different regions and at headquarters, increasing flexibility and cooperation across divisions around the world. The department's organization structure was changed to fit the new strategy. The government lending division, which reported to Newman, was disbanded and its work folded into the other divisions. New country sections and expanded existing sections were formed in the European, Latin American, and Asia-Pacific divisions. The Africa-Middle East division remained almost unchanged, since the IBD team concluded that in view of competition, growth outlook, and political risk, these areas did not present high-priority opportunities for Omnibank. The reorganization of the government lending division freed up personnel, providing much of the additional staff needed for the expansion in other areas.

The team had concluded that, because of turnover and reassignments, many of the bank's domestic officers who served U.S. companies with large overseas subsidiaries and trade were unfamiliar with IBD products, services, and personnel. The team developed a plan for managers at all levels of IBD to build close working relationships with domestic lending officers who worked with critical IBD clients. Procedures and data processing in London and New York were coordinated and upgraded, giving international banking customers more accurate, comprehensive, and timely service. Members of Newman's team then began to use knowledge-mode norms and methods in their own divisions. Each division leader introduced a lateral knowledge mode to plan and implement strategy within his or her own unit. Their subordinates then disseminated the lateral knowledge mode through IBD.

During the next ten years, as a result of Newman's and his team's formulation and implementation of the new strategy, top management rated IBD's growth and performance as outstanding. Newman was promoted to senior vice president, and one of his division leaders was promoted to Newman's former job. Word of Newman's accomplishments as a leader and his achievements at IBD spread, and he eventually left Omnibank to become CEO of another bank.

INTEGRATING KNOWLEDGE, TRUST, AND POWER

Knowledge

How did using the knowledge mode enhance knowledge among Omnibank's leaders? One can argue that the IBD might have formulated an equally good strategy without using a lateral knowledge mode. Recall, however, that Newman had tried unsuccessfully to formulate strategy with his leaders while they worked in their primary, production mode. He found that he did not have sufficient knowledge and that he could not get the commitment he needed from his globe-traveling, physically remote team if he formulated IBD's strategy without them. Newman concluded that the department's production mode had reached the limit of its adaptability and that it was poorly matched to the ill-structured tasks of formulating a global strategy in a rapidly changing environment and winning team commitment to that new strategy. He introduced the lateral knowledge mode, tapping into his team's distributed knowledge and imagination to formulate and implement an appropriate strategy. In the knowledge mode, Newman, his team, the task forces, and others in IBD who assisted the task forces learned the concepts and the application of strategic analysis. They created, synthesized, and applied knowledge of strategic analysis that was far superior to their initial ideas, which amounted to simply doing more of what they were already doing in their daily production mode.

Trust

Using the knowledge mode enhanced trust, as well. The leaders in the IBD team were bright and aggressive. Their well-structured daily work, however, had impelled them toward a production mode. (This did not mean, of course, that they did not care about one another, and about their subordinates.) They did have enough initial trust in Newman and in one another to enter and learn a lateral knowledge mode, and, gradually, their increasing trust permitted them to examine their department's future more deeply and comprehensively than ever before. This increased trust showed in their cooperation and coordination in formulating and implementing IBD's new strategy and in their day-to-day work across divisions. The leaders were clearly more trusting, open, and creative after using the knowledge mode than they had been before using it. In those days, their trust had consisted of confining themselves to leading their own division in a production mode.

Power

The knowledge mode augmented Newman's power through consultation, concurrence, and consignment, rather than through directive commands. It taught IBD's leaders to use power flexibly in their own divisions and increased leaders' self-confidence in their use of power.

Complex, ill-structured situations often arouse some enduring differences of opinion that test a leader's power. There were conflicts within Newman's team over the reports and recommendations of some of the task forces. These were discussed and most major differences were resolved in the knowledge mode through concurrence. Newman had to use his formal power to resolve some issues, but by the time he had to make a decision, the knowledge mode had given him and his team a comprehensive understanding of the issues, the options, and the risks. His team therefore saw his use of power to resolve stalemates as legitimate and proper, rather than as arbitrary and capricious.

The lateral knowledge mode also uncovered some deep personal and strategic conflicts that tested Newman's power. The manager of IBD's Paris office refused to contribute to the knowledge mode, obstructed its norms, and became a serious impediment to the teams functioning. He felt it was improper to discuss European strategy in the presence of other division leaders and was unwilling to let their views influence the formulation of that strategy. He also objected strenuously to forming alliances with other European banks and preferred to open more branches and offices, which apparently he hoped to manage throughout Europe. His arguments were not persuasive to the European task force, or to Newman and his team. Newman, after much effort, reluctantly concluded that he had to transfer this leader. On balance, Newman, and his team, learned to use power wisely and sensitively, tapping dispersed knowledge and building trust. The team learned to accept influence from knowledge, regardless of a person's formal power. It also learned how to link the power of new, strategic knowledge to people with formal power. It understood the different power attributes of the knowledge and the production modes and learned when to use each one.

When leaders introduce knowledge-mode norms, some leaders of neighboring departments feel threatened, fearing that the practice of asking questioning and supporting creative searches will contaminate their department's production norms. They use their power in an attempt to quash the knowledge mode before it spreads. Fortunately, this was not a serious power issue for Newman and his team, because IBD was an autonomous, self-contained unit, loosely affiliated with the rest of Omnibank. IBD's lateral knowledge mode raised few power concerns among other department leaders, except for curiosity about the exuberance of the IBD's leaders when they came back from their off-site meetings. IBD's prosperity and palpable team spirit under the new strategy had so increased Omnibank's senior management's confidence in Newman and his team that other than requiring monthly reviews of general performance, they refrained from modifying Newman's use of power and stayed out of IBD's internal affairs. If anything, they subtly encouraged other departmental leaders to find out more about Newman's leadership and his use of power.

THE KNOWLEDGE MODE AND TASK FORCES

Poor leaders assume that they can shift to a lateral knowledge mode simply by forming a task force. This is a serious misunderstanding. IBD's lateral knowledge mode used task forces, but with two critical features: Each task force used knowledge-mode norms and each was continuously and tightly tied to leaders in the formal organization.

Poor leaders form task forces that use the same production-mode norms as the formal organization. People in these task forces only superficially question goals and assumptions. They do not, and dare not, seriously probe the company's methods of and criteria for evaluation. They concentrate on discussing only narrow options that further their department's interests. They are often unrepresentative of the company as a whole, having been convened to recommend publicly the private decision a leader had already made. Such task forces suffer the same restricted inquiry and constrained flow of information as the formal organization. These task forces censor touchy issues and creative proposals that higher authorities ought to hear but that are deemed too controversial. Some task forces, responding to inordinate pressure from upper management, submit recommendations that use resources inefficiently or even unethically; others, operating with production-mode norms and working in isolation, often make unsatisfactory recommendations that senior managers do not implement. Poor leaders then convene a second task force, and sometimes a third, until they get the recommendations they want.

Because Omnibank's task forces used knowledge-mode norms, they were able to contribute creatively and enthusiastically. Omnibank's task forces were part of a comprehensive, inclusive knowledge system. There was constant feedback and review between the task forces and Newman and his team. Leaders and the task forces continually proposed new ideas, made necessary adjustments, and concurred along the way to a final decision. Omnibank's formal leaders with authority to approve and implement recommendations served on the task forces, tightly linking them to the lateral knowledge mode. Omnibank's task forces used the norms of a flat, explorative, knowledge network. They supplemented the power of formal leaders without interfering with production and integrated knowledge, trust, and power as they worked on their task.

THE PRODUCTION-KNOWLEDGE BLEND

Between the production mode and the knowledge mode there is a production-knowledge blend that combines the best features of the two modes. The knowledge mode is vital but delicate. It requires a leader's sustained support because it is easily overwhelmed by the directive norms and immediate results demanded by the production mode. In the production-knowledge blend, effective leaders use lateral knowledge-mode skills as needed in their production organization. Effective blend leaders are good listeners and team process observers. They are skilled interviewers and data gathers and cooperate with others in flat networks with varying memberships to diagnose situations. They skillfully install knowledge-mode norms as they form and guide task forces and steering committees. They weave knowledge-mode skills into the fabric of the production mode, enhancing and integrating knowledge, trust, and power to achieve a productive, adaptive organization that is responsive to both well- and ill-structured situations.

OPERATIONAL REALITIES

Effective leaders understand that enhancing and integrating the leadership triad by using a lateral knowledge mode has its problems. The number of meetings and the use of groups increase. There are new stresses on mid-level leaders. As a result, problems with individual flexibility and overoptimism develop.

Increased Use of Groups

In the early stages of the use of the lateral knowledge mode, leaders increase their use of groups or teams to find and solve problems that the primary organization has not solved. These teams include members from all parts of the company and represent a cross-section of the organization's distributed knowledge. Team meetings help people learn knowledge-mode norms and process. Leaders begin by asking teams to build an inventory of ill-structured problems. Knowledge-mode norms free the teams to identify problems previously known only to isolated individuals or suppressed.

Poor leaders mistakenly believe that using a team to develop a problem inventory increases the number of problems. This is not so. The problems have always been there, below the surface. The organization pays for these hidden problems with decreased effectiveness. Knowledge-mode teams do not create new problems; they simply report what has been underreported and enable people to identify and work on them.

Some problems have the potential to destroy the organization. Effective leaders know that knowledge-mode teams can identify and solve these high-priority organization-wide problems more effectively than can one person working alone. When knowledge mode teams function effectively, there is usually an initial increase in the inventory of problems. After the initial surge, the need for knowledge-mode meetings decreases as the problems are solved. Teams also reduce the need for meetings by referring any well-structured problem they find to the appropriate leader in the production organization. Only the complex, ill-structured situations go to the knowledge mode. The knowledge mode gradually reduces the number of unresolved, ill-structured situations, thereby decreasing the number of team meetings needed. After meeting weekly for several months, for example, Newman and his IBD team reduced the frequency of their meetings to once every two weeks.

Stress on Mid-Level Leaders

A lateral knowledge mode increases the stress on mid-level leaders because the flat, all-connected network permits high-level leaders to communicate directly with low-level leaders. Top leaders often discover that mid-level leaders have been editing, distorting, or suppressing information; low-level leaders find that their information and ideas can influence top management more easily than they thought possible. In one IBD meeting, a low-level operations supervisor asked why a certain loan form needed nine copies and six signatures when all but two copies were usually stored in dead files and, regardless of who else signed the form, the loans would never be made without the signature of two particular high-level leaders. Newman asked the team if there would be any objections to reducing the form to an original and two copies and eliminating four of the six signatures. There were none. Most people thought it was a fabulous idea; in fact, the supervisor had been pursuing this idea through the middle levels of IBD for more than three years, but mid-level leaders had hesitated to champion it for fear of offending peers and senior managers. The IBD meeting, using the knowledge mode, resolved the question in five minutes. High and low-level leaders clear away myths when the knowledge mode removes the mid-level filter. Leaders at the top and bottom discover that they are reasonable people, with a common interest in improving productivity and adaptability. They find that they each respond to accurate information and to sensible proposals and that they can quickly identify and solve problems that seemed intractable.

The flat knowledge mode prompts leaders to redesign the formal organization with fewer levels of authority. Reviewing the contribution and the role of mid-level leaders greatly increases their vulnerability and stress. Newman and his team, for example, reorganized IBD, eliminating the government lending division and making several mid-level leaders redundant. In this case, fortunately, the redundant leaders were absorbed in new growth areas, where they helped IBD implement its new strategy. The reduced number of mid-level leaders who remain in organizations after a knowledge mode has been successfully installed become critical members of the management team. During production-mode operation they become critical interpreters of top management's intentions. They also represent lower-level people in top-level forums. In the knowledge mode their ideas are essential to creatively transforming strategy into practical action. Mid-level leaders, albeit in reduced numbers, still perform a vital linking function within the organization.[2]

Individual Flexibility

Some leaders are comfortable working in only one mode, either the production mode or the knowledge mode. Production-mode people want certainty, stability, and consistency in their work. They need a structured, directive relationship with their superior. Knowledge-mode people, in contrast want freedom to explore. They get a kick out of ambiguity and the challenge of solving complex problems and need a loose, supportive relationship with their superior. The stable, well-structured markets and technology that production-mode people prefer, however, can quickly turn into ambiguous, ill-structured competition in a global world of intense rivalry. Effective leaders know that they and their subordinates must adapt. But they also know that they cannot force a knowledge mode on people who are rigidly fixed in a production mode and who mistrust a knowledge mode and will undermine it, if necessary, to preserve the status quo.

Organizations need flexible, triadic leaders who can use the mode that best fits the situation. Most leaders, fortunately, can work in both modes once they understand the knowledge mode and have personally experienced how it works. They need to know which mode they are operating in and when they are shifting from one mode to another. The flexibility of Newman and his subordinates was critical to the success of their use of the lateral knowledge mode. Many leaders have the flexibility to use a knowledge mode to create an adaptive strategy. Poor leaders misconstrue a person's initial skepticism about using a knowledge mode as a sign of deep-seated personal rigidity. Effective leaders understand, however, that the initial rigidity of most people dissolves as they come to understand the knowledge mode and experience how effectively it complements the formal organization. Then, leaders and their teams can be remarkably flexible.

Overoptimism

After leaders experience the lateral knowledge mode for the first time, they often react overoptimistically. Leaders feel that they and their team have broken through to a higher level of trust. They have reached a better, more sensitive use of power and communicate more directly than in the past, and they are more productive. Their enthusiasm propels them to overly optimistic images of future accomplishments. As the demands of daily, well-structured work intrude, however, they quickly take priority, pushing the lateral knowledge mode into the background. Meetings become infrequent and disjointed. Leaders and their teams solve some ill-structured problems, but the solutions take much longer to implement than planned. Leaders devote more effort to working through new, ill-structured problems than they expected. In short, leaders find that they must fight to protect the knowledge mode from being swamped by production operations.

After leaders learn to use the knowledge mode, they can better see the limitations of their hierarchical organization. They learn that using a knowledge mode does not mean that teams will degenerate into anarchy and chaos. Leaders can still take charge; they can still command. But they understand how using a knowledge mode integrates knowledge, trust, and power into their hierarchical organization.

SUMMARY OF THE KNOWLEDGE MODE

Effective leaders use a lateral knowledge mode to find, define, and solve ill-structured problems that have not been solved by the formal organization. When leaders in the lateral knowledge mode determine that a problem is well-structured, they refer it to the operating organization. Leaders use the lateral, knowledge mode to creatively complement the formal organization and operate it in parallel with the formal organization, choosing to use the production mode or the knowledge mode, depending on the situation. The lateral knowledge mode utilizes the people who work in the formal organization but without the reliance on hierarchy and formal power structure; instead it, temporarily rearranges people into new combinations. Leaders can approach and recruit people throughout the organization who can help solve a problem and are not limited to their formal subordinates. In the knowledge mode, leaders and specialists communicate freely, without being restricted to formal channels, allowing a rapid and complete exchange of information.

Knowledge mode norms—that is, expectations of how people will behave—differ from production-mode norms. Knowledge-mode norms expect people to question carefully and to analyze goals, assumptions, predictions, methods, and options. They facilitate new ideas and creative approaches to obstacles and promote new views of a problem.

Leaders of the formal organization are continuously linked to the lateral knowledge mode as members of the knowledge-mode network. They absorb and carry to the formal organization the reports and discussions they hear in the lateral knowledge mode. The knowledge mode does not act on its own; it makes recommendations to leaders with formal power. This tight coupling ensures that knowledge-mode outputs are used in the production organization.

Effective leaders construct teams with people who facilitate the knowledge mode and blend it with the production mode. They particularly seek leaders with formal authority to approve and support the implementation of decisions; experts with knowledge and analytic skills relevant to the situation; leaders who can represent the views of the people who will implement or be affected by decisions; creative people who challenge conventional notions and generate imaginative options; facilitators who initiate ideas, clarify, question, and maintain reasonable harmony within the team; and leaders who steer the lateral knowledge mode to identify new problems and work toward solutions. Many people need to learn knowledge-mode skills, having spent the majority of their working lives in the production mode. Effective leaders learn and disseminate the norms, skills and problem-solving behaviors of the knowledge mode. They blend the knowledge and production modes to integrate knowledge, trust, and power.

CHARACTERISTICS OF TRIADIC LEADERS

The leaders we have discussed such as Lee Iacocca at Chrysler, Sam Walton at Wal-Mart, and Fred Newman at Omnibank, have the characteristics of triadic leaders: wisdom, integrity, and courage. These characteristics foster and synthesize knowledge, trust, and power. Although most of our discussion has been about CEOs and other higher level leaders, triadic leaders at all levels have these three characteristics.

Wisdom

Triadic leaders have wisdom that combines knowledge, insight and judgment. They go beyond sterile facts to understand the underlying substance of their business, their market, and their competition. They can put into perspective the assumptions and the implications of what specialists and others tell them. With their staffs, they develop and implement an astute vision of a path into the future. Iacocca's vision, for example, upgraded the quality of Chrysler products, built minivans and Jeeps into market leaders, reinvigorated a moribund dealer network, and salvaged Chrysler from bankruptcy. Walton's vision positioned Wal-Mart stores in small towns, where store leaders honed their retailing skills, prospering for years without directly facing large competitors and propelling Wal-Mart to the front ranks of retailing. Newman's vision transformed Omnibank's IBD into banking guerrillas who cleverly outmaneuvered large competitors in Europe and preempted them in Latin America and Asia, where they were less well established. Triadic leaders often comprehend a vision before others do, and, like Newman, they have the wisdom to recognize and champion the vision they acquire from the insights of their colleagues.

Triadic leaders have the wisdom to use their power sensitively and properly. They know their colleagues' areas of competence and their shortcomings, their motivation and their degree of trust. They judiciously command, consult, concur, or consign, depending on the people involved, their relationships, and the situation. Triadic leaders use both the knowledge mode and the production mode wisely. They know how to blend the two to generate and synthesize knowledge, trust, and power.

Triadic leaders have the wisdom to ask questions that simplify complex situations. They know that concepts determine where people look and what they look for and understand that the way people see the problem is the problem, so they encourage probing questions that distill the essential issues and focus action on key priorities.

Integrity

Triadic leaders have integrity, which is the foundation of trust, the enduring reason underlying our willingness to share knowledge, and the basis for committing ourselves to act together to reach a common goal. Triadic leaders are authentic, accepting themselves and at ease letting others know who they are. Iacocca, Walton, and Newman were direct and honest. What they said was what they meant. They were dependable. People did not have to decipher hidden messages.

Triadic leaders trust their subordinates, willingly depend on them, and stay out of the way. They see integrity in others, so they consign responsibility as fast as possible, continually stretching their colleagues. Iacocca's trust of his people revolutionized Chrysler's product design process, making it perhaps the fastest, most adaptive, and least costly in the industry; Walton trusted young managers to open new stores successfully; Newman trusted his Omnibank team to shed its hectic, stupefying routine and to create a successful, new strategy.

Triadic leaders have the integrity to support their subordinates and do not demean them with vindictive uses of power. They are fair and give credit for a job well done, sharing rewards when the organization prospers and suffering deprivations with everyone else when the organization does poorly. The authenticity, trustfulness, supportiveness, and fairness of triadic leaders gives them integrity that wins the enduring trust of their coworkers.

Courage

Triadic leaders have the courage to take risks. They combine courage and wisdom to venture into uncertain environments. Their courage buoys other people, giving them courage to overcome the paralyzing anxiety that goes with failure. Triadic leaders have the courage to persist in their quest, steadfastly motivating others despite the uncertainty of the outcome. Iacocca had the courage to venture into minivans far ahead of his competitors, taking a risk that ultimately paid off tremendously. Walton's courage in merchandise promotion encouraged his store managers to take risks; their innovations gave Wal-Mart one of the highest ratios of sales per square foot in the retail industry. Newman had the courage to risk exposing his Omnibank team to conflicting views of demand growth, and imaginative strategic options. Although his subordinates were more comfortable doing their regular work, his courage led to a strategy that significantly increased productivity and adaptability.

Triadic leaders have the courage to risk using a knowledge mode, voluntarily relinquishing at times their power to make decisions unilaterally. They have the courage to be nondefensive and to respect the need of others to be defensive and to flounder while they learn. They also have the self-confidence to support their colleagues as they slog through an uncertain environment and to hear and to express controversial views.

In sum, triadic leaders have wisdom, integrity, and courage, and they impart these characteristics to others. Triadic leaders foster and synthesize knowledge, trust, and power, building productive, adaptive teams that share vision and commitment. We conclude with a poet's words describing the spirit triadic leaders instill in their people.

> *Fear not walking where there is no path,*
> *For where you walk the path will follow.*

Notes

Introduction: The Leadership Triad

1. This description of the early history of Allstate is based on G.L. Weil, *Sears, Roebuck, U.S.A.* (New York: Jove/HBJ, 1977), pp. 213–221.

Chapter 1. Leadership: The New Conditions

1. Maryann Keller, *Rude Awakening: The Rise, Fall, and Struggle for Recovery of General Motors* (New York: Harper Perennial, 1990); Jon Friedman and John Meehan, *House of Cards: Inside the Troubled Empire of American Express* (New York: Kensington Publishing, 1993).
2. Frank Rose, *West of Eden: The End of Innocence at Apple Computer* (New York: Viking, 1989).
3. R. B. Reich, "The Real Economy," *Atlantic Monthly*, February 1991, 37.
4. Rose, *West of Eden*, p. 62.

Chapter 2. Finding Knowledge

1. Jon Friedman and John Meehan, *House of Cards: Inside the Troubled Empire of American Express* (New York: Kensington Publishing, 1993); Leah N. Spiro, "Behind the Bombshell from Amex," *Business Week*, 21 October 1991, 124–126; Harris Collingwood, "AMEX Slips on its Optima Card," *Business Week*, 14 October 1991, 54.

2. "How Compaq gets there firstest with the mostest," *Business Week*, 26 June 1989, 146; "It looks like a PC maker, walks like a PC maker," *Business Week*, 12 December 1994, 106.

3. For more information about business strategy and related questions see A. C. Hax and N. S. Majluf, *The Strategy Concept and Process* (Englewood Cliffs, N.J.: Prentice-Hall, 1991); M. E. Porter, *Competitive Strategy* (New York: Free Press, 1980); S. A. Stumpf, *The Growth Challenge* (Chicago, Ill.: Enterprise Dearborn, 1993).

4. Alan Deutschman, "John Sculley: Odd Man Out," *Fortune*, 26 June 1993, 48.

5. Lee Iacocca with William Norak, *Iacocca: An Autobiography* (New York: Bantam, 1984), p. 175.

Chapter 3. From Knowledge to Action

1. The discussion of the Chrysler minivan case is drawn from Alex Taylor III, "Iacocca's Minivan," *Fortune*, 30 May 1994, 57–66, and from Lee Iacocca with William Novak, *Iacocca: An Autobiography* (New York: Bantam, 1984).

2. Ibid.

3. Richard D. Freedman and Jill Vohr, *American Express* (New York: New York University, Stern School, 1991); Leah N. Spiro and John Byrne, "A Quiet Coup at American Express," *Business Week*, 21 December 1992, 30–31; Leah N. Spiro, "Sandy Weill Strikes Again," *Business Week* 22 March 1993, 74–75; American Express Annual Report, 1993, 1994.

4. Taylor, "Minivan"; Iacocca, *Iacocca*.

5. The discussion of the Sears case is drawn from Gregory Patterson and Francine Schwadel, "Sears Suddenly Undoes Years of Diversifying Beyond Retailing Field," *Wall Street Journal*, 30 September 1992, A1, and from Susan Caminiti, "Sears' Need: More Speed," *Fortune* 15 July 1991, 88–90.

Chapter 4. Learning and Knowledge

1. Thomas A. Stewart, "Your Company's Most Valuable Asset: Intellectual Capital," *Fortune*, 3 October 1994, 68.

2. The description of Banc One has been drawn from Paul S. Myers and Rosabeth Moss Kanter, *Banc One Corporation, 1989* (Boston, Mass.: Harvard Business School Press, Case 9–390–029, 1990); *Wall Street Journal*, 13 June 1988, B1; 29 June 1989, A6; 30 June 1989, A3.

3. The discussion of 3M's leadership and the development of Post-it notes has been drawn from P. Ranganath Nayak and John M. Ketteringham, *Breakthroughs!* (New York: Rawson Associates, 1986), pp. 50–73; Thomas J. Peters and Robert H. Waterman Jr., *In Search of Excellence* (New York: Harper & Row, 1982), pp. 224–234; Russell Mitchell, "Masters of Innovation: How 3M Keeps New Products Coming," *Business Week*, 10 April 1989, 58–63; *3M Annual Report 1993* and company documents.

4. Maryann Keller, *Rude Awakening: The Rise, Fall, and Struggle for Recovery of General Motors* (New York: Harper Perennial, 1990).

5. Elizabeth Corcoran, "Green Machine: Volkswagen Gears Up to Recycle

Autos," *Scientific American*, January 1992, 140–141; B. Nussbaum and J. Templeman, "Built to Last—Until It's Time to Take It Apart," *Business Week*, 17 September 1990, 102–103; J.O. Jackson, "World Class Litterbugs," *Time*, 18 October 1993, 80.

6. For an introduction to these methods, see, for example, E. de Bono, *Six Thinking Hats* (Boston: Little, Brown, 1985), and W. J. Gordon, *Synectics* (New York: Collier Macmillan, 1968).

Chapter 5. Knowledge Stress and Knowledge Workers

1. Louis S. Richman "The New Worker Elite," *Fortune*, 22 August 1994, 56–66.

Chapter 6. Trust and the Decision Process

1. Various concepts presented in this chapter and parts of the Conrad case have been adapted from a research paper by the author that appeared in D.E. Zand, "Trust and Managerial Problem Solving," *Administrative Science Quarterly* 2 (1972): 229–239, and are used with permission. A general discussion of trust appears in Louis B. Barnes, "Managing the Paradox of Organizational Trust," *Harvard Business Review* (March 1981): 107–116.

Chapter 7. Determinants of Trust

1. The following discussion is based upon Lee Iacocca with William Novak, *Iacocca: An Autobiography* (New York: Bantam Books, 1984). The quoted material is from p. 4.

2. Ibid., p.3.

3. Ibid., p. 4.

4. Ibid., pp. 7–10

5. "Tinkering with Geneen's Growth Machine at ITT," *Business Week*, 15 May 1978 59.

6. The following discussion draws from Robert J. Schoenberg, *Geneen* (New York: Norton, 1985). Robert Sobel, *ITT: The Management of Opportunity* (New York: Truman Talley, 1982), is an additional source with details about specific acquisitions.

7. Schoenberg, Geneen, p. 23.

8. Ibid., p. 27.

9. Ibid., p. 32.

10. Ibid., p.47.

11. Ibid., pp. 82–101.

12. The following quotations and description of the ITT review meetings are based on Anthony Sampson, *The Sovereign State of ITT* (New York: Stein & Day, 1973), pp. 99–100.

13. Ibid., p. 100.

14. Ibid.

15. Schoenberg, *Geneen*, p.35.

16. Ibid.

Chapter 9. Legitimate and Decision Process Power

1. The following discussion is based on Ken Auletta, *Three Blind Mice: How the TV Networks Lost Their Way* (New York: Random House, 1991), and Robert Slater, *The New GE: How Jack Welch Revived an American Institution* (Homewood, Ill.: Business One Irwin, 1993).

2. See Steven Greenhouse, "Helms Is at Center of Storm After New Clinton Criticism," *New York Times*, 23 November 1994, A11; David H. Hackworth, "Soldiers Know: Helms Got It Wrong," *Newsweek*, 5 December 1994, 26.

3. Marshall Loeb, "Empowerment That Pays Off," *Fortune*, 20 March 1995, 145–146.

Chapter 10. Agenda, Staffing, and Review Power

1. The following discussion is based on David Kirkpatrick, "The Revolution at Compaq Computer," *Fortune*, 14 December 1992, 80–85; Stephanie Losoo, "How Compaq Keeps the Magic Going," *Fortune*, 21 February 1994, 90–93; C. Arnst, S.A. Forest, K. Robello and J. Levine, "Compaq: How It Made Its Impressive Move Out of the Doldrums," *Business Week*, 2 November 1992, 146–152; S.A. Forest and C. Arnst, "Compaq Declares War on the Clones," *Business Week*, 15 June 1992, 43.

2. This discussion of Sam Walton is based on Sam Walton with John Huey, *Sam Walton: Made in America* (New York: Doubleday, 1992), p. 115.

3. Ibid., p. 121.

4. Ibid., p. 54.

5. Kirkpatrick, "Revolution."

6. Walton, *Sam Walton*, p. 56.

7. Ibid., p. 62.

8. Ibid., pp. 61, 216.

9. The following discussion is based on Gary McWilliams, "At Compaq, Desktop Crystal Ball," *Business Week*, 20 March 1995, 96–97.

10. Derived from Cabell Phillips as quoted in David McCullough, *Truman* (New York: Simon & Schuster, 1992), p. 819.

Chapter 11. The Power of Leaders as Consultants

Some material in Chapter 11 has been adapted from Dale E. Zand, "Managers and Consulting: A Total Quality Perspective," *Journal of Management Development*, 1993, Vol. 12, No. 7, pp. 51–59, and is used with permission.

1. For further reading about consulting models, see G. Lippitt, and R. Lippitt, *The Consulting Process in Action* (La Jolla, Calif.: University Associates, 1978); L.E. Greiner, and R.O. Metzger, *Consulting to Management* (Englewood Cliffs, N.J., Prentice-Hall, 1983); C. Argyris and D. Schon, *Organizational Learning* (Reading, Mass: Addison-Wesley, 1978); C. Argyris, R. Putnam, and D. Smith, *Action Science* (San Francisco: Jossey-Bass, 1985); E. Schein, *Process Consultation: Its Role in Organization Development*, 2nd ed. (Reading, Mass.: Addison-Wesley, 1988); T.G. Cummings and E.F. Huse, *Organization Development and Change*, 4th ed. (New York: West, 1989).

2. For information about brainstorming, see A. Osborn, *Applied Imagination* (New York: Scribner, 1957); S.J. Parnes, *Creative Behavior Guidebook* (New York: Scribner, 1967). For information about synectics, see W.J. Gordon, *Synectics: The Development of Creative Capacity* (New York: Harper & Row, 1961); G. Prince, *The Practice of Creativity* (New York: Harper & Row, 1970). For information about six-hat thinking, see E. de Bono, *Six Thinking Hats* (Boston: Little, Brown, 1985).

Conclusion: Teamwork and Triadic Integration

1. The following discussion draws on a number of classic studies, including A. Bavelas, "Communication Patterns in Task-Oriented Groups," *Journal of Acoustical Society of America* 22 (1950): 725–730; L. S. Christie, R. D. Luce, and J. May Jr., *Communications and Learning in Task-Oriented Groups* (Cambridge, Mass.: Research Laboratory Electronics, 1952); H. J. Leavitt, "Some Effects of Certain Communication Patterns on Group Performance," *Journal of Abnormal and Social Psychology* 46 (1951): 38–50; H. Guetzkow and W. R. Dill, "Factors in the Organizational Development of Task-Oriented Groups," *Sociometry* 20 (1957): 175–204; H. Guetzkow and H. A Simon, "The Impact of Certain Communication Nets Upon Organization and Performance in Task-Oriented Groups," *Management Science* 1 (1955): 233–250; M. E. Shaw, G. H. Rothchild, and J. R. Strickland, "Decision Process in Communication Nets," *Journal of Abnormal and Social Psychology* 54 (1957): 323–330; T. Burns and G. M. Stalker, *Management of Innovation* (London: Tavistock, 1961); D. E. Zand, "Collateral Organization: A New Change Strategy," *Journal of Applied Behavioral Science* 10, 1 (1974): 63–89.

2. The linking role of middle managers is discussed in Ikujiro Nonaka and Hirotaka Takeuchi, *The Knowledge-Creating Company* (New York: Oxford University Press, 1995); Peter F. Drucker, *Management: Tasks. Responsibilities, Practices* (New York, Harper & Row, 1974); and Rensis Likert, *New Patterns of Management* (New York: McGraw-Hill, 1961).

Index